DOES IT YURT?

DOES IT YURT?

Travels in Central Asia
Or How I Came to Love the Stans

By Stephen M. Bland

HERTFORDSHIRE PRESS

Published in United Kingdom
Hertfordshire Press Ltd © 2016

9 Cherry Bank, Chapel Street
Hemel Hempstead, Herts.
HP2 5DE, United Kingdom

e-mail: publisher@hertfordshirepress.com
www.hertfordshirepress.com

Does it Yurt?
Travels in Central Asia Or How I Came to Love the Stans
Copyright © Stephen M. Bland 2016

English

Editors: Michael Bland & Ola's Kool Kitchen
Design Aleksandra Vlasova & Allwell Solutions

Excerpts from ChaptersTwo and Twenty were previously published in Caravanistan, Chapters Four and Twenty-Three in Eurasianet, Chapters Five, Eight, Fourteen and Seventeen in Open Central Asia, Chapters Six and Seventeen in IndraStra, Chapters Seven, Eight, Thirteen, Fourteen, Fifteen, Seventeen and Nineteen in Vice and Chapters Thirteen and Fourteen in Registan.

visit: www.stephenmbland.com

*British Library Catalogue in Publication Data
A catalogue record for this book is available from the British Library
Library of Congress in Publication Data
A catalogue record for this book has been requested*

ISBN: 978-1-910886-29-8

CONTENTS

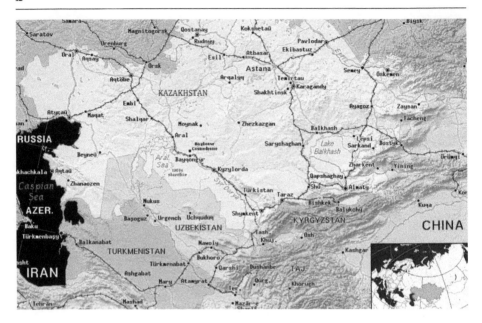

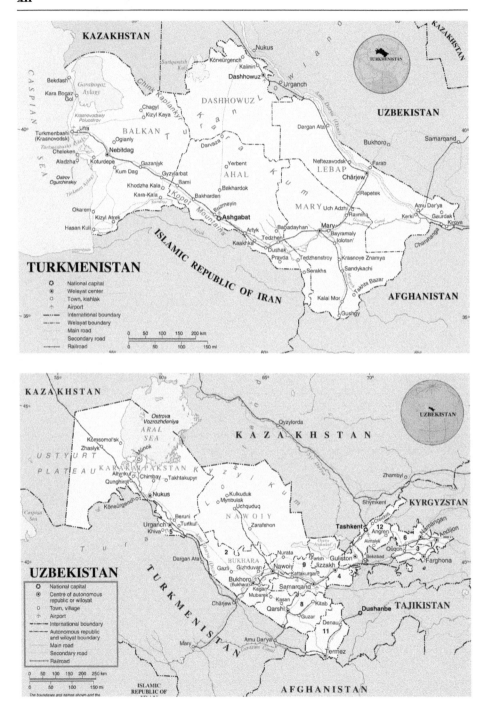

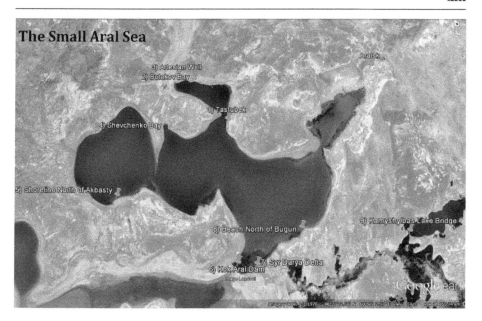

The Small Aral Sea

Prologue

Arrivals: Bishkek

We arrived at Manas International Airport in Bishkek, the capital of Kyrgyzstan to thunderous applause from the plane's passengers. It felt as if they gave every successful landing an ovation. Perhaps it was a bonus; the plane's emergency exit hadconsisted of a frayed escape rope. Conveying the impression that they wanted to prove they had a bus, but most likely a remnant of Soviet era full-employment, half an hour later the airport shuttle took us the twenty metres to the terminal building. Despite our arrival, however, our baggage wasn't so fortunate.

Inside the grey terminal building, futile lost luggage forms in Cyrillic were distributed and filed beneath a single flickering TV on which an advert for a local strip joint played on a loop. Our pre-booked driver having failed to materialise, we acquiesced to the hawker's insistent overtures and took a*taksi*, a beat up old Lada VAZwith a hole in the floor.

Approaching the urban sprawl, ahotchpotch of angular derelicts and half finished, stagnating Chinese construction projects lined the wide streets. Weaving their way around traffic on crutches, limbless men held out tin cans, begging in the middle of the road. A jigsaw of mismatched panels haphazardly cobbled together, the buses, dilapidated Mercedes Sprinters known as *marshrutkas* belched smoke as they laboured through potholes.

In the garden ofour accommodation, Gulnara's Nomad Home,sickly brown beans climbed a trellis towards thesummer sun, the sky already a bleached silver void at seven AM. Shrugging away the room reservation I'd printed out, the proprietor herded us into a yurt, the traditional, cylindrical tent dwelling of Central Asia. Latticework covered in *shyrdak*- handwoven Kyrgyz felt rugs- led to curved, blood red rafters which stretched to the *tunduk*, the 'door to the heavens,' a vented area at the apex which admitted no air whatsoever. At forty-one degrees Celsius, it felt like hell.

Jetlagged, we shuffled into the city centre, where garbedin turned-up jeans and tracksuit tops, posses of rude boys loitered beside fountains, arms wrapped around each other's shoulders. What you needed most in a region-blighted by water shortages, it seemed, was fountains, a symbol of defiance in the face of nature. Outside a defunct casino, a plethora of bored soldiers patrolled the empty square, sweat dripping from beneath their saucepan-like caps. The President was due to pass. As the leader of a new-born country, it was of paramount importance that people either have faith in you or fear you, preferably both. As the motorcade receded, though, the *militsiya* quickly melted away. There was cotton candy to be had from the babushkas in shady Panfilov Park.

PART I

CHAPTER 1

A Brief Background

W hen I told people I wanted to visit Central Asia, their first question was invariably 'where?' shortly followed by 'why?' Whilst neighbouring Afghanistan has become notorious, albeit as a barren wasteland where ill-conceived wars endlessly rage, twenty-five years after emerging from under the Soviet yoke, Central Asia remains an enigma, an area shrouded in mystery that people struggle to locate on maps. Even after I explained my reasons, most people's comprehension hit a brick wall after Kazakhstan. The size of Western Europe, Kazakhstan has only marginally wormed its way into the Western consciousness due to newsfeeds referencing its vast oil and gas reserves. So that was where I was going then, Kazakhstan.

Hailing from the graveyard suburb of Enfield, North London, a street market and festival trader at the time - largely because I can't abide having a boss - I've always had the propensity to become obsessed by off the beaten track places with bizarre histories. For nigh on a decade it had been Laos and Myanmar; now it was Central Asia.

A land of nomadic horsemen peopled by the descendants of Jenghiz Khan's Great Horde and a single nation of Persians, during the nineteenth century the once hugely important Silk Road states became a pawn in the so-called Great Game of expansion and espionage between Britain and Russia. With Afghanistan left as a buffer state separating these two empires, the rest of the region soon fell to Russia, disappearing for over a century behind what would become known as the 'Iron Curtain.'

The advent of the Russian Revolution of 1917 saw Central Asia's fortunes further reduced. Cloaked in the language of advancement and liberation, this second wave of imperialism followed the typical Soviet blueprint. Rubbing salt into the wounds, the Kyrgyz capital Pishpek - now Bishkek - was renamed Frunze after the locally born Bolshevik General who subdued parts of the region. Dushanbe would become Stalinabad, most large streets becoming Karl Marx Avenue and public spaces Lenin Square.

Closed off by Stalin from the thirties until his death in 1953 - even to the Soviet people - Central Asian's were made sedentary by a structuralism which saw nomadic traditions as random and backwards. Ruthlessly forced into communes known as *kolkhoz*, millions died, mostly as a result of starvation. Further degradations were to follow when the territory was reopened somewhat under Khrushchev's 'Virgin Lands' agricultural policy in 1954. As local experts predicted, nothing would grow, the desert soil simply blowing away.

Still the Soviets remained, bringing healthcare, education, greater gender equality, limited infrastructure and economic security as a counterbalance to their indiscretions. With the collapse of the Soviet Union in 1991, however, in most cases against their will, five new countries emerged from the husk of the last great empire: Kazakhstan, Kyrgyzstan, Tajikistan, Turkmenistan and Uzbekistan. Propelled to the centre of a new Great Game by a combination of their strategic location and the discovery of extensive oil and gas reserves, since independence Central Asia has seen one bloody civil war, two revolutions and seven dictators, one of who presided over arguably the most fully formed cult of personality the world has ever seen. For a keen student of history, or of the absurd, Central Asia has much to offer.

So in the summer of 2012, I head out with my brother, Stan, to explore these lands of breathtaking scenery, spectacular monuments, despots and crushing poverty. Scribbling down my first impressions, little did I realise that I'd keep returning for years to come, as travelling to a desert sea, a collapsed gas rig dubbed the 'Gate to Hell' and along the 'Heroin Highway' atop the roof of the world, I sought to unearth the stories of the people and places behind this fascinating region.

Shoestring Gorge

With Stan's luggage not forthcoming, our initial plans were soon revised. As we pulled away from Bishkek's west bus station in a shared taksi early next morning, every last hue of colour was sucked from the land, the capital unnaturally green by comparison. Obscured by clouds of dust, emaciated women with babies clutched tight to their breasts stood at roadside yurts, their stands teeming with plump pomegranates and watermelons.

In the first village outside of Bishkek, comprised of a thin strip of corrugated shipping containers surrounded by achromatised boulders, we picked up a family who crammed their possessions into the car. A kettle, two blankets, three cardboard boxes and a pushchair with a wheel missing were loaded under the watchful eye of an underemployed shopkeeper. After a few attempts at slamming the boot shut, a string solution sufficed and we were off. With babushka in the front, us, mother, father, son and a wailing infant in the back, over-encumbered we limped along the one lane highway. Quickly asleep, the teenage son rest his head upon my shoulder.

Adjusting his Champions League Football cap, our driver twirled the silica diamond encrusted gearstick with his thumb, the asphalt ahead of us shimmering like an oily mirage. The Kyrgyz flag - an airbrushed red and gold Soviet relic revamped - flapped against the cracked windscreen festooned with fluffy dice. Every automobile, it appeared, had a cracked windscreen.

Away from the highway, parched farmland spread out, melting into the horizon. In the yards of mud-walled compounds, men were piling up mounds of dung cakes, fuel for the coming winter freeze. Weaving our way past a jaywalking puppy and a broken down lorry, we passed a goat market. With business winding down before noon, unsold animals were being reluctantly herded back into giant wire cages. Rising farther into the mountains, white markers like gravestones lined the road. In a gorge at the bottom of a blind corner lay a glut of shattered vehicles.

Three hours into the journey, we pulled over at a truck stop diner, the Kyrgyz equivalent of a Denny's or a Little Chef. The windblown grit of

Shoestring Gorge stinging like mosquito bites, all around bulldozers were busy carving a wider artery for Chinese imports. Spray paint not having made it here yet, adverts and graffiti were daubed in matt emulsion on the scrub beige hillsides.

Deciding to give the food a miss, I headed for the toilets. Behind a crumbling wall, a line of grinning men were hunkered down, shitting in a ditch. It was three Kyrgyz som for the privilege. The three som coin might well have been invented specifically for *tua-let* wallahs standing guard over these reeking holes. As I'd come to discover, getting change was a bitch.

Cholpon Ata

Dropped in the middle of I didn't know where, we dragged our bags along, chalky white clouds rising in our wake. The search for a homestay leading only to packs of dogs, eventually a chestnut brown-eyed young man with a broad, round face took pity on us.

'*Zdravstvuyte!*' he greeted us with a mild, vodka-fuelled enthusiasm.
'*Vy govorite pa-Russki, da?*'
'*Niet* Russki,' Stan and I chorused.
'Niet Russki?' he echoed, the smile slipping from his face as his interest waned. 'Uh…*nomir*… ruhm,' he proffered, placing his hands together to form a pillow upon which he lay his head.

At the homestay, where the owners two-wheeled Lada sat elevated upon stacks of bricks, the standard response to not understanding the language was in full swing; the bristling moustachioed grandpa repeating the same phrase ever louder. Finally conceding that this approach was doomed to fail, he drew the sun and the moon in the dirt with a stick and rotated his outstretched arm round and round until the penny dropped.

'Three nights,' I answered, holding up my fingers.

We were staying in Cholpon Ata, literally translated as 'Venus Father,' birthplace of the black plague which fleeing Genoese traders had carried all the way to Europe, wiping out sixty percent of the population. Those rats really knew how to party. A donkey munching garbage marked the beginning of the muddy trail to the lakeside beach. Dotted along the track, old women recumbent on blankets knit woolly socks to sell, ramshackle huts with peeling walls offering inflatables, misshapen melted ice creams, buckets, spades and bottles of vodka.

On the burning sand as coarse as glass, raucous, pot-bellied Russians stood greased up and bronzing evenly. Each tourist crammed into their allotted inches in parallel lines as close to the shore as possible, to sit for these Russian sunbathers was a sign of weakness. The freezing waters of Lake Issyk- Köl - 'Lake Naturally Warm' - presented no challenge to these hardened souls. Some were used to the Siberian tundra, where they'd chisel their way through the ice for a morning dip.

Along the beach, oxidised, burnt out rubbish bins which doubled as barbeques spilt empty bottles and watermelon rinds onto the brown grass and sand. Obscured by *shashlyk* fumes - grilled meat on a stick, the national and regional delicacy - camel and eagle hawkers lazily patrolled this Kyrgyz Blackpool, looking for, but failing to find novelty seekers. Outsized umbrellas lining the water's edge, children frolicked in the shallows on splintered wooden pedalos, like park benches on giant skis. The dazzling sun reflecting off the rippling, expressionless expanse, ominous clouds sat immovable atop the dark, enveloping peaks.

The lightly salted Lake Issyk-Köl, riviera of Central Asia, sits at sixteen hundred metres, ringed by the four thousand metre plus Tian Shan Range, the 'Celestial Mountains.' In 1998, courtesy of the Canadian-owned Kumtor gold mine - the country's largest and practically only industry - two tonnes of sodium cyanide had found its way into the Barskoon River which feeds Issyk-Köl. Bleaching powder was dumped in as the solution. These days the lake doubles as a torpedo testing site for the Russian and Indian Navies. The Indians are particularly keen; it being a closed environment they can collect their missiles and recycle them.

With noon approaching, lunchtime was upon us, vendors at their grills donning Stetsons and knock off wrap-around Ray-bans. Fanning the flames with sheets of cardboard, they sharpened their knives and flashed grins, beautiful as their gold teeth caught the sun. Only poor relations had silver teeth, or worse still their own decaying, yellowed teeth. They were truly to be pitied.

Swathed in the billowing emissions escaping from square Soviet ZIL 130 trucks which thundered through the one road town, we chowed down on a layered cake of cold white rice, raw potato, egg and mayonnaise and a bowl of oily french fries swimming in ketchup. Scooping up a lump from my plate, I offered it to a hungry, sad-eyed tripod mongrel that was hovering underneath our table. Tail between its legs, it fled with a mournful yelp.

In this holiday getaway, after lunch if not before, it was without fail vodka time. It aided digestion and much-needed forgetfulness. Like a sugary Eurovision soundtrack on a loop, Russian pop poured from the bars speakers. Occasional forays into Western music were even more horrific; the singing DJ's rendition of "Tears in heaven" could have made the angels weep.

'Kazakhstan? *Ot* Kazakhstan!' the DJ-Compare cried with a false bonhomie as he moved onto hosting a Miss Central Asia pageant in miniature.

The losers looked resigned to their fate, their drunk and angry boyfriends less so.

Having imbibed a healthy dose of Baltika Seven lager, I tottered off to the toilets, where a bowl haired man blocked my path.

'Where from?' he began.
'England. *Angliya*. London,' I replied.
'Ah, Olympics!' he rejoined, a wide smile spreading across his boyish, freckled face.

The Olympics were hugely popular. Unfortunately, I hadn't watched a single event.

Through a process of rudimentary sign language, we were invited to join Tilek, his friend Tilek and their curvaceous dates, Cholpon and Bululu. It was the two Tilek's birthdays, both of whom were turning thirty-two. One Tilek wore a shell suit top, the other the matching trousers. It was a popular look. Perhaps they'd bought one outfit and were sharing it; you rarely saw the whole get up on one person.

Tilek Abdulaev worked as a driver at the Kumtor gold mine; beyond that he didn't want to talk about his job. As I'd come to discover, to say that the mine was a touchy subject which solicited volatile reactions was to put it mildly. He'd once had a large family based around Cholpon Ata, Tilek told me, but as the years went by, one by one they'd moved away in search of gainful employment.

'One of my brothers, he is very clever, now he works on building site in Russia. Many of my relatives go to Bishkek, but no work there,' he concluded.

Weary of this depressing subject, Tilek ordered another bottle. I'd read that the Kyrgyz were the most laid back of the Central Asian people and I would learn that this was true. In many cases, they were Muslim-lite, for although if pushed they spoke of having one hand on the Quran, in the other hand they were waving around a drink whilst laughing boisterously. It being rude not to finish an opened bottle, which always had the lid thrown away, the vodka terrorism continued late into the night, toast after toast being required.

'May you live a hundred years,' I slurred, raising my glass and sticking to the Soviet classics.
'A good toast,' Tilek number two responded, a metallic brightness in his eyes; 'but no,' he added, shaking his head and unleashing a disarming smile, 'ninety years is enough.'

In the main hall, Russian and Kazakh tourists shoulder danced, the rest of their bodies remaining perfectly still. Mushroom cuts were clearly in fashion; nearly everybody had one, including a large proportion of the ladies.

> 'Our Kyrgyz women so beautiful, no?' Tilek number one repeatedly asked me over the blasting music, indicating his girlfriend with the aid of her linguistic skills.
> '*Da*,' I agreed, though she looked more like a bowl of plov than the Goddess of Love incarnate.

At this juncture, things got hazy. I have a vague recollection of being dropped off in a jalopy stuffed with the six of us as dogs set each other off for another all night howling session. Rolling off Cholpon's lap, I stumbled away with promises to meet in the morning for what their miming led me to believe would be some sort of dirt bike adventure.

Boris and the Mountain

Awaking bleary eyed at one PM, the scratchy writing in my notebook confirmed our missed rendezvous and my wallet told me I'd paid a fair chunk of the bill. Exiting the homestay in urgent need of water, I ran straight into a local named Boris. Like all of the vodka casualties in town, the question I'd asked myself the first time Boris approached me was: is that red-faced man coming at me with grievous intent or just staggering in my general direction?

Boris lived in a rusted railroad car hemmed in by abandoned, roofless shacks at the bottom of a boulder-strewn mountain. Unfinished building projects littered the land. The intentions were good, the finances and the will less solid. Taking me in a bear hug, Boris flew straight into his word soup. He wasn't going to let the fact that he knew I couldn't comprehend a single word deter him. A cloud of flies surrounding us, we did the ritual three-minute handshake, his monologue broken only by my futile interjections of 'niet Russki.'

With Stan emerging from the homestay to rescue me from Boris's grasp, we set out to ascend a massif to the north of town, hoping to get a better look at what we presumed to be a weather station, but may have been some bizarre ex-Soviet military installation. A third of the way up, though, in a gulch filled with empty beer cans, Stan doubled over holding his stomach.

'Oh, my guts!' he cried, inching back down the slope with an awkward, clenched gait.

To the receding cries of Boris and a tuneless muezzin in the turret of the local mosque, through a series of dead ends, I finally reached the summit. At the pinnacle of the jagged ridge, all you could hear were distant dogs barking excitedly; the view of tiny plumes of smoke rising up from myriad shashlyk grills all over town. I may have been none the wiser as to what the installation that had piqued my interest was, but I did discover a surprising array of discarded knickers up there.

Bridging the Kyrgyz-Kazakh border, thirty kilometres north lay the micronation of Hasanistan. Founded in 2011 by self-declared dictator Hasan Çakar, Hasanistan claims to be the successor state to the Great Seljuk Empire. Since its declaration of statehood, the enclave has seen largely unremitting turmoil due to an ongoing power struggle between Çakar and his ally Shady Morsi and the Sufi Legion, the so-called 'Hasani Mujahedeen.' Despite this, the authorities are looking to expand their territorial claims into Bahrain and Algeria. As of October 2016, the micronation has declared itself a constitutional monarchy, the Imperial State of the Empire of Pavlov, Shahdom of Hasanistan and Rum under the rule of Iskander IV of Pavlov. It's possible to submit an application for citizenship via their government BlogSpot should one feel the urge.

A purple sky settling over the distant Tien Shan at sunset, distant thunder rumbled, threatening rain which would never arrive. Completing my descent to Cholpon Ata in the dark, back at the homestay I found Stan getting stoned behind the outhouse with two teenage boys who, though eager to share their weed, boasted not a word of English between them. The act in itself provided a universal language.

Back to Bishkek

Travelling through grazed red peaks, the corroded cages of graves cast in the shape of yurts lined the highway, melding nomadic tradition with the Hanafi Muslim faith. They knew how to take a theme and run with it. Weaving in and out of the middle of the road as we overtook in dead man's lane, our marshrutka repeatedly avoided high-speed collisions by a matter of millimetres. It kept the journey interesting.

Gridlock and a cacophony of horns welcomed us back to Bishkek, the city's name meaning 'the ladle that beats the mare's milk until it ferments.' Toward the end of the nineteenth century, the mildly alcoholic uber-sugary mare's milk drink *kumis* had a strong enough reputation for its medicinal qualities to support a cottage industry of 'kumis cure' resorts. Tolstoy and Chekhov were amongst those to try the treatment. Long-suffering from tuberculosis, Chekhov drank four bottles a day for two weeks, gaining twelve pounds, but no cure.

Tailed by taksi drivers at the west bus station, we endeavoured to find out about the marshrutka to Shymkent, Kazakhstan, but at each new window, we met with the same response.

'Da, da, Shymkent,' they'd nod indifferently, directing us back to the counter from which we'd just come.

Giving up on the bus station of misinformation, we instead tried to get a ride back to our accommodation; more difficult than anticipated considering the gaggle of drivers. Pointing at the desired location on a map proved futile. All cabbies were map illiterate. Never available during Soviet times, maps were a new phenomenon. Navigation in Central Asia was still about naming a well-known landmark near your destination; if there didn't happen to be one, well that was tough.

Eventually, we got lucky, the fourth driver understanding at the sixth attempt where we were trying to go.

'Da, da, EAST bus station,' he roared, repeating what Stan had been saying for the last ten minutes, but with more conviction.

Across the grid of concrete blocks and statues, leafy parks and marigolds planted on traffic islands added a splash of colour. A conversationalist, seeing that we didn't speak any Kyrgyz or Russian, our driver delighted in telling us the name of every street we passed.

'Shevchenko, Manas, Erkindik, Prospektesi, Soviet!' he bellowed.

Sipping a drink at dinner that night, I chanced upon a copy of The *Times of Central Asia*, an English-language newspaper produced by an Italian-born businessman, proprietor of the *Adriatico Paradise* Restaurant. The only country in the region to wear more than a modest shroud of democracy, Kyrgyz politics is still an incendiary cocktail of clans and vested interests riven by a north-south divide. Whilst President Atambayev was in talks with the leaders of Azerbaijan, Kazakhstan and Turkey about future regional prosperity, the Kyrgyz government, it transpired, had collapsed on the day we'd arrived. The government's official website was offline, having been brought down by a group identifying itself only as 'Group PHhack.'

Chaos seemed to be in store. Demonstrators - most likely bussed into Bishkek and paid off by rival elites - had stormed the Embassy of Belarus demanding the extradition of former President Kurmanbek Bakiev, who was now living in exile in Minsk. This was the same man protesters had been plied with vodka to storm the decidedly grey White House and put in and then ousted in a second reportedly psychotropic enhanced revolution. Just months later, they voted his cronies back in again.

Recently unveiled outside parliament, a new monument to those that died during the second revolution portrayed youthful figures pushing away a dark mass to leave only the light, but in Kyrgyz politics, nothing was as simple as black and white. Shortly after we left Bishkek, parliamentary proceedings ground to a halt amidst allegations that a member of the Ata-Meken Party had stolen a rival MP's son's bicycle. The ritual slaughter of seven sheep in a bid to drive evil spirits from the building appeared to have failed.

Heading back to the city centre, accompanied by the belch-like 'burfph' of militsiya sirens, the President's motorcade whizzed past us. Lingering in Ala-Too Square, we watched the famed light show and dancing fountains. Half of the lights were broken and the jets of water which worked "danced" out of time for a full six minutes.

Around the square, animated locals were showing off their prize peacocks, pigeons and rabbits. Long-legged, raven-haired beauties in short sequinned dresses paraded up and down the *ulitsa*. Slouched on eiderdowns, old ladies attempted to sell their trinkets and mementoes. For a som, you could weigh yourself on your choice of scales which rows of peddlers manned, or for a whopping ten som, you could go for the luxury of new-fangled talking scales.

This was the place to dust off your blades, myriad roller-skaters whooshing around. Awed pedestrians threw three som coins at the tallest man in Kyrgyzstan, a sorry, deformed figure measuring maybe six feet nine. In shows of strength that never lasted long, men hung from gymnastic high bars, counting the seconds until gravity inevitably defeated them.

In season, this was the city of brides, identikit weddings everywhere. The yurt-shaped World War II monument in Victory Square was a particularly popular spot, couples queuing for their moment at the eternal flame, which served the dual purpose of keeping drunks from freezing to death in the winter.

Wedding receptions involved a stroll around funfair filled Panfilov Park and a stick of candy floss, snow white brides standing out against the gaudy colours of the Climbing Wall, Toy Town Train and a Shooting Range filled with eager young boys. After dark, laughing or grimacing new brides in puffy gowns were to be photographed for posterity striking old-school electronic punch bags along Prospect Street. Weddings were so popular and found in such abundance that I had to wonder how many of the brides were kidnapped.

Simpler than courtship and circumventing the bride price, *Ala-Kachuu* – 'take and flee' - is a ritual form of bride kidnapping prevalent throughout much of Central Asia. The Soviets having done what they could to destroy local identity, debate rages as to the ethnographic roots of the practice, but what is certain is that it's on the increase.

Whisked away on horseback, or these days more likely stuffed into the back of a car by the prospective groom, future in-laws then try to calm the girl and coax her into putting on the *jooluk*, the white wedding shawl of submission. Whilst the waters are muddy as the appellation covers both abduction and elopement, the *New York Times* conservatively estimates that over half of Kyrgyzstan's married women were snatched from the street by their husbands, hence the adage 'every good marriage begins in tears.'

Back at Gulnara's Nomad Home, the luggage shenanigans continued.

'To-mor-row,' the voice at the end of the telephone line brusquely stated before the receiver slammed down.

Emerging from behind the yurt, the elder Gulnara - Gulnara Major – informed us that our reservation for Independence Day had been cancelled.

'Maybe for you sleep on ground outside?' she smiled. 'You have tent?'

Shoving us from her path, meanwhile, the teenage Gulnara - Gulnara Minor - was huffing and puffing about having to bring a guest a blanket.

Leaving her to her sullen mood, a wave of trapped heat struck me as I entered the yurt. It was time for a quick cold shower before the water ran out. Early next morning, we would set off for the Ala-Tau Mountains.

CHAPTER 2

The Rat-Sick Hut

We rose at the crack of dawn, but regrettably, our driver didn't. Only two hours behind schedule, though, we were on our way, the once whitewashed breezeblocks of Bishkek's outskirts fanning out as we ascended past donkey carts, leaving the screeching traffic behind.

At the Alplager, foot of the Ak-Say Canyon leading to the Korona Glacier, numerous thinly trodden paths wound their way into the mountainside, the only problem being that there were no signposts and no one to ask. After a few false starts, we found a weathered babushka in the sole building and asked her. Giving us a look somewhere between bemusement and suspicion, she turned her back and teetered off down an unlit corridor. Some moments later, she returned with an old man wearing the tallest *kalpak* - the traditional Kyrgyz felt hat designed to resemble a peak from the Tien Shan Mountain Range - I had ever seen.

'Ak-Say?' Stan asked, indicating the myriad trails.

The whitebeard screwed up his wizened face into a ball of incomprehension.

'Ak-Say?' Stan ventured again, pointed towards a footpath and making a walking motion with his fingers.

Grandpa's face settled into a blank canvas. We were clearly deranged.

'Ak-Say?' Stan enquired for the third time.
'Ah, *Ak-Say!*' the old man yawped, repeating exactly what Stan had been saying.

Breaking into a smile which lifted his flat cheekbones, he waved his arm in a general direction. Repetition appeared to help.

We'd been told by a bloke from northern England called Andy that this trek was 'a cakewalk.'

'From the Ratsek hut, there's a really easy glacier,' he'd said. 'You could do it in an hour in yer sandals.'

Unfortunately, as we were later to discover, Andy was a professional mountaineer who'd led expeditions up K2.

With this unbeknownst to us, we set off towards the Ratsek hut at Base Camp One, climbing steeply eastwards towards the peaks. It all began pleasantly enough, the air cool and fresh, a thin, white stream rippled over grey boulders at the foot of the valley. Pines covered the hillsides, wild lupines, sky blue cornflowers and redcurrants peeking from beneath the mottled pink tips of tawny grass to soak in the brilliant sunlight. Within a couple of hours, however, it became abundantly clear that stocking up on so many provisions - our bags weighing twenty-five kilos a pop – hadn't been a good idea. Stan's replacement rucksack from the TSUM Centre already starting to disintegrate, his new boxers from the underground bazaar were fraying at the seams as they chafed.

The trail deteriorating into a death-trap of ancient, twisted, sheer rock faces, slippery gravel ledges less than thirty centimetres wide separated us from precipitous drops. I've trekked over the Himalayas, but there's trekking and then there's climbing. This was climbing. On top of this, having not seen a soul since the Alplager, we didn't even know if we were going in the right direction.

With the sun setting behind the silhouette of a ridge, it was too late to turn back.

'We're going to die out here,' I moaned melodramatically, apprehension in the pit of my stomach as I hauled my dust-caked form ever onward.

Vegetation thinning as we rose through a veil of mist, I was beginning to lose all hope when three figures appeared on the horizon, steaming down the mountainside and leaving clouds in their wake.

'Ratsek hut?' I panted at the first two, who completely ignored me.
'Rat sick?' the third one replied without stopping. 'Twenty minutes.'

Swooshing his waist-length dreadlocks, he turned to toss a trekking pole at me.

'Give this to Imfi. The guy with the big backpack,' he shouted, before vanishing below a rapidly darkening crag.

Finally emerging onto a plateau surrounded by frozen escarpments, a trickling rill surrounded by a slither of green cut a swathe through the rocks. With me barely crawling at the rear of our party of two, we arrived at the Ratsek hut an hour later. Beyond the tin-roofed lean-to, last vestige of civilisation, a moonscape led to ice fields and snow-capped peaks.

Shown into the basic dorm by a surly teenager, we dumped our packs down.

'Tua-let?' I asked him.

Taking a break from our papers - which he couldn't read – the blotchy, jaundiced-looking boy indicated a track leading over a sharp incline obscured by mist, which plummeted to a dilapidated metal outhouse on stilts tilting precariously over the edge of a cliff. Garnering after a few attempts that we could speak no Russian, running a hand across his mousy buzz-cut, our welcoming party decided we weren't worth the effort. Losing interest and discarding our permits on the floor, with a tut and a frown he melted away.

'Imfi?' I asked a couple of Russians wreathed in buckles, expensive ropes, North Face fleece jackets and insulated pants, but they just looked at me like I was mad. The guidance I'd been given – 'the guy with the big backpack' - proved useless; everyone had a large bag, all stuffed to the brim with hardcore alpine gear.

Directed to a plyboard shed, the tourist manager offered us a warming cup of Kyrgyz tea - *chay*. A broad-shouldered, middle-aged German, he'd been staying at the Ratsek hut for three-month stints for many years. Still clinging to the idea of scaling the glacier the next morning despite our aching muscles, I enquired as to which ascent was the easiest. Looking mightily confused, he asked his comrades, who were equally dumbfounded. Arms shooting out in various directions, evidently this wasn't going to work.

Our stilted conversation turned to buzkashi, *Ulak Tyrtysh* in Kyrgyz, the traditional, but notoriously difficult to track down Central Asian horseback sport which roughly translates as 'goat grabbing' due to the fact that a headless goat, the *buz* is used as the ball.

'Yah, I went once many years ago,' said the German, his voice tapering off as he and his colleagues returned to staring into space, a pastime at which they were particularly adroit. Perhaps from the constant lack of oxygen, they glazed over as if naturally stoned.

Our search for buzkashi had begun in Bishkek some days ago at a Tourist Information Centre which had no information. Passed up the food chain, we ultimately graduated to the manager's office.

'Maybe buzkashi, maybe not,' the stout woman decked in a leather jacket despite the heat shrugged from behind her desk. 'I don't know,' she added, shaking her crimped black hair, 'I stay at home.'

In search of the elusive goat, we were variously told that the games would definitely be on and most assuredly wouldn't be. They'd be held on Thursday or Friday, starting at ten in the morning or in the evening. We both would and wouldn't require advance tickets. Attempts to glean any nuggets of wisdom regarding Independence Day festivities in general were equally unproductive. Replies ranged from there'd be a parade, but no one knew when, to Independence Day had been cancelled altogether this year.

Back at Base Camp One, long-horned, bearded ibex had gathered on a bluff to inspect the humans. With the light failing, the mountains briefly glowed blood orange, before the forms of the goats turned to silhouettes and the valley was lost to shadows. The air biting, the temperature fell below zero by seven PM. Retiring to the dorm, we broke out the vodka. With no heat or electricity, it would be a long, cold night in the pitch darkness of the canyon.

Rising at dawn from the wooden bunks unfestooned by mattresses, our stiff muscles made it known there would be no ascent of the glacier. Five hours later, soaked in perspiration and utterly shattered, we emerged at the Alplager to the scene of some sort of sports day taking place, grandmas and grandpas gleefully foot-racing around chay yurts. Given the sheer descent, the trekking pole I'd gained had proved to be a godsend. Falling flat on his arse repeatedly, the bruised and battered Stan hadn't been so lucky.

Back at Gulnara's, Andy asked how it had gone.

'Fookin' 'ell,' he cried at our explanation. 'It's just as well yer didn't try for the glacier.'

The Raid

Stan's luggage having theoretically been located still stuck at the airport in London, we headed to the National Telecoms Office in an attempt to expedite its arrival. Inside the crumbling Soviet monolith, rows of bored, starch-permed women in matronly uniforms sat in airless cubicles behind smudged glass. Notwithstanding their underemployment, however, it remained difficult to get served. A case of seizing the moment or losing out, appearing from nowhere there was always someone ready to stealthily shoehorn themselves in front of you at the window. If that didn't work, they'd find a vantage point, a chink of light between you and the counter from which to talk over you.

An hour and a half later, unable to procure enough change for the duration of the call, Stan exited the phone booth none the wiser.

'I just kept getting cut off,' he sighed.

Jostling through a stifling bazaar situated in an underpass, old women blew smoke from bunches of burning herbs into our faces, an ancient rite said to ward off *Koz Moichok*, the evil eye. Escaping their outstretched hands, we emerged onto Chuy Prospektesi, ambling past statues of idealised workers, fictional heroes from epic poems and a rifle-toting man riding a bull. Opposite the main square, two guards ready to protect the honour of the Kyrgyz flag stood marooned and motionless in glass cases, like tiny mechanical men waiting to be wound. Adorned in thigh-high, shiny leather boots, skinny black ties and outsized hats, when their shifts ended, they goose-stepped away in slow-motion.

Vying for meagre scraps of business, sketch artists and photographers with bulky vintage cameras stood ready and willing, boards displaying their work filling the pavements. Street vendors with wooden trays hung from their sunburnt necks hawked sweets, glue and single cigarettes. Their hands fixed upon each other's shoulders, pubescent boys slurping Shoro from plastic cups perambulated aimlessly.

Peddled on every intersection from red and blue barrels emblazoned with a handlebar moustachioed man in a pilot's cap who seemed to have stepped straight out of the thirties, Shoro came in a choice of two flavours. *Chalap* Shoro was essentially sour fizzy milk, whilst *Maksym* Shoro was an interesting sparkling bread based drink.

Across the street in Dubovy Park, elderly women in headscarves and floor-length gowns waddled past a Lenin statue which pointed to the ether dreaming of better days. Moved from Ala-Too Square - formerly Lenin Square - he had initially been replaced by the fictional character Erkindik, who represented freedom. A voluptuous winged creature in a flowing gown perched upon a globe, Erkindik held aloft a tunduk, the circular frame that forms the top of a yurt. She, in turn, was dislodged in 2011, some Kyrgyz believing that a woman holding a tunduk would awaken the evil eye. Now a statue of Manas, the national folk hero from the epic poem sits there astride his trusty steed, covered in birds and caked in shit.

Languishing in permanent shade in its current less glamorous location, this was the last Lenin monument on a grand scale remaining in Central Asia. In nearby Oak Park, a sculpted Marx and Engels sat upon a bench debating the nuances of dialectical materialism, Marx's hand firmly planted upon Engel's chiselled butt. Senior citizens in tall felt kalpak hats emblazoned with rams' horn motifs lounged upon low walls beside them, cracking sunflower seeds between their teeth and grinning blankly.

'Zdravstvuyte,' they slurred at us.

They'd been at the hooch, a fine way to sterilise the potential risk of food poisoning. It was a good excuse anyway.

Saddled with the now familiar sensation of diarrhoea about to erupt, we inched a path into Pele, a shady sports bar where the ubiquitous music of the video channel blared from multiple TV screens. Despite the difficulties at other venues, lines at Kyrgyz tua-lets, stretching for what felt like city blocks, were a different animal altogether. Even if the lavatory was obviously occupied as they'd just seen you go in, angry young men would still yank at the flimsily locked door with a blind fury.

'*Atkriyti, ya shrit!*'

You quickly learnt to become more assertive. Here it was kill or be killed, and everyone was firing on all cylinders.

Back at Gulnara's, we joined a group of travellers who were tucking into a crate of *pivo*, the Proto-Slavic word adopted throughout the region for beer. The loudest of the guests by far, gossiping Gertie, a portly twenty-something English girl who'd recently been fired from her job explained the purpose of an establishment which had been something of a mystery to us.

Ambling along the potholed streets to town and back, we'd been passing the Moulin Rouge VIP Club, its consistently locked pearly gates guarded by two fig-leafed, granite Adonises. Curiosity had finally gotten the better of some other travellers, who'd knocked upon the door and been ushered in, only to discover that it was a "Natasha joint" filled with high-class hookers charging 3,200 som a pop.

'Jeez, forget it,' they'd told the Russian madam. 'We'll just buy some beer and snickers for three hundred som instead.'

Everyone was in high spirits at Gulnara's, the alcohol flowing freely until the militsiya poured in through the iron gates.

'*Politsei!*' the Estonian contingent shrieked.
'Da,' the head honcho confirmed, plain clothed yet unmistakable in that manner that only undercover officers can achieve. 'Everybody all tourist?' he asked, all smirking self-importance as he scrutinised the crowd, a lackey with a minicam to hand filming our every move.

The backpackers nodded their heads with a phoney fervour.
The militsiya, it transpired, had come to drag away a bunch of Germans we'd met during our second luggage hunting stop at Gulnara's. Driving from Munich to Bishkek, they'd suffered numerous run-ins with the mercurial Kazakh authorities along the way. Bishkek was the end of the road for them, and they were selling their car before flying home.
Belonging to an exceedingly friendly large boned chap called Hano, one of the sacks of clothes they'd brought to give to needy Kyrgyz had, in the absence of his own, ended up being the rake-like Stan's ill-fitting new wardrobe. Having started out in his own garments before moving into mine and then into Hano's charity cast-offs, by now Stan was having something of an identity crisis.

'Maybe we see you again,' the militsiya commander exclaimed as they left, pointing firstly to his beady black eyes and then to each of us in turn, saving a particular eye-popping glare for Stan.

As my brother sat there in his shapeless, hand-me-down German fugitive clothes, Gossiping Gertie gave her authoritative spin on events. Apparently the police had searched the German's car and found a breadknife stashed in the door lining, which made perfect sense given that they'd been living out of the vehicle and self-catering for the last five weeks. What were they supposed to slice bread with, spoons? It seemed to me that having seen the 'For Sale' sign in the window, the militsiya had taken quite a shine to the mud-spattered Hyundai. They'd no doubt been amongst the tyre kickers looking it over that afternoon.

Independence Day

Independence Day was here at last, a source of great excitement for me, if not so much for the Kyrgyz people, who'd never sought their freedom from Soviet bondage. What had nationhood given them, after all, but the withdrawal of Russian subsidies, revolutions, economic collapse and untold hardships? Unwelcome independence must have felt like being orphaned, the bygone colonial era now looked back upon with nostalgia by the older generation as a golden age. On the noticeboard of Fatboy's Café where we sat for breakfast, a poster advertised a yurt for sale under the heading 'Does it Yurt?' I imagine it did.

A nomadic people forced into a sedentary life by their overlords, the Kyrgyz had been unceremoniously cut adrift, left with only what lay on the ground. A few notoriously dangerous Aeroflot planes - banned from landing at European airports because of their safety record - became the national airline. There was the odd tank and forty mothballed ships slowly eroding on Lake Issyk-Köl, which constituted the landlocked Kyrgyz navy. A century and a quarter after the fall of Pishpek, the Russians, who'd created the arbitrary landmass called the Kyrgyz Republic, were gone. Pinned to the noticeboard, this photograph of a dilapidated yurt for sale felt poignant, emblematic of a past which could never be recaptured.

As the sound of car horns began to rise with the heat of the day, we set off in search of the lesser spotted buz. With preparations for Independence

Day celebrations well underway, the city centre was blocked off by barricades, trolleybus cables hanging limp and redundant. The driver of the neon blue toy train which normally circumnavigated Bishkek's streets during daylight hours was rather put out by the detour he was being asked to make. Disgruntled, he sat there with his arms folded, stubbornly refusing to budge.

We stopped for a bottle of water, but this as did every transaction, led to a prolonged process of procuring change. From taksi rides to cigarettes, dorm beds to meals, it was always the same. Anyone who had precious change would hoard it with a maniacal zeal. Small change was worth more than the noughts printed on banknotes.

Along Chuy Prospektesi, tweenies proudly swigging pivo were the first to be seen staggering. It was ten AM. In Dubovy Park, drained bottles lay discarded beneath oak trees in the long, unkempt grass beside a waterless fountain. *Gamburger* pitches - a burger, but not as we know it, more like a kebab - and *got-dog* stalls were springing up on the kerbside. (There is no 'h' in Russian, it being replaced by a 'g.') Games of *ordo* had begun, the aim being to throw a goat's knee bone, the *alchik* at som notes weighted to the road by stones; a bit like a fairground coconut shy. To the yelps of unfortunate bystanders being struck by the bone, they played with great gusto, but not much skill.

In Ala-Too Square, troupes of dancers in flowing red and gold gowns and tall domed hats emerged from the dressing yurt and took to the stage. Moving with poise and grace to traditional music, they glimmered in the bright morning sunlight. Despite the feverish build-up given them by the two Eurovision style presenters, however, they and the performers which followed were greeted with a deafening silence. Even the Russified pop acts met with this fate, each descending from the stage without so much as a ripple of appreciation. Outside of planes, applause was not the Kyrgyz way.

Leaving the festivities behind, we reached the far end of the barricades and set about looking for a taksi to the horse games at the Hippodrome, but no one would drive there. When they worked out where we were trying to go, driver's eyes widened, filling with fear at the thought of the tailbacks before they sped away. It clearly wasn't going to happen. Having seen what we presumed to be the Hippodrome on a map in the Tourist Office a week before, we decided - given no other option - to walk in the vague direction we believed it to be.

It was thirty-eight degrees Celsius in the shade as we walked through the shadeless city and on into the sprawling suburbs. Gradients of Lada, from wrecks to souped-up, tinted windowed racing machines with streamlined spoilers idled on the humid streets. The farther from the centre one travelled, the more ramshackle things became, neglected Soviet era high-rises lifting from piles of trash scattered by the desperate looking for food or things to sell. Abandoned factories with broken windows decayed in overgrown yards, vehicle parts corroding in the dead yellow grass.

We'd been traipsing for twelve kilometres beneath a cloudless sky, the top of my head starting to blister when we heard the faintest whisper of what sounded like cheering. Lumbering towards the noise, we reached a fence. Through cracks in the wood, there was the Hippodrome, its flags fluttering gently. The roar of the crowd - tantalisingly close, yet still so far away - told us that the games were on; and they were good.

Following the perimeter for another hour of heatstroke-induced delirium, we eventually reached the fabled white arches of the Bishkek Hippodrome. It was a beautiful moment. There was even some tree cover, for which we didn't have time to linger.

This being a ticket free affair, we shambled into the main arena. For an event nobody could tell you anything about, there were sure a lot of people there, a heaving throng of rowdy men in hats made from newspapers quickly turning their attention to us.

'*Sahdytsah*! Sit down!' they jeered.

Unable to see anything standing, let alone seated on the baking concrete steps, I was buggered if I was going to sit.

My view of the backs of heads and yesterday's news was interrupted by a railbird insistently beckoning. The people around us prodding and pointing, indicating that there would be no choice but to go and speak to him, we reluctantly waddled in his direction.

'Where you from?' the shaggy-browed, tracksuit-clad man questioned us through his soup-strainer moustache.
'England. Angliya,' Stan replied.
'Ah, American,' he nodded sagely, flicking a stray piece of meat from his facial hair. 'You want to buy car?'

Given the experience of our German friends, we politely declined.

Coated in a veneer of sweat, with no chance of seeing anything we retired to a dappled spot beneath a tree near the entrance. No sooner were we settled than we had a new friend, Stanbek, who also thought that England was part of America. It was a common misconception.

'How about horse?' he asked, beaming eagerly as he flattened down his bowl of hair.

We gave the thumbs-up of approval.

'Your name?' he asked.
'Stephen,' said I.
'Stan,' said Stan, which sent Stanbek into tremors of ecstasy.
'Like me, like me,' he laughed, doing a little jig.

Stanbek worked as a waiter at the Obama Bar & Grill, an overpriced diner frequented by children of the moneyed classes. Soon after we left, this establishment would find itself challenged by the karaoke stylings of the Putin Pub, in an uneasy local version of wider geopolitics.

With the language barrier ensuring that our conversation was all but exhausted, Stanbek decided to follow us, my search for a better viewpoint leading to a hole in the wire mesh fence behind a militsiya truck. Stan and Stanbek looked worried, but undeterred I clambered through. Passing the stables, I emerged on the side of the bone-dry field of play, where a thin ring of people were situated. This was the vantage point I'd been looking for.

A game popularised by Jenghiz Khan - though his horde preferred to use a human torso for a ball - buzkashi is historically an every man for himself game, the brouhaha of rearing horses sometimes measuring over twenty metres in diameter. The 2001 finals in Dushanbe, Tajikistan left twenty-two dead and hundreds maimed, lying in pools of their own blood as they reportedly grinned madly. Banned by the Taliban, the game has now returned to Afghanistan, whose players -warmly regarded for their bush-league enthusiasm - have been known to carry AK-47's, which although considered vulgar, is not against the rules per se.

Whilst still brutal, the Kyrgyz version, Ulak Tyrtysh was a tamer affair, two teams of four competing to carry the buz around posts before hoisting it into a walled concrete circle; quite a feat considering the cauterised goat carcass weighs some twenty-five kilos.

The stampede producing a great wall of dust, the majority of the game consisted of players decked in old tank helmets preventing their opponents from picking up the buz. A scrum of whips and sweating horses snorting stringy snot, occasionally a horseman would emerge, swinging the goat by a leg. A game of honour not renowned for its recompense, if the carcass were to be the prize, it would at least be well and truly tenderised.

Shortly though, the moment came, a roar rising from the stands as with seven horsemen in hot pursuit, a jockey from the red team emerged from the pack, charging towards us with the buz laid across his steed. With the other riders gaining ground, yanking at the reigns of his mount as they punched and whipped him, the jockey with the precious goat lost control of his horse. Teeth bared, the chargers headed straight for us. The crowd breaking, each fled for their life as the surging animals engulfed us. This was a sport that spectators could get up close and personal with.

Leaving the arena, I turned to see Stan rearing back with a horrified expression as - trainers bringing their horses for the next event - a whinnying stallion's head bore down upon him.

We walked back into town past men lying in bushes, presumably uncon-scious, not dead. In the quads of tower blocks, bag ladies were chuntering at their children. As we ate at the Cyclone Restaurant, an inebriated old-timer teetered like a tightrope walker on the high-wire, mumbled something at me before falling into an *arik* - a deep drainage ditch.

Being the only man in town with anything approaching long hair, I attracted a lot of unwanted attention; except, that was, from waiting staff. For their skills having been learnt from the Russians, the Kyrgyz was not a service economy. There was a singular intensity to the blinkered way in which staff could walk straight past you without even glancing in your direc-tion, no matter how hard you might try. They were masters of the art of looking busy whilst doing absolutely nothing. In addition to this, only the waiter who took your order in the first place would subsequently serve you. Should they go on a break, Allah help you.

The sun setting low behind the mountains, we ploughed into the nucleus of the celebrations, where some power pop was threatening to get the crowd going. At last, it seemed the revellers had something they could sink their teeth into. Having graduated from Speedos into their formal evening wear, shorts that disappeared up the arse crack, a smattering of Russians had joined the locals. Honest men; they left nothing undisclosed.

With the headliner, a balding, suited and booted crooner drawing to a crescendo, the choreographed fountains kicked in, and as a special Independence Day treat, danced for a full ten minutes. Sporadic fireworks sputtering into life, the low eighties synth 'boing boing thwack' of punch bags being struck was the soundtrack for our walk to the Pele. It had been a long, hot day and it was time for a few cold Baltikas, which came in a range of 0, 2, 3, 4, 6, 7, 8 or 9, which I presumed vaguely corresponded to their alcohol content. Sticking with tradition, we chose the seven, stronger than the three, but wiser than the nine.

As the festivities wound down, the bar quickly filled. Behind us, a bespec-tacled teenage girl sat with arms folded, absolutely mortified that a woman with a young boy had gatecrashed her table. Sipping her pivo through a straw, she cast an evil eye at the mother, whose child stared back at her tits.

Flaneuring the night away, we kept a firm grip on our drinks, as the one thing that bar staff were very efficient about was taking your glass away, be it empty or not.

With the time approaching midnight, it occurred to me that there might be a curfew at Gulnara's. A single attempt sufficient for us to grasp that negotiating a taksi would take longer than walking, we scuttled away through the increasingly deserted outskirts. Still lit up like a grounded UFO, silhouetting men as they reeled away, the circus on Frunze Street cast an unnatural glow across the poorly lit city's open sewers. In our befuddled state, I persuaded Stan we should take a shortcut through *microrayon* thirty-two, the sub-district now filled by the sprawling Hyatt Hotel. It was a bad idea. Half an hour later we were still circling forlornly around the umbrellas on the veranda, the starch-suited night guard presuming us to be guests and saluting us in military style with each pass.

Our concerns had been well founded, for finally tottering into the darkened alleyway full of feral dogs and abandoned roadworks where Gulnara's was situated, we were greeted by the sight of the tall metal gate resolutely locked before us.

Eight pints of Baltika Seven leave one in a rather sorry state for climbing. I still have the scars to prove it. Leaping, I'd cling to the top struggling to pull myself up, only for gravity to down me over and over.

'You can do it, man,' the disembodied voice of the younger Stan, who'd already hoisted himself over encouraged me.

It was gone one in the morning on the pitch black street, the dogs were closing in and I was pissed up. Realising that it was this or the ditch, with a superhuman effort, I hauled myself onto the top of the gate, tottering perilously for an interminable amount of time. Perched up there, a memory of my first proper job came to me. Working at a water-sports company - though I can't even swim - my boss, Phil had been a West Country farm boy whose life philosophy fused new age ideas with the sickest animal porn imaginable. At a trade fair in Hamburg, having had one drink too many, he'd decided to scale the fence rather than walk the two hundred metres to the exit. Crashing to earth, he'd broken both his legs. As I cautiously lowered myself to the welcoming ground, visions of filthy Phil swam before my eyes.

The next evening we recounted our escapades to a posh, foppish English boy called Richard who was slumming it at Gulnara's.

'Really?' he scoffed. 'Why didn't you just ring the bell?'

Chicken

I'd awoken at six thirty AM to the sight of Stan hugging his rucksack.

'It came!' he cried, unearthing his happy meal bag of pills and potions; 'it came!'

Now it was noon and we were still at the marshrutka station, fleets of vans - mostly Sprinters doubling as buses - spewing dark fumes into the airless air, but rarely moving. Wide-eyed and shouting appeared to be a conversational norm and this held especially true at transport hubs, where tempers quickly spilt over. Throughout Central Asia, if not globally, bus stations brought out the worst in people.

Two and a half hours later, we finally had enough passengers to depart for the border and from there onto Taraz, Kazakhstan. So with my knees crushed up against the seat in front, wedged between two headscarf-clad babushkas who were soon asleep with their noggins resting upon my shoulders, we clattered away from Bishkek.

I had a knack for becoming the meat in the sandwich, ball cupping fat men, old ladies and mothers with inquisitive infants being naturally drawn to me. When we stopped, I'd disembark with sweat patches on my forearms from the close contact.

Swerving violently in the no man's land in the middle of the unmarked asphalt, travelling with the fastest driver on the road had its pros and cons.

On the plus side, you'd reach your destination sooner, assuming you got there at all. It also enlivened the monotonous hours, though it didn't help that the driver had his mobile phone constantly pressed to his ear.

'Ullo? Ullo?'

Some of the overtaking manoeuvres were scarcely believable, breathtaking in their audacity. Veering single-handedly out of a particularly hairy game of chicken, we shaved the paint off the side of an oncoming open back truck overloaded with horses, goats and cows. Tumbling headfirst, my neighbour fell from her chair, landing unceremoniously in the footwell. Unmoved by the experience, she dusted herself off and was shortly asleep again, drooling down my front as she snored. It was par for the course.

The cause of any infrequent slowing was immediately apparent. Only at the sight of militsiya vehicles did we go under 140 kph. The checkpoint soon a bad memory in the rear view mirror, we tore up the flat brown distance once more, hollow silhouettes of the hazy Ala-Tau Mountains haunting us as we left Kyrgyzstan behind.

CHAPTER 3

Inauspicious beginnings

Throwing sparks onto the waiting throng, power lines buzzed above the narrow, prison-like confines of Kazakh immigration. In the stifling, sun-baked queue, giving an inch meant a wave of people shoving past you. Standing my ground, I blocked off any space with my luggage, attempts to scramble over it eventually desisting.

It soon became manifest why locals had been so eager to push in front of us. Kyrgyz and Kazakh citizens not requiring an exit stamp, digging out her underused equipment, the woman at the Kyrgyz border post had stamped the wrong date in my passport. Evidently, we were the first Westerners of the day, but at least she'd cocked it up with a smile, asking to borrow a pen with which to correct her error.

The sign at the cubicle window on the Kazakh side of the border read 'Passport Control Makes Corporal Telemov Termhamedikov.' Obviously Corporal Termhamedikov was nothing without his job. Drowning beneath his ludicrously outsized green felt cap, Comrade Termhamedikov's piercing amber eyes probed me.

'Vy govorit'e pa-Russki!' he demanded.
'Niet Russki,' I replied.
'Russki!' he repeated.
'Niet Russki,' I replied again.
'Niet Russki?' he spluttered in astonishment, aghast at the idea that anyone could possibly not speak the language.

Perplexed by the dust-jacket on my passport, patently Comrade Termhamedikov couldn't fathom my country of origin. Wholly unaware that there was no longer a Kyrgyz visa requirement for many nationalities, even the Kazakh transit visa seemed to confuse him. The disgruntled file of people behind us growing ever longer, he fingered his way back and forth through the dizzying array of stamps, mooching a biro to take notes.

'English cigarette?' he asked weakly, but I didn't have any.

Resignedly, with a gesture akin to defeat, he ushered me through, his disappointment compounded when I indicated that I'd like my pen back.
    Worse was to follow at the green 'Nothing to declare' channel at customs, where the bald, sweaty officer became extremely animated at the sight of my laptop.

'*Komp'yuter!*' he yelled, springing to his feet.

Pot-belly wobbling, he tapped his index finger on the polycrilic countertop, motioning for me to turn the device on.

'Islamic materials?' he hissed, half question, half accusation.

Trawling through folders, he first chanced upon a novel I've been working on, the cover of which is an illustration of a skeleton wearing a General's uniform. He didn't like that one iota.

'Niet! Niet! *Problema!*' he barked disapprovingly, shaking his head, jowls swinging like distended udders as he prodded at the screen.

I scrolled down to show him the text, attempting to explain the nature of the document. Indicating myself, I mimed typing, but his brow just settled into a cavernous frown.
    Striking upon an idea, I pulled a random paperback from my bag to use as a prop.

'Me; *moy*' I said, indicating myself and then the book, before simulating the act of writing.
    'Da,' he responded cagily.

I had the feeling we were making progress.

Opening the novel, the Customs Officer landed upon a photo of its author, a young William Kotzwinkle. Running his fingers over the picture, his obdurate gaze hardened. Not looking a jot like William Kotzwinkle, I was clearly a fraud.

Continuing his inspection, he struck gold, chancing upon a folder filled with downloaded images of Central Asian dictators, military parades and Polygon weapons testing sites. Not having any money on me, I didn't even have the option of offering up a bribe. The Customs Officer babbling furiously at me, both of us were becoming increasingly frustrated.

'Keep calm and keep smiling,' Stan whispered, pulling me to one side.

It was sage advice, if difficult to follow.

Face contorted in suspicion and rage, accepting at length that repeating himself in a language I didn't understand would bear no fruit, sausage fingers thrust his mobile phone at me.

'What is your purpose?' a flat, monotonal voice asked.

I explained that I was a tourist and had a transit visa.

'Huh,' the discarnate man grunted disbelievingly. 'Now pass phone my friend.'

This scenario played itself out four times, on each occasion my account being met with a prolonged silence broken only by static. At the fifth time of asking, the voice at the end of the line became more strident.

'Now I must ask your exact purpose,' he catechised. 'You must tell me truth why you come my country? What you do your country? What is your job? You must tell me everything,' he insisted.

'I'm a tourist and I have a valid transit visa. I'm headed to Uzbekistan. In my country, I'm a market trader. I buy and sell things,' I elucidated.

'Da? Market... bazaar... sell like goat?' he asked, his interest piqued.

'Yes, I sell goats,' I agreed.

'Da, da, da,' he chirped, his tone warming now he had something which fit within his frame of reference.

'I'm also a student,' I lied to account for the photographs. 'I study Asian History and Development with a special emphasis on Central Asia.'

'Da, da,' the voice said. 'Now I speak my friend.'

'Stu-dent. His-to-ry,' the shiny headed Customs Officer repeated, phone pressed to his hairy earlobe, undoubtedly glad that he'd signed up to his provider's unlimited minutes package.

It was at this juncture that a man in a long white thobe with a skullcap and mildew coloured Mullah Omar beard appeared.

'Islamic materials!' the Customs Officer hollered, beckoning him over and vigorously indicating his leather briefcase.

Dismissed with a disparaging wave of the hand, I was quickly forgotten, disappearing as fast as my bag would wheel into the vast, flat emptiness of the Kazakh scrub.

Thankfully, our bus, for which we'd been paid a foreigner surcharge, was still waiting. Time had little value here, it seemed. Crossing the border, the road became the M39 and suddenly even the tumbleweeds were bigger and brasher. Shortly asleep, the babushkas rest their heads upon my clammy shoulders once more. Three more hours, checkpoints permitting, and we would reach our destination.

Wooden Ships

We caught the marshrutka from Taraz to Shymkent, or at least we thought we'd caught it. In hindsight, it was all too quick and easy. Maybe we were tired, perhaps the border crossing had taken its toll, but we should have known better. No bus in Central Asia ever leaves half empty. Yet there we were, barely having had the time to pee behind a rusted fence, on the move once more.

Welcoming us on board, Didar and his chums Tselmeg, Artyom, Can and our driver Chargerman were a jolly bunch.

'Friend, friend,' the round-faced Didar repeated demonstratively, grinning wildly as he made himself heard above the blasting throb of Loreen's Eurovision-winning "Euphoria," which had functioned as the soundtrack to our journey so far.

'Friend, friend...' his buddies mimicked.

'American friend,' Didar added emphatically, showing off his language skills.

'English,' we protested. 'Angliya. London.'

'Ah, London!' he repeated, his face lighting up. 'Rooney! American Olympics.'

It being a commonplace misapprehension that England was part of America, therefore it followed that the 2012 Olympics had taken place in the United States, a mistake I had neither the fortitude nor the will to correct. It'd been a long enough day already, and all I really cared about now was reaching our terminus.

Unfortunately, fifteen minutes into our two and a half hour journey to Shymkent, we pulled off road and drove down a dirt track into a field, where we came to an abrupt halt. We'd grown used to buses stopping for no discernable reason every kilometre or so, but generally speaking this hadn't happened in a furrow on the edge of the steppe in the outskirts of a town where an Islamic extremist had killed seven people just six months before.

Disembarking and motioning for us to do likewise, our hosts sat in the shade of a lone tree. Looking happy as lunatics, they proceeded to point out the various animals that could be seen on the flat brown expanse. On the steppe where they were first domesticated some five and a half thousand years ago, it was apt that we had horses, but there were also pigs.

'Oink! Oink! Friend, ha ha!'

Lambs, cows and goats.

'Baa. Baa,' the acne scared Tselmeg bleated, his gold overbite glinting in the dappled sunlight.

It was an added dose of random.

Whilst this show and tell was going on, Chargerman had gotten back on the bus where our luggage sat and was busy drawing all the curtains. Leaving Stan to the farmyard impressions, I watched over our bags through a chink in the windows.

Seeing that we were getting restless; the bonds of our companionship stretching thin, Didar got an associate on the phone, pressing the device tight to his ear to listen and moving it in front of his mouth when it was time to speak.

'*Pahlavon,*' the ever excitable Didar explained, a term widely used in Asia for wrestlers.

'Olympics,' he added, throwing a strongman pose and intimating his friend on the end of the line as he passed the chunky black Nokia to Stan.

'Mr. Stan? Don't be scared,' a deep, droning voice crackled before the line went dead.

It wasn't the best thing to have said.

With the connection eventually regained, between being told not to be afraid we gathered that we were perhaps waiting to collect some freight, which might be due to arrive in twenty minutes or so.

Two hours later, we were on our way, discovering on a sandy alley on the outskirts of town that our freight was ornately carved wooden model ships;

lots of them. So many that another two hours elapsed as the jigsaw pieces of our delicate cargo were repeatedly loaded, removed and reloaded. At last, as the pink light of evening settled over the land, packed to the rafters we were ready.

The first thing you notice about Kazakhstan is its size. The sweeping emptiness exacerbated by a population of only seventeen million, power pylons broke up a triptych of road, scrub and sky. Occasional silhouettes of distant mountains flitting in and out of view, hours could pass with nothing more to see.

'How is Kazakhstan?' Didar asked every ten minutes, as we weaved our way along unfinished stretches of highway, taking unfailingly ineffectual shortcuts.

We were thirteen hours into our supposedly seven-hour journey, having taken a wrong turn and rumbled along a rut past another of the numerous militsiya checkpoints when the bus broke down.

'Huh,' Didar exhaled. 'The King is dead.'

I don't know if he picked up that snowclone from a movie, but considering he'd only spoken a couple of words in English beforehand, it came as somewhat of a surprise.

The wheezing engine coaxed back to life, ten minutes later we stopped again. My arms crossed in a huff, Stan could see that familiar black look of impatience settling on my face. Clambering back into the front, Didar and Tselmeg turned and smiled broadly.

'Friend,' they chorused, passing us a plastic bag full of succulent Aport apples the size of grapefruits, cold sugary Apple Kok drinks and melting ice creams.

Beneath a moon like a misshapen ball, we juddered on towards Shymkent. Sparks flying from its undercarriage, the marshrutka emitted a sorrowful sound as we ground over concrete barriers on unfinished sections of highway. As many vehicles had no lights, night driving was particularly hazardous. This didn't deter high speed overtaking, though, hence we rumbled past cars so dust-caked it was a wonder their drivers could see at all.

Handed a phone every few minutes, we spoke to a plethora of helpers who attempted to find us a hotel. This was despite the fact that we'd repeatedly said we had specific accommodation in mind; although we'd now be arriving so late we wouldn't have enough Kazakh tenge - pronounced *'den'gi,'* as in the Russian word for money - to pay for the room. We were an event for our new friends, but their kindness was starting to kill me. We'd been on the road for sixteen hours; then we started dropping off the boats.

Circumnavigating ill-lit back roads, delivering our cargo to animated young couples with pushchairs and prams in dusty lay-bys, we stopped in the village of Sayram. Greeted by the cast with whom we'd confabbed on the phone, the colossal wrestler explained that Didar had paid for our ride.

'Friend,' Didar beamed, man hugging us affectionately and shaking our hands one last time, before we disappeared from his life forever, into the still, cool night.

Flies in my Porridge

Crashing face down, I slept the sleep of the dead, waking to a breakfast of flies dotted like raisins in my porridge. Our two and a half hour ride from Taraz having taken over eight hours, we'd disembarked outside the Hotel Turist, Shymkent at half past midnight. A notorious dive, the area at the front of the *gastnitsa* was filled with shady characters on the prowl. Hauling our bags in, we explained to the person on the front desk - a stone-faced woman whose face had been chiselled from the ugly rock - that having just arrived in Kazakhstan, we had no tenge and would need to go to the bank first thing in the morning. That, we thought, was that.

A healthy mixture of damp and jutting pipes, the fetid, peeling walls of the room were scored with knife etched graffiti. Adorning the room, two outsized paintings depicted horses doing the closest approximation they could to cuddling. Baked after our journey, we ventured out for a cigarette, getting as far as the lobby before being accosted.

'Den'gi, den'gi, den'gi, den'gi!' rock-face squealed, all blind fury, her tall, dark helmet of hair quivering as she wagged a sculpted cerise fingernail.

Old rock-face seemingly suffering from den'gi fever, it was clear that if we didn't pay up pronto we'd be spending the night on the streets; a most unpalatable end to a very long day. Only when we returned an hour later having found a working ATM did she flash the slightest glimmer of a smirk, a fang-like incisor inching over her chapped lips as she thrust out her hand.

The Road to Nowhere

Over breakfast, we met a middle-aged Turkish fellow with a bristling grey moustache who was in town on business. He'd been coming to Kazakhstan for thirteen years, he told us, giving lectures in tourism and hotel management. He had to admit, though, that his teachings hadn't proved a great success.

'They just don't get it,' he sighed wearily. 'They don't see why they should make the effort.'

My lukewarm, sugary Nescafe and all thoughts of food quickly forsaken, I took an anti-diarrhoea tablet – a prerequisite for any journey - and paid the curmudgeonly proprietor for the room. Behind the counter a flickering television was blasting out part one of the President's new epic biopic trilogy, a movie called *The Sky of My Childhood* about Nursultan Nazarbayev's youth

– 'an endless winter night of hunger and cold' - growing up in a yurt in the Tien Shan. They still had parts two and three, *Iron Mountain* and *Fire River* to look forward to.

The most integrated of the former Soviet Republics and the last to cut the umbilical cord, upon independence the Kazakh economy had collapsed. There was no money to pay salaries, no petrol and no gas for heating in a country where every existing oil and gas pipeline ran north into Russia for processing. With the Kazakhs over a barrel, in order to permit them to join the new rouble zone, Russian President Yeltsin set stringent stipulations including control of the Kazakh budget and money supply. Ex-Communist turned independence leader Nazarbayev capitulated, but still the new roubles failed to arrive. Deliberately engineered, this financial uncertainty allowed millions of old, invalid Soviet banknotes - much of it gangster money - to flood the country, pushing inflation up to three thousand percent.

Nazarbayev, though, had a backup plan. A secret decree having been issued that a new national currency be readied, the Kazakh government sent huge Ilyushin-76 transport planes to Germany and the UK. Under cover of darkness, they returned to Almaty stuffed with new coins and banknotes, a top secret operation underway to deliver supplies of tenge throughout the land. The President announced it on television on a Friday night; by Monday the era of the rouble would be history.

After a stuttering start, with the discovery of substantial mineral deposits, reserves of oil and natural gas far outstripping all previous estimates, Kazakhstan boomed. That Nazarbayev remained genuinely popular as long as the economy continued to grow was undeniable, but the global downturn had recently led to previously unheard of pockets of protest against endemic corruption. Revenues from oil and gas being pumped from the Tengiz Field in the Caspian Sea - the world's fifth largest oilfield - had enabled Nazarbayev to construct a space age new capital city in the middle of the empty steppe, but this felt far removed from the daily experience of many being left behind. Dealt with ruthlessly efficiently, any dissent never lasted long. In Kazakhstan, even the President's electoral rivals voted for him. Thus it came as no surprise when in April 2015, Nazarbayev secured an unconstitutional fifth term in office, winning a purported ninety-seven percent of the vote.

In every faceless concrete block that lined the route to Shymkent bus station, the fact that the country was far more developed than Kyrgyzstan was immediately apparent. The baton waving *politsiya* setting the tone, it was also more Russified, surlier and edgier. Ever present pictures of the President and his watchful paramilitaries filled shop windows. Government loudspeakers littered street corners, wires dragging along the perfect pavements. Black wall plaques in Cyrillic showed sketches of suited, unsmiling men radiating white light like halos. Cardboard cut-outs of schoolchildren skirted a zebra crossing where a perplexed, head scratching man had driven his car off the side of the road and into a ditch. Chassis wedged against the embankment, his attempts to reverse weren't working out.

Planted on a traffic island in the heart of the city, a giant tulip-shaped fountain forged from sheets of metal painted in green and red served as a focal point. Cruising the patch of grass encircling it, hipsters in white trousers and reflective silver sunglasses tried chat-up lines on girls whose bangs obscured their bushy eyebrows. At the entrance to the Bazar Samal Marshrutka Station, a chronically shaking beggar with plastic bags tied around his hands played air guitar as he leapt from foot to foot.

The main purpose of our passing through Southern Kazakhstan was to visit the Yasaui Mausoleum in Turkistan, a Timurid era Sufi shrine dedicated to the first great Turkic Muslim holy man. Supposedly Kazakhstan's most beautiful building; its inner sanctum contains a two-ton cauldron filled with holy water. Siphoned off by the atheist Soviets in 1935, its hallowed H2O was not returned until 1989.

We were on our way soon enough, cutting across a flat, barren dual coloured wilderness of semi-desert and sky, Rothko-esque in its unyielding focus. The ability to fall asleep at will being a regional trait, my neighbours heads pin-balled with every bump in the dirt track which had replaced the road. Frequently awoken, sleepers were required to participate in the pass the parcel of handing phones back and forth, an integral part of the journey. Mobiles were the in thing. A sign of relatively new affluence, they spilled from a tangle of charging leads which sprouted from the dashboard.

'Ullo? Ullo?'

Southern Kazakhstan was a maze of abandoned roadworks; I rarely saw a construction worker, just piles of rubble and idle machines. This was indeed *Roadworkistan*, but instead of finishing one stretch before starting on another, they'd dig up a hundred metres, leave the next stretch and excavate the following hundred ad infinitum, the upshot being that you were constantly scaling banks between dirt track and road. The only sign that any progress was being made was that none of the marshrutka drivers knew where they were going. With the roads in a constant state of flux, circling back was a frequent occurrence.

So four hours into our theoretically two-hour 120-kilometre journey, we drove on across myriad bridges, signs naming rivers which were nothing more than arid gullies filled with plastic and cans. Giving the thumbs-up to every other marshrutka we passed, our driver quietly seethed if his gesture was not reciprocated. It was all part of the sign language used to warn of impending checkpoints. Seatbelts were only for show, to be briefly held across your chest when others indicated the authorities up ahead.

A billboard of President Nazarbayev sniffing flowers welcomed us to Turkistan. A sandy backwater which obviously didn't get many visitors, it was one of those places where as a tourist you become the attraction. Children giggled shyly at our alien appearance, adults eyeing us with varying degrees of suspicion. Even by Kazakh standards, it seemed an acutely joyless town, schoolboys dressed in black bow ties and girls in frilly black and white costumes, like milkmaids in mourning.

The fact that we couldn't find the supposedly impressive, historic Sufi pilgrimage site in this sleepy hamlet didn't bode well, our requests for directions met with evasions and gruff dismissals. Set adrift in a brown field, when the sun bleached Yasaui Mausoleum limped into view, apart from the obligatory wedding party, it was deserted. Rows of sleepy traders doing no business, a murder of crows circled above the scaffolding.

Exit strategies

Back in Shymkent – oddly twinned with the town of Stevenage in England - we walked for some ten kilometres in search of a restaurant called Kok Saray, but the search for Kok proved fruitless. Settling instead for several one-litre cans of Baltika Seven and a bottle of Kretchet vodka, our change arrived in the form of a half full box of matches. This, along with sticks of gum and liquorice based sweets were popular forms of change, though often you could count yourself lucky if you got anything at all.

I awoke the next morning having vodka terrorised myself. From origins unknown, with a bottle of Legend of the Kremlin having appeared at the side of my bed, we'd missed the bus to Tashkent. The two-tone handbell shaped container reflecting me in warped convex, Stan was not happy.

Late that afternoon we made it out for food, the very thought of which set my stomach to churning. Ordering a salad, I stirred a spoon around a skinned, cold cup of Nescafe as columns of shashlyk smoke wafted into my face. It reminded me of a saying I'd read which was attributed to President Nazarbayev: 'In Kazakhstan meat is destiny. It will always come after you - you cannot avoid it.' This held true for the entire region. When my *salat turist* of tomato and cucumber arrived, it was garnished with small pieces of random meat and sprinkled with sugar.

Opposite a popular MIG monument and a display of Soviet era tanks and field guns lay the Museum of Victims of Political Repression, the curator of which looked both shocked and displeased to have her nap disturbed. Yawning, she switched on the spotlights which picked out the centrepiece, a sculpture depicting freedom striving figures alternately being gagged by a hammer and sickle banner or decapitated upon the Red Star of Battle. The first museum of its kind in Kazakhstan, fading portraits of men with toothbrush moustaches commemorated casualties. Including the famine caused by collectivisation, up to one and a half million Kazakhs – nearly half the population - perished during Stalin's time alone. "The broom of revolution must sweep up the Kazakh village," the party had sloganeered.

After dark, the politsiya disappeared and boy racers ruled the roads. It was a young country and the youth were bored and unfulfilled. Full of piss and vinegar, sullen teenagers idled with knives protruding from their pockets. Walking back to our digs we had no choice but to pass dimly lit Fantasy Park, a shadowy mesh of metal, grass and concrete filled with archaic funfair rides that smelt of violence waiting to spill over. Jeering as he advanced, a crew cut malefactor shook his fist, spraying our faces with spittle as he unleashed a string of expletives which his girlfriend found hilarious.

Along eight-lane Respubliki, men wrestled in bars to the sardonic clamour of other patrons. At the metal tulip, man hugs were taking place, hands on shoulders for an arm's length handshake, often followed by spitting on the earth at each other's feet whilst slamming one's knuckles into the open palm of the other hand.

The alarm clock beeping before dawn the next morning, the fact that our transit visas were set to expire only added to our determination to leave. Forsaking the breakfast, we vacated the Tenge Palace and made a beeline for the bus station, from where supposedly 'frequent' marshrutkas departed for the border. This proved to be purely theoretical, however. Sure enough, there was a man shouting '*Tosh-Kent!*' who shepherded us into his vehicle, but three hours later we were still the only ones aboard. Appearing to lose faith in his ability to rustle up any more passengers, wilting under the merciless sun, even the would-be driver quietly slipped away.

I'd already circuited the station looking for alternative modes of transport on numerous occasions - as much for some air and to pass the time as with any real hope - and now Stan had gone to do likewise. He'd been gone for a while already when three rat-faced, acne ridden boys appeared at the back of our marshrutka. Something felt wrong, and it wasn't just my dodgy guts. I was busy keeping an eye on their surreptitious battle with our bags padlocks, when two bulky politsiya officers descended upon me, standing in the doorway of the vehicle and blocking out the light.

Dismissing my claim that I was a tourist, they gabbled at me for a spell.

'*Pasport*,' they demanded, the owl cockades on their caps bobbing in unison.

I handed them a photocopy of my documents, but they were having none of it.

'Niet, niet, niet!' one cried, flinging my papers down with evident disdain and grinding them into the ground with his black leather boots. '*Vash documenty!*' the other spat, steadfastly oblivious to the boys battling with our luggage.

Reluctantly, I fished out my passport. Holding it upside down, they flicked back and forth through its pages, murmuring in evident disappointment. Presumably either everything was in order or they couldn't understand a single word of it.

Giving up on the idea of extortion, they sighed and settled for asking me how great their country was.

'Kazakhstan?' they enquired, giving me the thumbs-up.
'Da, da, good,' I nodded, mirroring their gesture and grinning back through clenched teeth.

With the politsiya sidling off, the rat boys boarded the marshrutka and surrounded me. Their skirmish with our bags having proved abortive, they were going for a more direct approach. It was at this point that Stan reappeared. He'd found a cab to the border for fifty US dollars, which was daylight robbery, but by this juncture I didn't care. There are some situations it's better to just extricate oneself from; so barging past the marauders we grabbed our gear and fled, the bus driver emerging to wring his hands in our wake.

We'd barely left the station when the taksi driver started badgering us for the money we'd agreed to stump up upon reaching the border. Not content with fifty dollars, he preceded to short change us at the petrol pump, his attempt to drive away with the nozzle still inserted in the car leading to a furious screaming match with the attendant.

'It's like nearly everyone in this country's only a step away from going all fists of fury,' I commented.
'Perhaps they're all bark and no bite,' Stan replied, 'but I really don't want to find out.'

Drawing away from Shymkent, we passed sculptures of lions and fish bones distending from the low hillocks. Occasional donkeys stood roasting by the roadside, a hint of colour returning to the land as we headed south. Approaching the border, we passed a giant billboard of President Nazarbayev, smiling broadly as he waved us goodbye.

CHAPTER 4

Border shenanigans

On the Kazakh side of the border, we were met with grimaces. Sensing that our presence meant a long delay was in the offing, sprinting locals steamed ahead. After the inevitable scrutiny, the Passport Control Guard eventually snorted, barked 'visa,' and crossed his arms in a big, final, X-shape before pointing towards Uzbek territory.

On the Uzbek side of the border - there being forms to be filled in, but with nobody knowing where the English language copies might be - confusion reigned supreme. A Presidential edict to move from Cyrillic to Latin script seemed to have had little impact. There were positive omens to be found, however, in the fact that people were not so hell-bent in their desire to push past us. Slowly but surely, we approached the counter, where the guard smiled wryly.

'*Angliyskiy?*' he asked, fondling our passports. 'Maybe you give me something to remember you… like… one hundred dollar?'

There was a moment's pause before he and his cohorts broke into a hearty laughter and settled for a pen to share. They had their comic timing down pat.

'Welcome to *Oz'bekiston*, Mister Stans,' they chorused, waving us goodbye.

Entering Uzbekistan was carnage; no sooner had we exited the customs compound and began the two-kilometre walk through no man's land than we were swarmed upon. Vagrants and children greeting us, they stroked our arms and raised their hands to their mouths.

'*Den'gi die; den'gi die,*' they repeated like a mantra.

Quoting absurd figures which they pulled from the air and typed onto their mobile screens, luggage grabbing taksi drivers emerged from the ether with an increasingly voracious dog-eat-dog quality. Reaching the border village of Gisht-Kuprik - where the first marshrutkas sat idly waiting - was out of the question, it was difficult enough just to stay on one's feet given the pulling and shoving.

Shaking off the most insistent harassment, I agreed on a price to the Sobir Rahimov Bus Station and we ploughed off towards the centre-less sprawl of Tashkent. Fleets of Daewoo ruled the roads; even the ambulances were squat little Daewoo Damas vans, impossible to lie down in. As part of a trade-off for cotton rights, the South Korean-financed UzDaewoo plant in Andijan had been churning out these autos for over a decade, pouring over a billion US dollars into this joint venture before declaring bankruptcy. The only way the factory had stayed in business this long was through prohibitive government tariffs on imported vehicles. Thus whilst a small Daewoo, now rebranded as General Motors Uzbekistan, cost ten thousand US dollars in Uzbekistan, in neighbouring Kyrgyzstan a far superior foreign model could be had for under half the price.

The air heavy with power and telecoms cables, billboards advertised beauty parlours and new apartment complexes far beyond the reach of the average Uzbek. The dulcet tones of the dictator's pop star daughter, Gulnara 'Googoosha' Karimova spilling from the radio, we zipped past the National Soccer Stadium, the Pakhtakor, home of Pakhtakor FK, which aptly translates as the 'Cotton Picker.'

Delivered to a new scrum of drivers, I endeavoured to arrange a twenty dollar ride with a meek, portly man who communicated by writing his price in the dust on the back windscreen of a Sedan. This was not to the liking of an English speaking boy with clumps of cowlicks sprouting from his bean-shaped head, who wanted forty dollars.

'You stop talking,' bean boy threatened our prospective driver, who actually hadn't said a word.

It was at this point that Stan snapped. Tired of his shoulder being endlessly tapped by hawkers and no doubt wondering what I'd gotten him into, he unleashed a vicious snarl. The gaggle surrounding us jumped back in surprise, emitting a collective 'whoa,' noise as they raised their hands in the internationally recognised 'jeez, alright mate, calm down' gesture.

We pulled away across the Hungry Steppe which had drunk all of the land's water, and it was the Karakalpak region which was paying the heaviest price. Bouncing us into the taksi ceiling, potholes were the only interruptions to the unerringly flat land. After Kazakhstan, the abundance of agriculture was a novelty. There were corn and barley fields, but mostly there were endless acres of Uzbekistan's white gold, little cotton balls ripening beneath the fierce sun. Picking season would soon be underway.

I later spoke to Aidan McQuade, head of Anti-Slavery International.

'Year on year hundreds of thousands of Uzbek citizens are forced by their government to pick cotton for the benefit of a narrow political elite,' he told me. 'If they refuse they'll suffer punishment, including harassment, detention, loss of their jobs or expulsion from schools and universities.'

Calling for an end to compulsory labour and demanding unfettered access for the International Labour Organization, McQuade attempted to deliver a petition to the Uzbek Embassy in London, but with no one willing to come out and accept it, he could only toss it over the railings.

'The fact that no one had the courage to meet us shows that they know how wrong slavery is,' he said. 'It has no place in the twenty-first century.'

Stopping at endless checkpoints, we rolled on along the Russian-built M39. Passing the debris of fallen car parts, we weaved our way around the odd calf in the centre of the carriageway, languid and unmoved by the commotion. Where there weren't checkpoints there were wooden facades of militsiya cars and cardboard cut-outs of *militsiyamen* waiting to fool the uninitiated. Our driver, though, had an ingenious solution to this problem. I wasn't sure how it worked, but he had a contraption wired into the dashboard which unfailingly, a minute before every speed-trap, emitted a high-pitched bleeping at which we would slow our pace.

Edging towards Samarkand, the land took on a golden quality. The hazy hills of the Zaamin National Park drifting into view, we rose through craggy bluffs past roadside vendors of *dizel* and petrol, honey coloured in the afternoon light. Roadside stalls were always grouped, a hundred metre stretch of colour coordinated apples followed by a hundred metres of water stands, all run by head-scarfed women in bright floral frocks who lay perfectly motionless on rusting iron frames, endlessly waiting. As we descended onto the outlying plains of Samarkand, I wondered how there could conceivably be enough *bizniz* to go round on this sparsely used highway. I was musing on this as we clattered past a cluster of donkey carts, the fabled city coming into view.

The Golden City

Having checked in at the leafy Bahodir B&B, our first task in Samarkand was to change money. Uzbek banknotes come in only four denominations, the rarely seen one and two hundred, the five hundred and the one thousand som. With the highest value banknote being worth less than forty US cents, the Uzbek version of 'how much does it cost?' involves jazz hands. Black market moneychangers lugging overflowing bin bags around, the currency comes in stacks. Their location a movable feast, these marketeers hung in packs and - in our experience at least – were only ever found after their services were no longer required.

Cutting through a low metal gate fashioned into towering walls, we entered the labyrinthine alleyways of the Old Jewish Quarter. A once thriving community of fifty-thousand, the Jews of Samarkand were ghettoized by the strictures of Muslim rulers who forbade them from living beyond the confines of the district. Today, with the Jewish population of Central Asia in terminal decline, less than two-thousand remain in Samarkand. Of the thirty synagogues present in 1917, only one, the Gumbaz remains functional. The menorah and Star of David adorning its wall, decked in a *kippah*, a lone child on a bicycle circled its padlocked entrance.

The homely smell of freshly baked bread wafting on the thin breeze, after hitting numerous dead ends we emerged at the odours source, the Siob Bazaar, where girders held aloft a two-tiered corrugated monster of a roof. Surrounding this, an overspill of traders hunkered under bleached gazebos and parasols, selling a wide array of goods. From children's toys to hard, round, bagel-like *lepyoshka* - unleavened bread with intricate patterns printed upon it, revered as holy - it was there. Chinese instant noodles piled high upon pitches, necklaces of wolves teeth purported to ward off the evil eye were laid out on pelts. Stout old grannies wearing bright sequined dresses with socks and sandals sat about waiting for business. In whole sections devoted to bulbous *arbuz* melons, skullcap-clad men were occupied in hacking up balls of phlegm, for whilst blowing one's nose in public was considering rude, spitting balls of snot was just dandy. Nearly everything imaginable was there, except black market moneychangers.

We enquired at an official exchange booth, where the infrequently called upon staff were shocked to be asked about currency conversion. It took three of them a lot of shrugging to come up with a measly rate. Leaving them behind, they returned to staring at old school green monochrome computer monitors.

Back at the Bahodir, a member of staff called Igor - who brought to mind a hybrid of Lurch from The Addams Family and the cartoon character Ren, his bulging eyes about to give up on the idea of staying in his skull altogether - went to change money for us. He soon reappeared with two black bags loaded to the brim with two hundred dollars' worth of som.

'Here, Sir. Please count it, Sir' he said, indicating the piles of banknotes held together with rubber bands.

, we gave up on the accounting. It was probably all there.

Night fell swiftly in Samarkand. The streets deserted by eight thirty PM, stragglers from weddings held in the shadows of towering monuments drifted away. Finishing up their plov in the Platen Restaurant, high-end French and German coach parties were whisked away to overpriced accommodations. Cordoned off beyond broken faux-marble paving slabs, the silhouetted husk of the desolate Afrosiab Palace Hotel was an eerie presence. Outside the Registan, kids with pit bulls loitered listlessly before dispersing into the darkness. By ten PM, the doors to the Bahodir were locked. Yanking on a drawstring which was attached to his big toe, the drowsy doorman was raised from his hammock to admit us.

Stolen Cities

We set out early to see the sights of the culturally Tajik city, the brilliant early morning light resplendent on the tapering turquoise minarets of the Registan. Encircling these age-old monuments, however, the Tourist Zone felt plastic, pedestrianized Tashkent Avenue's sightseer perfect walkways having not a sand coloured slab out of place. Open-air vehicles resembling golf buggies were the only transport here, silently gliding through the streets they appeared ludicrous against a backdrop of imposing, Timurid facades. Everything was too smooth, the Xeroxed trees identical distances apart, the whitewash souvenir shops interchangeable, all the rough edges of life rounded off.

Nestled behind the main drag, its high tympanum coated in cobalt blue tilework, the Bibi Khanym Mosque stood in a grassy courtyard around a large, marble carving of the Quran. Commissioned by Timur and named for his Chinese wife, local folklore tells how the architect fell in love with her and stole a kiss. Escaping the wrath of Timur by jumping from the minaret, he sprouted wings and flew to Mecca.

Crossing the six-lane highway, we made our way up a brown, weed-covered rise to Shah-I-Zinda, the 'Tomb of the Living King' and the avenue of mausoleums. Dotted across the hillside, portraits were etched upon the subsiding gravestones of those not important enough to be buried inside its fêted walls. Originally dating from the ninth century, the necropolis is purported to be the final resting place of Qusam Ibn Abbas, a cousin of the Prophet Mohammed who brought Islam to the area in the seventh century. The name is derived from a legend which tells how when Ibn Abbas was beheaded by raiding Zoroastrians, he tucked his head under his arm and escaped into a well to return on an appointed future date.

Samarkand's most impressive sight, Shah-I-Zinda was rebuilt under Timur after being sacked by the Mongols. Having been subject to a dogmatic restoration programme since 2005, whilst some of the work may have been well executed, the untouched buildings remained far more evocative. Still, relative to some of Samarkand's other sights, the complex has gotten off lightly.

Boasting some extraordinary majolica and terracotta tilework, Uzbeks and Westerners alike were entranced by the evocative shapes and colours of the domes and minarets and the precision with which each detail had been executed. The tiny doorways to the mausoleums ensuring by design that bowing to Allah was compulsory, the plain white graves laden with pilgrim's gifts of banknotes for comfort in the afterlife were conspicuous in their simplicity against glittering backgrounds of infinite blues, greens and yellows. The sheer scale of the site's majesty, the busyness and the minutia of the architecture was dizzying, as was the dry heat. In one of the mausoleums, a placard translated into English quoted Timur:

'If you have doubts in our might and power, look at our monuments.'

You couldn't argue.

It was the vicious warlord Tamerlane - Timur the Lame, buckled by a birth defect and an enemy arrow - who transformed Samarkand into the 'threshold of paradise.' Slaughterer of the Uzbek people to who the quote 'If you see an Uzbek, kill him' is attributed, Soviet historians began airbrushing Timur into a national hero in the forties, preventing the natives from seeking out their real ancestors, the hated Golden Horde of Jenghiz Khan. Sparing artisans in the cities he razed - as Jenghiz Khan before him had done - Timur shipped them back to Samarkand, creating a fusion of architectural styles ranging from Azerbaijani to Indian, Persian to Caucasian. At the pinnacle of Timur's reign, a single public garden in Samarkand was so large that when a diplomat's horse went missing in its grounds it was not found for six weeks.

Leaving Shah-I-Zinda, we decided that rather than go through the rigmarole of haggling for a taksi up to the Ulugbek Observatory, we'd rather walk. This proved foolhardy. By the time we reached the observatory atop Samarkand's highest point, we were panting and dripping with sweat, an ice lolly Stan had stopped to buy dyeing his fingers luminous green as it melted. At a distance from the centre, things were less sanitized up here. As soon as they caught sight of us, pointing mothers set their children upon us to beg.

'Den'gi die; den'gi die!' they tap, tap, tapped.

Across the parking lot, a queue of expressionless grooms and distracted brides, the hems of their gowns swishing through the dust, were waiting to complete their vows in front of an equally distant and unhappy looking statue of Ulugbek, the astrologer-King. If not the result of kidnappings, the majority of weddings we'd seen had most likely been arranged marriages. Diverting couples from their dismay, however, we soon became the centre of attention, attracting waves, giggles and glares from wedding guests, out-of-towners and schoolchildren on mandatory field trips. Their interest piqued, ticket officers began to follow us, vociferously indicating that we needed to buy a *billet* to be in this locale, whether we intended to visit the observatory or not.

Abandoning our whigmaleerie in the face of these aggressive tactics, we decided to navigate our way around via the local bus network. This turned out to be a rather laborious process. Stopping for five minutes every fifty metres to enable the conductor to hang from the door and bellow in the hope of procuring more passengers, each bus caused a huge traffic jam. A cacophony of horn rage ensuing, motorists battled over non-existent inches of space. There was no room whatsoever on board either - the term 'sardines' doesn't do it justice - yet somehow every time we pulled up, a few more people managed to squeeze themselves in. After a while it was impossible to know where you were, any sight of the windows, let alone out of them, a distant memory.

Emerging from the bazaar district, we disembarked in the faceless new town, all freshly laid pristine streets and empty storefronts. Cutting through the western edge of town, we emerged at the National Bank of Uzbekistan, where Formica counters bent under the weight of piles of banknotes so high it made your eyes spin. Doubled over under the strain, whitebeards lugged boxes and laundry bags stuffed with cash to their cars, the suspension groaning as they loaded it in.

Upscale Dining

The heat of the day having receded, the streets were filled with people taking late afternoon sabbaticals. In Navoi Park, toddlers played on a rusted swing set under the watchful eyes of cooing grandmothers. Glistening in the low sun, full sets of gold chompers abounded, but sadly the monobrow had fallen out of vogue. Some persisted though, certain that this once popular mark of great beauty would come back into fashion.

Emerging from the park, we were accosted by a friendly fellow with dark circles spreading from his armpits down his taut white shirt.

> 'You guys is from England? No way! I's like used to live in Muswell 'ill,' he gushed, shaking our hands with great enthusiasm. 'My name is Aziz, it mean mighty man, but everybody call me Alex.'

His Pidgin English littered with cockney slang, the gangly Alex had worked in the hospitality industry during his sojourn in London, and whilst he'd loved England, he hadn't been so keen on his employers.

> 'Guv'nor Dave was alright,' he mused, 'but guv'nor John, he was a right wanker.'

Now on the payroll at the Uzbek Ministry of Justice, Alex was trying to find a way back into the UK, which had recently tightened visa regulations for citizens of Uzbekistan. It was a gripe we'd become all too familiar with.

'Why you even wanna come 'ere?' he asked, indicating Samarkand. 'Is a bleedin' shithole, mate.'

As I politely disagreed, looking about ready to wilt his female companion steadied herself against a lamppost. Oblivious to her plight, eager to continue our conversation, Alex invited us to his party the following evening.

'You see a film called *Hostel*?' he asked.
'Erm… yes,' Stan replied tentatively.
'Donor worry,' he beamed, all gesticulating hands, 'is nuffin' like that. We just have a drink and smoke some pot 'innit.'

Whilst I wondered if it was such a good idea to smoke weed with a relative stranger from the Uzbek Ministry of Justice, Alex excitedly scribbled down his contact details.

'Be a great laugh. Me parents go away 'innit,' he raved, adding with a wink and a nod toward his consort; 'Donor worry, I lock me wife and kid in the basement.'

Having passed a cellar bar called the UK Pub earlier, as fair-weather patriots it felt only right after this thirsty work that we should pay it a visit. Our entrance met by a good-humoured astonishment, I was unsure whether it was the fact that we were British or that they had any customers at all which was proving so novel. A cleaning frenzy kicking in, one of the passel of teenage boys followed me into the toilets with a can of air freshener and a toilet brush. Pretty soon, though, the furore subsided and they returned to watching a dubbed version of *Firefly* on an Uzbek TV channel, one guy doing all the voices.

'The unauthorised reproduction or distribution of this copyrighted work is illegal...' ran the constant warning blotting out the bottom third of the screen.

Choosing the Italian themed Venezia Restaurant from our limited dinner options, we skirted back past the National Bank. Its doors now shut, on the street out front people were still stuffing swollen bags into the boots of their cars. Entering the deserted restaurant, we sat on the terrace and settled for the last bottle of warm pivo to share. That the napkins were folded in the uniform fancy pattern was a semi-promising sign; it was a poor restaurant indeed which couldn't be bothered to arrange their napkins ornately. It was pleasant enough, until all too soon, the food arrived.

I've eaten some foul things in my time. From Hungarian hamlets to the Thorong-La Pass in Nepal and roadside stands in Cambodian backwaters, I've had ketchup pizzas, cauliflower dhal and unidentified objects swimming in grease so thick you couldn't cut it with a knife. As a vegetarian, though, my culinary adventures in parts of Central Asia took the biscuit. The fact that in most restaurants three-quarters of what was on the menu wasn't available was a blessing in disguise.

There was no olive oil; salads came drenched in recycled cotton seed oil and sweet mayonnaise. If for some reason there was no mayonnaise, it was common to find your salad had been sprinkled with sugar. Anything claiming to be a Thai dish came covered in processed cheese and ketchup. Nothing ever contained any spice. There were generally three, sometimes four dishes. *Dimlama* was random meat with dill, onion, carrot and potato in a juice akin to watery vegetable soup as served in a hospital. *Plov* was random meat with dill, onion, carrot and sometimes raisins spilt sparingly over lukewarm rice. *Shishtovli, laghman* or equivalent was random meat with dill, onion and carrot on thick, tepid noodles; and shashlyk was random meat on a stick, sometimes served with dill and prized cubes of fat. Whatever you chose to order, if it didn't include a generous helping of shashlyk, that was cause for quizzical looks.

The food at Venezia was no exception, the pasta sauce a hybrid of diced onions, hard carrots and soy sauce. Our money swiftly dispatched into the restaurant's counting machine, at least the bill came to less than fifty banknotes.

'Which side do you want?' the rather green looking Stan asked as we visited the establishment's twin toilets.
'I'm easy,' I answered. 'They both smell as bad.'

Sure enough, we barely made it back to the Bahodir before the spasms struck.

'I don't feel so good,' Stan's voice reverberated from the bathroom as he started firing from both ends.

New Friends

Stan having been up all night with vomiting and diarrhoea, I break-fasted with a Californian called Christopher and his Malaysian girlfriend Maimunah, with whom I discussed the latest developments in Tajikistan. Shortly after we left the UK, fighting had broken out. Whilst on the road, we'd come across a few travellers who'd gotten stuck in the town of Khorog, capital of the Gorno-Badakhshan Autonomous Oblast and gateway to the Pamir Mountains. Holed up in their homestays and hostels, they'd watched bullets from helicopter gunships whizzing past their windows.

Various accounts regarding the cause of the conflict had been advanced. What was certain was that the Regional Security Chief had been ambushed and killed, pulled from his limousine and stabbed. With phone and road links severed by the authorities, locals had built barricades, calling the government's actions an invasion. Tit-for-tat battles followed, most likely for control over lucrative smuggling routes snaking their way through from Afghanistan. Over a hundred people were said to have been killed.

'We met a dude who got caught up in all that,' Christopher told me. 'Man, he'd cycled through Iraq and he said it was worse. Outside of Dushanbe, the shop shelves are all bare. I mean, you can't even buy bottled water.'

It was something to look forward to.

With Stan still in bed, I sauntered towards the old town. In the blink-ered tourist zone's cafés, big plastic bottles of Fanta, Sprite and Coke ruled supreme. Order any soft drink in Central Asia and you'd end up with two litres. Conspicuous by its absence, all signs of alcohol were kept away from the ageing, big buck French and German coach parties. Not long after we left, Coca-Cola would also disappear from menus, its Uzbek directors – Gulnara Karimova among them - embroiled in a corruption scandal.

Along the sanitized main drag, frivolous sprinkler systems were wasting water. Confused by the heat, pails of wasps buzzed languorously around, bouncing off mirrored surfaces. Women with insistent eyebrows gossiped in the striped sunlight outside storefronts, all bling and glitter in their sequined gowns. The men, by comparison, in uniform nylon trousers and short-sleeve shirts were distinctly understated.

Reaching the edge of the tourist zone, I let myself get lost in the maze of Old Samarkand's winding lanes. The sky a mess of fizzing cables, the hazy gravel streets were calm and unoccupied save for the odd waddling babushka and her bashful wards.

Back at the rustic and spacious, but dilapidated Bahodir, the immensely slow moving yet ever busy Igor, who seemed to be everywhere at once, was absorbed in some task or other set to ensure the happiness of his guests.

'Good aft-er-noon, Sir,' he said in his hissing fashion, somewhere between a snake and a breeze whispering through the trees; 'How are you to-day, Sir?'

Venturing up to our room and finding Stan in a marginally better state, I persuaded him to give the Registan - visible from the guesthouse - a look. The centrepiece of the city, the Registan is a triad of madrassas. Meaning 'Sandy Place,' its Tajik name refers to the sand which soaked up the blood from countless executions held here until the beginning of the twentieth century. The plaza outside originally having been medieval Central Asia's main bazaar, the commerce had now moved into the former student cells inside the walls of the complex.

Stan didn't last long. As we approached, a tour guide and a soldier got into a spat about who was going to pocket our entry fee. Winning the argument by virtue of his loosely holstered pistol, the militsiyaman led us through tunnelled passageways into his tucked away 'ticket shop.' By the time we'd refused the second-hand tickets he was hawking, Stan had relapsed.

'Enough, enough,' he moaned, parking himself on a bench out front.

Having found the real ticket booth, as I neared the entrance the docent sidled up to me again.

'Your friend not coming?' he murmured conspiratorially.
'He's sick,' I replied.
'But,' he mouthed, rubbing his thumb and forefinger together, 'I make him special price.'

This encapsulated the trouble with the Registan; despite its magnificence, it was a ginormous web of commerce, every nook and cranny filled with hawkers. Whilst the restoration project had been overzealous, sucking away at the sense of history, it was difficult to transport oneself to the past when the present was tugging at your sleeve. Its mosaics a Zoroastrian hangover flouting the Islamic prohibition on the depiction of animals, the sun setting on the Sher Dor (Lion) Madrassa was a stunning sight, but hard to take in when set beyond a foreground of caterwauling vendors.

Returning to the bench where Stan was sitting, I wasn't surprised to see he'd acquired a throng of new friends, chief amongst who was Og'abek. A tourist in Samarkand for the first time himself, Og'abek was an ebullient nineteen-year-old with a big, acne-pocked Turkic nose, a pointy chin and a tall, moussed quiff of jet black hair. A door-maker from the town of G'uzor, some 130 kilometres south, he'd come to Samarkand to practice his English. In keeping with an increasing array of young people we'd meet, his dream was to study at Oxford University, seen as the apex of education; if only the British government weren't so intransigent about handing out visas.

Despite his desire to go to Oxford, Og'abek was unwavering in his assertion that Europe was in decline and Asia on the rise, an assertion which, like everything else, he repeated ad infinitum in an attempt to find the right words. Despite the faltering power of Europe, he admitted that Western culture had become a huge influence on the younger generations of Uzbeks, so much so that it had created a generation gap between those who spoke Russian as their second language and those who spoke English. This further complicated an already problematic linguistic soup.

When Stalin decided to follow through with Lenin's policy as regards the 'self-identification of working people' by unilaterally dividing Central Asia into Soviet Socialist Republics, facts on the ground weren't going to be allowed to get in the way. In a classic divide and rule play, the culturally Tajik cities of Samarkand and Bukhara were set adrift within Uzbek territory, whilst in return, newly formed Tajikistan gained the inhospitable Khojand land mass surrounding the Fan Mountains. The Tajik's had been shafted. As late as 1989, the leader of the Tajik Soviet Socialist Republic petitioned Mikhail Gorbachev for the 'return' of Samarkand and Bukhara.

One of the upshots of this carve up was the abundance of languages extant in Samarkand and Bukhara, meaning that Uzbek-speaking Og'abek was rarely understood in this once Tajik city. Having decided to accompany me and the wilting Stan in order to try out his English, Og'abek was determined to take charge, stopping to ask every other person the location of the restaurant we were after. Most of them stared back at him blankly, but a true pachyderm if nothing else, he pressed on.

Between pausing every thirty seconds to scan our map uncomprehendingly and ask for directions, Og'abek continued to practice his English, calling attention to every conceivable landmark with a childlike sense of glee.

'Look, bank! B-A-N-K, bank. Look, look university! Un-i-ver-si-ty,' he chirruped happily, pointing and rolling his cranium up and down and side to side like a nodding head dog.

Interspersed with this litany of repetition, pearls of wisdom surfaced.

'Money makes the world go round' and 'if wishes were horses, beggars would ride,' appeared out of nowhere with a metronomic movement of the head.

The ashen-faced Stan flagging badly, each eatery we stopped at had invariably changed hands and become a shashlyk joint. Milling about us with menus boasting pictures of fleshy skewers they couldn't begin to understand why our mouths weren't watering at the thought of, the eager staff attempted to entice us in. Looking longingly at the grills, evidently vegetarian was a word Og'abek had neglected to learn.

'Tomorrow morning, we shall be together,' he declared cheerily. 'What shall we do then?'

I told him we were leaving for Bukhara.

'Oh, that's so great!' he cried, reshaping his quiff. 'I've never been to Bukhara. I can come with you!'
'Um,' I erred.
'Um,' he scoffed, indicating his groin; '*Um* is Uzbek word for lady parts.'

Lolloping off to ask for directions, Og'abek re-emerged with bottles of Apple Kok for each of us.

'Gift,' he beamed, 'how you say, "Don't kick a gift horse in the teeth".'

Stan took a sip and dry heaved a little.
I'd barely begun to contemplate our Bukhara adventure when we were halted in our tracks by a jovial hollering.

'Yo, hey, *shalom aleykum*! Where you dude's from?'

We paused to chat with a scar-faced, bearded Chelsea supporter called Terry – 'John Terry' - real name Toychi. Having lived in Maidstone, England for eighteen months before spending the last four years in California, he'd developed a pretty interesting accent. As he and Stan staggered for different reasons, smelling like poteen, Terry bemoaned recent changes to visa regulations for Uzbeks wanting to visit the UK. Og'abek's face clouded over. He didn't want to share his new mates; especially not with someone who spoke better English.

Taking our leave, we ploughed on.

'Later dudes,' the weaving Toychi called as we started down Ulugbek Street, Og'abek once more engaged in asking for directions.

Rattling traffic roared along the cracked tarmac, billowing exhaust fumes as we circumnavigated ditches and Daewoos parked on the pavement, jaywalking our way to the Z'Praha Restaurant. It was here that Og'abek's tenacity finally paid off. With the joint closed for a wedding reception, located next door was the Café Romantic, a deserted, grizzled husk of a place, its television blaring out a Russian game show. I didn't really understand what was happening by this point, that is, until the chef appeared.

Extremely heavy on hair product, the portly, striped-shirted Henri - real name Hoshnaut - was an Arsenal fan who'd just returned home to Samarkand from a four-year stint living in Edgware, North London, where he'd apparently trained as a chef. He missed his host family, the football, pretty much everything about London, in fact, and was consequently very happy to meet some natives.

'Now I's stuck in this dumpy crapper,' he moaned, indicating the confines of the café. 'I tries to get some Olympics tickets, come back for a visit like, but they wouldn't give me a visa. Fuckin' bastards!'

Henri went off to the kitchen the Café Romantic shared with its neighbour, soon reappearing with a specially prepared dish - there was nothing non-meat based on the menu - of greasy fried vegetables. Taking a sniff, Stan went outside to get some air whilst I tucked in, offering to share the dish with the troubled looking Og'abek.

'No, no,' he said, putting his palm up in a dismissive motion. 'It's only vegetables. Veg-e-ta-balls.'
'This is the best meal I've had in Samarkand,' I complimented Henri.

I wasn't lying, but it wasn't saying much either.

Beaming at my praise, with three hundred guests arriving imminently, Henri withdrew to the kitchen. My plans to meet Alex seeming ever less likely to come to fruition, I sent a text making my excuses. Discovering that there was yet another English speaking local we'd met, the discomfited Og'abek scowled at the news.

It was time to get Stan back to the Bahodir. Weaning the attention of the waitress from the game show, she slammed the bill down in front of Og'abek, whose jaw dropped.

'No, no, no,' he wailed in great agitation. 'Is wrong, wrong!'

Prising the bill from his grasp, I discovered that it came to less than a dollar.

'It's okay,' I said, attempting to soothe him.
'No, no, no,' he shouted. 'Is too cheap!'

Confirming with the waitress that the bill was indeed correct, much to Og'abek's continued consternation, we said our farewells with an unlikely pledge to meet again tomorrow. Two minutes later, however, our having failed to get a taksi, Og'abek resurfaced, stuck out his arm and flagged down a passing car. In Uzbekistan any vehicle could be a cab; so loading us in and explaining our destination to the driver, he negotiated a price and waved us off for the last time.

We sped away into the night in grandpa's surprisingly fleet old Hulk-green Lada. The go-faster stripes were clearly working, the traditional folk music blasting from the tinny speakers making a welcome change as we clattered along. Soon enough we were back at the Registan, where the toothless, unintelligible driver, presumably in the process of 'golding up' became extremely animated. It was the generic con. We'd agreed on a fare of two thousand som, but all along, of course, this had meant two thousand each.

Furious, Stan stormed out of the cab. Forgetting I was behind him, he slammed the door, a rush of wind blowing my hair back as it missed my face by an inch. Paying the driver, I disembarked, Stan slamming the door for a second time so that it came off its rusted hinges slightly. It looked like the old man would be spending the money fixing the car instead of his teeth.

Bye-bye Bahodir

Back in the airy, laundry draped courtyard of the Bahodir, materialising from all possible angles, Igor filled my cup with immense frequency. Idling on a *tapchan* - a raised platform seating area like a fenced in four poster bed - we talked to a pale-faced Japanese boy named Kazuki. Noting that the guesthouse was teeming with Japanese backpackers, with whom Samarkand was immensely popular, we'd tried to ask a few of them what had led them here, but had met with only shy smiles and navel-gazing.

'I know. I thought I was getting off map coming here,' Kazuki confided, 'but is full of Japanese,' he added with disappointment as he scuttled off to the toilets.

That was the last we saw of him.

It was only upon checking out early next morning that we realised why Igor had seemed to be everywhere at once.

'Were there two of them?' Stan asked, unsure if he was seeing double from his bout of sickness.
'There were,' I confirmed.

Igor had an identical twin.

The Sharq

Our taksi pulled away towards Samarkand train station, or *vokzal* as it was in Russian. This word had entered the Russian lexicon when, eager to introduce the railway to his own country, Tsar Nicholas I sent a delegation to Britain to study the mode of transport. Travelling the south-west line, the party noted that every single train stopped at Vauxhall, thus concluding that this must be the word for a rail network.

Reaching the outskirts of Samarkand, policemen wielding outsized orange batons like novelty vibrators became more prolific. At roadside checkpoints vehicles were being searched, their owner's documents combed through. Luckily for us, President Islam Karimov having ordered his militsiya to leave tourists alone, they largely ignored us. It was widely accepted that taksi drivers now preferred to have tourists in their cars, as this helped them avoid shakedowns.

We'd been to Samarkand's hulking, concrete train station two days previously, finding the ticket office - which was an obvious afterthought - tucked in a shed round the side. Here we were sent from queue to queue as the staff behind the windows argued amongst themselves as to which unfortunate soul should serve us. Once inside the main building and through the airport style security, though, proceedings took on a more sedate nature. Soldiers outnumbering punters, an eerie stillness reigned, broken only by the clomping of jackboots.

Inside the dolphin-nosed Sharq Ekspress locomotive replete with stewardesses, it was pretty comfortable bar the heat. As we drew away and I sank back into my sweaty seat, music videos flickered into life on TV screens, bad pop and dance routines for tweenies playing to a carriage filled with middle-aged, middle-class people. A conservative bunch, our fellow passengers reserve was only interrupted by the distant howling escaping from another compartment. Their clothes a toned down affair, gone were all the colours so gaudy they could have poked out Hispanic eyes. Colour, it seemed, was the preserve of the poor.

I was brought back from my drowsy reverie by the bleeping of my phone. It was a text from Aziz.

'i revise your massage estterday u shuld cum estterday was god I hope we will moet each other a gin let me now if u stile in Samarqand'

The air-con kicking in, our hermetically sealed netherworld rolled on towards Bukhara. Peeking through shades drawn tight against the blinding sun, bleak, mono-coloured low-rise industrial towns occasionally reared into view. Their whitewash brickwork crumbling, chimneys belched smoke into a blanched expanse of sky. Quickly forgotten, they were like mirages strung together by telegraph poles.

Scene of weddings, Victory Square against a backdrop of the Ala-Tau Mountains, Bishkek

Boris's converted railway sleeper, Cholpon Ata, Lake Issyk-Köl

Ride it, drink its' milk, eat it: the well-loved Central Asian horse.

Vegetarian Haute Cuisine Cholpon Ata style.

The Ak-Say Canyon

The Ala-Tau Mountain Range.

A local celebrity sporting a kalpak being interviewed for TV on Independence Day, Bishkek.

Dancers in traditional costumes perform as part of the Independence Day celebrations, Bishkek.

Buzkashi riders in action, Bishkek.

A muster of crows circle above the Yasaui Mausoleum, Turkistan.

Afternoon gossip on the streets of Samarkand.

Lepyoshka for sale in the Siob Bazaar, Samarkand.   *The Shah-I-Zinda complex, Samarkand.*

The Sher Dor (Lion) Madrassa, the Registan, Samarkand.
In a definitively Uzbek twist, the lions are actually tigers.

The Mir-I-Arab Madrassa, Kalon Mosque and Minaret, Bukhara.

Children playing in the streets of Bukhara.

Papier-mâché Stoddart and Conolly in the Zindon, Bukhara.

Travels with Stan, the last of the warm beer, Bukhara.

Wedding at the Kalon Minaret, Bukhara.

The Khiva Silk Carpet Workshop.

One hundred US dollars' worth of Uzbek som.

Tua-let Kyzyl-Kum Desert style.　　　　　*Dawn breaks over the Ichon-Qala, Khiva.*

The wall of vodka, most important part of any shop.

Trader at the Markaziy Bazaar, Nukus. *Abandoned construction site, Nukus.*

Chaikhana with the Portrait of Lenin *by Aleksandr Volkov, Savitsky Gallery, Nukus*

The bus ride to Moynaq.   *Tumbleweed crossing the main road, Moynaq.*

The ship graveyard, Moynaq.

Timur mounted upon his castrated steed, Tashkent.

CHAPTER 5

Devil Wagon

M uch to the consternation of the assembled taksi drivers, we did the last sixteen kilometres from Bukhara Vokzal - located in the village of Kagan - to Bukhara on a local bus. By this point, I was so overheated that only in retrospect did I realise I'd been wandering around asking about transport to Khiva.

Bukhara train station owed its obscure location to the Mangit Dynasty, slavers and charlatans who kept their people in ignorance and superstition. When the Russians laid the tracks for the Trans-Caspian Railway in the 1860s, under pressure from mullahs, the Emir demanded that this 'devil wagon' not pass within sixteen kilometres of the city. This was the era when the mullahs also endeavoured to ban the bicycle, tomatoes and the potato.

A thirty-minute journey with my luggage loaded on my lap and an elbow in my eye led us to the old town, the main road so intensely quiet and still you could hear distant goats bleating and naturally spoke in whispers. One of the Igor's at the Bahodir having recommended we stay at their friend's place, the Madina & Ilyos, sure enough, the only person out in the midday sun was the proprietor, an unsmiling matriarch in her mid-fifties with her black hair immovably permed. Walking us part of the way to her accommodation - just far enough so there were no other hotels around - she returning to the desolate centre, hoping to sniff out any other slim pickings of backpackers.

Upon arrival at the silent, sky blue house we were met by Ilyos, who was very pleased to discover that I had a Nokia charger, as it meant he could get his phone to work for a few days at least. It was the beginning of a series of minor skirmishes in which his countenance would darken every time I asked for it back. Informed that only the most expensive air-con room was available, at these temperatures we didn't much care. In the overpowering heat of the day, the firmament vast and glaring, it was too hot to move or think and we flopped down on the beds in pools of perspiration. The room was clean, cool, had an odourless indoor toilet and a TV that could only pick up the Islamic channel. It was by far the nicest accommodation we'd stayed in.

Plague Ponds

The centre of the old town was Lyabi-Hauz - 'around the pool' in Tajik - a partially shaded square where a wooden model of the Kalon trinity – madrassa, minaret and mosque - floated in the middle of a pond. Fountains occasionally pumping out a vague mist, at the stagnant water's edge stood a six-hundred-year-old Mulberry tree, food of the silkworm, atop which perched a great white papier-mâché bird. Once home to a hundred such pools, now only two survive in Bukhara, the others having been bricked over by the Soviets to stop the spread of disease. Plague was not completely eradicated in Bukhara until the 1960s, when the government drained Lyabi-Hauz only to discover a plethora of dog carcasses.

In a city boasting a world-famous minaret, a sight so awe-inspiring that even Jenghiz Khan couldn't bring himself to destroy it, the most popular attraction for locals was a statue of holy fool Sufi savant Hoja Nasruddin mounted upon his ass. Skirting Lyabi-Hauz, it offered something different from the grand, austere Muslim monuments of antiquity and was a favourite climbing apparatus for schoolchildren, who liked to hang from the donkey's neck.

The square was the only place to be after dark, middle-class families gathering to gorge themselves around the pond and its minor league dancing fountains. The lines on their faces telling a thousand stories, elderly women laughed under the soft moonlight. Tipsy on vodka, their husbands and sons offered increasingly loud toasts. Serving up shashlyk and drinks, the pick of the waiters was the coolest kid in town, a teenage boy with a tilted Michael

Jackson fedora and a single silver glove who repeatedly attempted to moon-walk his way across the cobblestone plaza.

After the music we'd heard throughout Central Asia, the sounds here were a veritable delight, a heady mix of Persian folk, traditional Turkic and Hindi pop. A young boy who carried the speaker around on his shoulder ensured that this feast was also moveable. Sipping on his pot of choy, the DJ rocked things out, songs stopping in the middle should his cell phone ring or he happened to fancy a plov break. His silky voice double-tracked to the tunes, occasionally he would pick up the microphone and belt out a number. There was no Loreen's Eurovision-winning "Euphoria" here, rather they were content to be mildly entertained. Favoured by babushkas, Bobomurod Hamdamov's classic "Kim Ekan" rang out nightly, though to our untrained ears - as not even the DJ could tell us what the ditty was called - it sounded like Bobomurod was asking someone to "give me jam."

Ensconced in the cheap seats by the doors of the main restaurant, we'd sit of an evening surrounded by wood carvings and plastic statues, kitschy and cartoon-like. The pintsize camels attracted hyperactive children, whilst a turban-clad sculpture of a water waiter occupied the staff. Something was amiss with the water pressure; every time the employees turned their backs, a cascade would jettison from the figures silver canteen and saturate the ground, but for the life of them they couldn't work out what was making the floor wet.

It was this wet patch that led us to witness our first shashlyk maiming, when the gloved waiter emerged through the restaurant doors with a spread of precariously balanced platters. Slipping in the puddle, he sent his keen-tipped skewers soaring into the air, where they pirouetted before gravity took hold. Michael Jackson Junior barely had time to panic, a look of quick dread spreading across his features before, legs akimbo, he cried out what sounded like it should translate as 'my eye!'

As he lay prone, the deadly dish induced a brief flurry of animated chatter.

'Hgmh,' an avoirdupois German gent at the next table grunted towards me. 'We have not seen you before. Which coach are you from?'

I explained that we were travelling independently.

'Not on a tour?' he scoffed. 'This is not possible! It is dangerous, yah?'

I opined that although often inconvenient, it was certainly not particularly hazardous. Eyeballing me with a mixture of incredulity and disenchantment, he returned his attention to the tour group.

The incident with the skewers led my conversation with Stan onto a subject with which he'd become a little obsessed. In the course of our trip, we'd only seen two people wearing glasses, a ludicrously low number which Stan thought he'd figured out the reason for. In Soviet times, he explained, the cure for any degree of poor eyesight was to spend one week in pitch darkness, followed by a week of injections which left one totally blind for three weeks before one's eyesight gradually returned.

'The practice wasn't the least bit effective,' he explained as the unfortunate young waiter was led away holding a wad of tissues to his bloody oculus, 'but it was so awful that patients would proclaim themselves healed. They'd live with the problem rather than face any more treatments.'

Commerce

Broom-wielding women in high-viz orange jackets and headscarves cast bulbous shadows as they swept the dust from side to side on the pedestrianized lanes of the old town. The headwear was practical, it stopped the top of your skull from catching fire in temperatures of fifty plus Celsius, but it also served to emphasise a generation shift. The youth weren't down with it, preferring the latest out of date Chinese made Western logo fashions.

Every day we'd stop at a tiny wooden wheeled stall on the main drag behind Lyabi-Hauz, its sign proudly proclaiming it to be a 'Super Mini-Market,' despite the fact it sold nothing but cigarettes, bananas and a detergent called

Barf, Tajik for snow. Behind its counter perched a prune-like grandma in a heavy *chapan,* an outdoor dressing gown that glistened like a thousand gold teeth, though she looked so old it seemed likely she'd remember the days when it was à la mode for women to blacken their choppers.

'*Yesht,* banunchki bamunchki' she'd urge, offering up bunches of bruised bananas and their attendant midges.

Seeing that, as always, we weren't going to buy them, she'd shrug her scrawny shoulders.

'*Puz-ne-yeh,* to-mor-row!' she'd purr in a sing-song manner.

Commerce here was a force for female empowerment. Stuffing their takings into their bras, women stopped their husbands from frittering it away.

We trailed through the *Taq-I-Sarrafon,* one of Bukhara's four remaining domed bazaars, the oldest commercial structures in Central Asia. Resembling the desert cities of Star Wars, the edifices dated back to the functional reign of Ubaidullah in the early 1700s. Traders crouched behind stall after stall of mock silks, ceramics, glazed pottery and hats with indeterminate animals' feet dangling from them. Military headgear was found in abundance here, a superb array of mid-sixties to late eighties SSRU tank drivers and pilots helmets available, which had fallen into disuse in double quick time.

Herded swiftly from sight to sight, the old town was geared towards coach parties. This flashbulb tourism flourished for a couple of hours a day for less than two months of the year, then the season was over. The Bukharans had to make their living whilst they could. Tour guides exchanged their charges money, doling out som at breakneck speed whilst retaining a healthy commission. Whilst in Kyrgyzstan the slightest mark made US dollars unacceptable, in Uzbekistan such was the desire for foreign currency that notes could be dipped in dog shit and nobody would bat an eyelid.

'Hello! Shalom aleykum, my friend! What country you from? You come my shop. Just for looking,' echoed the refrain from every doorway.

By the second day, the peddlers started to recognise you.

'Mister Stan! Now you look my shop,' women with their wares spread upon blankets that lined Hoja Nurabad, the track outside the Kalon Mosque cried.

I swear we'd never seen them before, but they remembered us.

Draped in a dress with a pattern of autumn leaves, a chubby hawker in her mid-thirties whose plain features were offset by a shock of dyed ginger hair locked arms with Stan and marched him away. I observed, chortling from a safe distance as introducing herself as Nazokat, she began to festoon Stan in a rainbow of shawls.

'You tell me your price; how much you wanna pay meester? If it's a good price, I let it. What colour you like?' she rattled through her spiel, holding up a flesh pink mock silk polyester shawl.

'Silks for girlfriend,' she stated, indicating me.

I was the madam; the missus. As a man with middling length hair, I'd gotten used to it. I didn't see a single Central Asian male with remotely long hair, but the fact that they thought that I was female still reflected rather poorly upon the local ladies.

Stan clarified to Nazokat that I was actually his brother and he didn't currently have a girlfriend. Inspecting me with a raised eyebrow, a look of disbelief flashed across her face.

'Uh, okay,' she continued undeterred, 'for you then.'

Stan tried to explain that where we came from, he'd get lynched for wearing a pink shawl.

'For your Mother,' Nazokat insisted, certain she must be on steady ground here. 'Everybody has a mother, and you have only one. Come on, come on!'

Having repeated this pitch ad infinitum and failed to make her sale, Nazokat changed tack. She was good. She had her patter down to a tee.

'Wait, wait, wait meester! What you do in your country? What is your job?' she asked Stan, who answered that he was currently a student. 'Me too!' she chimed. 'I am student too. I wanna go Oxford, but I sell nothing all day,' she added mournfully. 'That's why I pushing like mosquito for tourist. How can I go Oxford if I sell nothing? So you tell me your price. How much you wanna pay? If it's a good price, I let it. Maybe you buy more.'

Unfortunately for Stan, having seen that he'd reluctantly bought two items in order to secure his escape, the next trader grabbed him by the arm and wouldn't let go. Initiating a thumb lock, she physically dragged him against his will towards her blanket. Nazokat may have had the patter, but this one had the force. And she could smell blood.

The Bug Pit

Seven times rebuilt, each new incarnation erected upon the ruins of its predecessor, Bukhara's Ark - the former Royal City - had grown ever higher. Finally bombed out by the Russians in 1920, the last Emir fled the city after learning of the Soviet army's advance under General Frunze via Bukhara's only telephone. Thus ended the last vestige of Bukharan independence. With the Ark closed for refurbishment, we circled its extensive ramparts, finishing our peregrination in empty Registan Square, where the British agents-cum-explorers Stoddart and Conolly had met their fates in the summer of 1842.

Coming to power in 1827, Emir Nasrullah Khan is widely accepted to have been the cruellest of the Mangit Khans. Numbered among his body count were twenty-eight of his close family, including three of his daughters he had killed to ensure their virginity. He once cut a member of his court in half with an axe because they'd annoyed him. Enforcing Sharia law, Nasrullah had his men stop citizens at random and ask them to recite suras from the Quran. The penalties for failure were unforgiving, to say the least. Meanwhile, he encouraged the poor to sell him their children for the purpose of buggery.

At the peak of the 'Great Game' waged between Britain and Russia - the nineteenth century equivalent of the Cold War - into the court of the Bukharan Emir rode Colonel Charles Stoddard. His mission twofold, Stoddart was to convince the Emir to free Russian slaves - thereby eliminating the Tsar's justification for the annexation of Bukhara - and to procure a treaty of friendship with the British. Little was known about the Bukharan court at the time, but one thing that had been established in the writings of Alexander Burnes, cousin of the Scottish poet Robert, was that only Muslims were allowed to ride a horse within the city walls.

Be it through hubris or folly, unfortunately for Stoddart, he failed to dismount his steed. He also brought no gifts, refused to bow and lashed out at an attendant who attempted to hasten his supplication. His letter of introduction wasn't signed by the Queen and compounding his misfortune a dispatch from the Emir of Herat had just reached Nasrullah, denouncing Stoddart as a spy who should be executed. Thus began Stoddart's long incarceration in the Emirate's dungeon. Known as the Bug Pit, the diseased hole into which a fair proportion of the city's sewage ran was filled with scorpions, rats and other 'specially bred vermin and reptiles.'

The British, the Sultans of Turkey, Khiva and Kokand, even the Russians all wrote to the Emir asking that Stoddart be released, but to no avail. When Kabul fell to the British in July 1839, fearful of invasion, Nasrullah gave Stoddart a life or death ultimatum, convert to Islam or face execution. Bloody, chewed up and desperate, Stoddart agreed. Bathed and circumcised, he was installed in the chief of police's home and finally had some freedom of movement, often going to pray at the Kalon Mosque. He even managed to sneak letters out, writing to his family in Norwich, 'This Ameer is _mad_.'

With the British not advancing on Bukhara and his letter to Queen Victoria going unanswered, Nasrullah threw Stoddart in and out of the Bug Pit according to his whims for the next year. Most outraged of all by

Stoddart's treatment was Captain Arthur Conolly, who coined the phrase 'Great Game.' A fanatical Evangelical Christian, he dreamed of uniting the region against Russia under the British flag, abolishing slavery and civilising 'the wogs.' Thirty-three years old and recently jilted, he was certain that at the very least he could persuade the local potentates to accept British overtures over those of their Russian counterparts.

Finding backers plentiful once Stoddart's cause had been added to his plans, Conolly tartly dismissed Burnes advice that the only thing which could unify the Central Asian landmass was 'the wand of a Prospero.' His scheme was finally given the go-ahead by his cousin, William MacNaughton, the British envoy in Kabul who would do nothing a year later as the esteemed explorer and Britain's most knowledgeable man on the region, Alexander Burnes was ripped limb from limb. MacNaughton fared no better himself, his torso hung from a meat hook in the centre of Kabul whilst his arms, legs and head were 'passed round the town in triumph.'

In September 1840, Conolly set off for Khiva, where though well received he procured no assurances, but was warned to stay away from Bukhara. He travelled onto Kokand, where though hospitably entertained, he obtained no treaty and was told in no uncertain terms to avoid Bukhara. At this juncture, a packet of letters from Stoddart reached him. 'The favour of the Ameer is increased in these days towards me,' Stoddart wrote. 'I believe you will be well treated here.'

Conolly arrived in Bukhara in November 1841, almost three years into Stoddart's detention. Unbeknownst to him, Nasrullah's spies had been tracking him for weeks, finding it most curious that he'd visited all of their worst enemies. The Butcher of Bukhara hedged his bets, however, receiving Conolly cordially and asking where his long awaited response from the Queen was. Conolly assured him that word would soon arrive; he was, after all, the sovereign's representative.

Whilst Stoddart and Conolly languished under house arrest, word finally arrived - not from the Queen, but from Lord Palmerston - confirming that the Emir's correspondence had been received and transmitted not to the Queen, but to the Governor General of India. Nasrullah was furious at this slight, and this was before another message arrived from Herat denouncing Captain 'Khan Ali' as a spy. Hence, Conolly got his first taste of the Bug Pit. As for Stoddart, by this point, he'd no doubt lost count of his incarcerations.

When the Governor General of India finally wrote to demand the liberation of Stoddart and Conolly, he referred to the pair as 'private travellers,' diplomatic language for disavowed agents. This combined with the ignominious British retreat in Afghanistan left Nasrullah convinced he could do as he pleased.

Returning from a resounding victory over the Khanate of Kokand in murderously high spirits, on June 24th, 1842, four years into Stoddart's captivity, Nasrullah had the duo led into the Registan, where they were made to dig their own graves. In front of a transfixed crowd, the bleeding and emaciated Stoddart and Conolly, with 'masses of flesh having been gnawed off their bones,' wept in each other's arms. Nasrullah's drummers beat a dirge as their hands were bound behind their backs and they were forced to their knees. As a convert, Stoddart most likely had the luxury of having his throat slit. Promised by the executioner that Nasrullah Khan, 'the shadow of God upon the Earth,' would spare his life if he converted to Islam, perhaps yet another trick, Conolly replied 'I am ready to die,' and was swiftly beheaded. Their remains lie buried in an unmarked grave beneath the Registan.

With no news of the officers forthcoming, friends back in Britain raised the money to send their own emissary, an oddball clergyman called Joseph Wolff. Arriving in 1845, Wolff only escaped death because the Emir found him hilarious in his full canonical garb, so amusing in fact that he summoned his 'musical band of *Hindoos*' to play Wolff a rendition of 'God Save the Queen.' Nasrullah Khan went on to rule for another fifteen years, dying peacefully in his sleep.

We visited the Emir's mud-brick prison, the *Zindon*, home of the infamous Bug Pit, now a museum where rusting manacles and faded photographs of the latterly executed are hung on display. A pitch-dark, seven-metre deep hole beneath a slim, squared-grate, at the bottom of the pit lay misshapen papier-mâché models of Stoddart and Conolly, bound by leg and neck irons and dyed a bloody hue.

The Shadow of History

In the orange early morning light, women holding parasols walked their children to school down uneven gravel alleyways filled with the ever present hum of air-con units. As the sun arced towards its zenith a haze developed, the heat so overpowering that even hawkers lost the will to sell. From noon through to four PM, if you had to be outside you stuck to whatever shade there was, and if that happened to be in the middle of the road, so be it. Veering around strollers, the few drivers on the road understood.

Weaving our way past the scant pedestrians, our bus headed out of town towards the glittering Summer Palace of Bukhara's last Emir, the outsized Alim Khan. I'd been wondering how many people you could fit in a transit van including a conductor hanging from the door by his fingertips, and I was about to find out that the answer was twenty-three.

Beyond the imposing majolica tiled gateway of the Russian-built *Sitora-I Mohi Khosa* – Palace of the Stars and the Magnificent Moon - the banqueting hall contained an elaborate bronze chandelier from Poland weighing half a ton. To gasps of awe, Bukhara's first electric light had shone from it during the 1910s, thanks to a fifty-watt Russian generator.

An avenue of quince trees led to an ostentation of peacocks parading around a voluminous pool where the Emir's harem used to frolic. Raised on a platform high above them, he would sit upon his gilded throne, bejewelled and decked in golden threads, choosing his lucky lady for the night. Escaping the conflict between reformers and imams, ever more dependent upon the overlords who would inevitably bring about his downfall, Amir Khan spent his last years as ruler cocooned in the Summer Palace, sating his gluttonous appetite from a glass fronted Russian refrigerator.

From the ninth century Pit of the Herbalists to the Ismail Samani Mausoleum and the bird market, Bukhara wasn't about its separate sights, though, it was the sum of its parts, the timeless city permeated by an air of antiquity, an unspoilt window into the past.

Avoiding hawker row, we took to the cobblestone back alleys. Decked in *dopys* - four-sided black skullcaps - striped robes and knee-length rubber boots, revered white-bearded elders - *aksakals* - were idling the afternoon away over pots of choy. From terraces where their mothers were hanging lines of laundry between buildings, the playful cries of children rang out. Climbing a darkened spiral staircase, we found a vantage point from which to watch the sun set over the Kalon Minaret.

Built as an inland lighthouse for desert caravans, the Kalon Minaret - 'great' in Tajik - was probably the tallest building in Central Asia upon its completion in 1127. The third minaret to have been built on this site, previous incarnations had caught fire and collapsed onto the mosque below, officially because of the 'evil eye.' Also known as the 'Tower of Death,' over the centuries the minaret has seen countless bodies sewn into entrail catching sacks and tossed from its forty-seven metre high lantern. Particularly popular during Mangit times, this practice survived until the 1920s.

Home of the first recorded use of the now ubiquitous blue tile in Central Asia, the fourteen distinct bands of the minaret were majestic in the pink light, its scale and intricacy remarkable. The sense of history lingering, everyday life went on unabated at its stout base. Nazokat and the other traders were beginning to pack down for the night, transferring their goods into storefronts. The heat of the day finally having abated, head-scarfed babushkas sat chit-chatting on the cool stone steps of the Mir-i-Arab Madrassa. In the square, a Daytona yellow, three-wheeled Del boy van which managed to invade all of my photos was again circling where other drivers feared to venture. At the foot of the minaret, the requisite wedding was taking place, only this time the bride and groom were smiling for once.

The Pivo Centre

At dusk, in leafy Samani Park opposite the Ark, we finally found the legendary Pivo Centre, where a head sized tankard of beer cost one thousand som, less than thirty English pence. Pleased to see us, the horseshoe moustached proprietor hovered around our cracked plastic table. Making thumbs-up signs and grinning excitedly, he endeavoured to entice us into trying the shashlyk, which congealing lumps of cream coloured fat were dripping from as it released dark plumes across the bottle strewn garden.

Pleased to have ultimately located the place, we had a couple of drinks and played with a kindle of scraggy kittens that milled about at our feet. Pre-occupied, we failed to notice the arrival of a drunk who'd wandered in and collapsed face down upon a tapchan. The proprietor and his barkeep were vainly attempting to revive the lush with a combination of shakes and tiny slaps to the face. Interrupting them out of sudden necessity, I asked for directions to the tua-let. Guided toward a malodorous underground passageway with no light and disintegrating steps, I smashed headfirst into its entrance lintel.

Re-emerging the worse for wear, I discovered that whilst the staff may have given up on rousing the drunk, the boisterous posse on the table behind us had taken up the baton and were howling with laughter as they taunted him.

'Shashlyk! Shashlyk!' a young man scoffed as he waved a kebab skewer in the prone fellow's face, much to the amusement of his friends.

The sot squirmed. The belly was game, but the rest of the body was unwilling.

Soon more joined in the jeering, until the call of the shashlyk proving too much, the carouser finally awoke and reeled away into the night. Unfortunately for him, he'd left behind not only his bag, but a stack of som tucked under the *kurpachas* - patchwork mattress-cum-cushions – he'd been passed out upon. Red and blue lights suddenly flashing as if a disco beat were about to kick in, it was then that the militsiya turned up. It was time to leave.

With all three restaurants in town fully booked by coach parties, it became apparent that there would be no dinner. Vowing to have a nightcap at Lyabi-Hauz Square, we cut through dentist's row, where *Stomatologiya's* placards advertised cartoonish pictures of giant molars and approving mullahs. A pounding beat welcoming us through the last of the winding alleyways, we arrived at our normal haunt as the DJ's plov break finished.

At the Lyabi-Hauz Chaikhana, freed from their parent's supervision, a bunch of sullen, underage Russian kids in skin-tight stonewash jeans and leather waistcoats were sprawled out swigging bottles of *Sigma* and smoking thin, black cigarettes. Sat at the table next to them, a mother with two young children performed the *amin* in gratitude to Allah, cupping her hands and passing them in front of her face in the Muslim gesture of grace as her order of a bottle of Coke was set down. With its imitation red and white stripes, the locally produced bottle of Libella that had arrived was, in appearance at least, barely distinguishable from the real thing. Sneering secure in the conviction of their cultural superiority, the Russians sauntered off.

Presently the coach parties pulled up, German pensioners who'd had a glass of Riesling too many dancing with their tour guides in some arm flapping interpretation of an imagined local style. Feeling sorry for the guides, who had to endure this on a nightly basis throughout the short tourist season, I was pleased to be distracted by the dulcet tones of "Kim Ekan," and this time one of the locals knew what the song was. I thought I'd finally cracked it, until his attempts to write down the artist and the title proved to be no more than an illegible scrawl.

We later tried to find this track and a song that's chief refrain sounded like "Alan John" in the record stores of Tashkent, but the staff just gave us funny looks.

'Why do you want Uzbek music? We have Russian and European dance-pop,' a baffled assistant asked.

The lack of food and mounting pivo count beginning to take their toll, I staggered to the tua-let about ready to call it a night. Passing the Lyabi-Hauz Chaikhana's immensely disturbing taxidermied swan, I managed to bust in on a hunkered down babushka who, having failed to lock the door, screamed at my intrusion. With the image of her roosting indelibly scratched into my retinas, we stumbled back to the B&B. I had a phone charger to reclaim.

CHAPTER 6

Across the Kyzyl-Kum Desert

At the Karvon Bazaar, the gateway for westbound transport, old women sat wrapped in thick chapans despite the heat. Broad-shouldered men in horizontally striped t-shirts clustered around plastic tables in the shade of gazebos. Given the intense sunlight, it was impossible to tell if they were squinting or scowling. Wandering somnolently, soldiers in dusty asparagus green uniforms seemed unsure of their purpose. Even when handbags broke out over a driver poaching a fare, they turned their faces away.

There being no public transport, we waited for a shared taksi to fill up. Asked when we might depart, the driver's response was '*hozer*,' which literally translates as 'any moment now,' but in practice means an indeterminate amount of time, maybe never. So with the scent of diesel and dill thick in the air, we sat drinking choy as the laborious process played itself out. Every forty minutes or so, a potential passenger would arrive and linger for a while before giving up and disappearing, at which point another new hopeful would materialise.

After two and a half hours, there was a flurry of excited activity and we were suddenly ready to depart. It was a relief to finally be on the move, a soothing breeze whistling through a crack in the window. A mere four minutes into our journey, however, we pulled off the main road, jouncing between rows of ramshackle *Khrushcheby* which looked as if they'd been placed by giant hands.

Built in haste during the Khrushchev years in response to a dire housing shortage throughout the USSR, the Khrushcheby took their slang name from the Russian word *trushcheby*, meaning slum. A mixture of grey and beige - part of what has been described as 'an economy of planned shortages' - each of the apartments in the five-storey blocks had the usual defective air-con unit jutting from it. As we juddered to a halt in a pothole, a rotund woman decked in slippers who'd taken the final spot in the Lada trudged off through a playground filled with rotting garbage, faeces and a swing set with a single seat left suspended. The armpits of his shirt already stained with sweat, our driver kicked his tyres disinterestedly whilst the militsiya, more conspicuous and emboldened in the suburbs, eyed us with a cold, hard suspicion.

An hour passed, the marbled sun climbing ever higher. The female passenger had returned, but we were still no closer to leaving. Emerging from a passageway, a shady looking skinhead we'd evidently been expecting slunk towards us. His eyes darting like stag beetles, the gaunt stripling handed the woman an envelope bulging with banknotes. As if smelling the som, the militsiya descended, the youth disappearing into a tenement as we pulled away in an urgent cloud of dust.

Wedged in the back - Stan pressed up against a big-boned fellow fondly fondling his balls - we made good progress for two hundred metres, until spotting a friend, our driver stopped for a chinwag in the middle of a roundabout. Away again on the burning road, we made five kilometres before pausing for food. Lumbering resignedly out of the car, I realised we were back at the Karvon Bazaar. In over four hours, we'd gone precisely nowhere. As we finally set off in earnest, however, the large woman turned to face us with a disarming smile, offering to share the plastic bag filled with yoghurt she'd just purchased. In an instant, all was forgiven.

Passing through a checkpoint near an isolated town, lorries loaded with massive pipes bound for oil and gas projects queued whilst the militsiya riffled through our luggage. Cotton fields and donkeys were giving way to desolate, patchy scrub. A sunburnt arm resting out of his open window, our loquacious driver and his two Uzbek passengers gabbed ceaselessly on their phones. It was good to talk. Even when we reached the desert and the signal dropped out, it didn't stop them checking for reception and looking mildly disappointed.

As we journeyed farther from Bukhara, the initially colourless sand lining the road turned a deep golden yellow, but never the red - *kyzyl* in

Turkic - that had given the desert its name. Stopping at another checkpoint in the middle of nowhere, a wooden shack offered shrivelled plastic bottles of petrol and lukewarm cans of Fanta at vastly inflated prices. Rusted barrels, scrap metal and discarded road signs lay strewn across the sand and gravel, out of place pigeons bobbing their heads as they strutted. Ostensibly abandoned, hulking containers loomed, but offered no shade to the conscripts stationed at this posting in hell. Cut a hundred metres adrift in the flat emptiness was possibly the worst toilet in Central Asia. To expect running water, any water at all, or even a door may have been extremely hopeful, but there wasn't even a hole, just excrement smeared litter on the desert floor.

At yet another roadblock, our driver and passengers struggled to conceal their annoyance as bored inductees pawed through our belongings once more. Then, without warning as we approached the town of Turtkul, a river spawned a belt of vegetation all the lusher after six hours of unbroken wasteland. In fields full of fibrous cotton, people were hunched over, picking at lobed-leaved bushes with bleeding hands.

In the faceless, Soviet grid town of Urgench, a frenzied crowd had gathered to goggle at a car crash. Visibly exhausted, our driver palmed us off on a taksi full of boys slow to desist in their rubbernecking. With "Euphoria" blasting from the stereo of the boxy, but surprisingly fast Moskvitch 412 aggrandized with a slick spoiler and tinted windows, the shaven-headed crew posed barely audible questions for the remainder of the ride to Khiva.

Khiva -
Boiler Room Blues#1

Madina and Ilyos having forwarded us onto their friend's digs in Khiva, we were delivered like a clammy gift upon the steps of the Alibek. The journey having taken eleven hours, I was happy to hand over our passports in order to receive registration slips and be shown to a room. Attempting to enter the tiny, windowless cubbyhole proved no mean feat, however, the door being wedged shut by the unavoidable proximity of a bed. When I say bed,

I mean a sheet of hardboard with a blanket on it. From within the walls, an ominous clanging and whirring emanated.

The chill of the desert night having descended, we head out in search of a supermarket, of which there were three in a row, each featuring crates of vodka stacked precariously high. Securing a stash, we ventured up to the terrace of the Alibek, where we were joined by the proprietor's son. A boyish, well-spoken fifteen-year-old, Dilshod's ambition was to study at Oxford, though he couldn't say when or where he'd first heard of the prestigious university. The wind whipping stinging grains of sand around the balcony, the only other guest was a balding, middle-aged Austrian with misty round glasses who looked well lubricated. Waddling over, he settled at our floor table. He had an interesting story to tell.

Whilst standing atop the West Gate the previous evening, he'd spotted hectares of downy cotton fields receding into low dunes in the distance. Resolving to take a stroll, this very morning he'd set off, sharing his packed lunch with beaming cotton pickers along the way. The farther he got from town, however, the less genial a reception he'd received.

'People started pointing back the way I came, but I didn't understand. I waved at them and carried on,' Holger explained, waving his hands and pressing on. 'I just reach the dunes when the militsiya come running at me pointing their guns. I froze. I was terrified! They were trying to take my camera, but it is expensive, yah. So we are on top of the sand dune having a tug of war over the camera. They tackle me to the ground, put me in handcuffs and take me to the military hut. One of the soldiers speaks a little English, so I tell him how I have seen the dunes and only want to take a walk. They laugh a little and give me some plov and some vodka.'

I poured Holger a drink as he warmed to his tale, the gusting wind causing his comb-over to dance. In the street below us, a disturbance was taking place, a gang of boys wrecking something whilst barking and baying. The commotion closing in on the guesthouse, Dilshod peered through the carved wooden balustrade, excused himself and went to see what was happening.

'So, forty-five minutes later,' the rosy-cheeked Austrian continued, removing his grit covered glasses and wiping them on his sleeve, 'a car arrives and they take me to the Passport Office in Urgench. I spend another hour and a half explaining what happened to different officers, each of them feeding and pouring me vodka. Finally, I speak to the Captain in a very big office.

'"Mister, you are very lucky," he explained to me. "You were about to cross the border into Turkmenistan, and here there are landmines. Still, the Turkmen soldiers would probably shoot you before you got that far."

'So they delete the pictures from my camera and give me a lift back here. They even give me a souvenir,' he concluded, pulling a bottle from his knapsack and smirking as Dilshod made his way back up the stairs.

'Very bad, very bad,' Dilshod frowned, jerking his head towards the hullabaloo on the street. 'They are drinking so much they forget where they live and cannot speak. Now they only fall over and howl like wild dogs.'

As the squall increased, the night grew bitter. It wasn't even ten thirty and the streets were uninhabited. This was no party town. Leaving the yowling to actual packs of strays, a sound augmented by the high-pitched shrieking of bats, even the drunks had dispersed. Withdrawing to our poorly lit room, the rumbling of the boiler seemed heightened by the still of the night. Whilst partial deafness and earplugs shielded me somewhat from the death-rattle, they could not save me from the pain of the bed.

'We've got to get out of here,' Stan groaned at four AM.

I agreed, but we had to get our passports and registration slips first.

The Museum City

Sleep being a distant dream, we set out for Ichon-Qala - the walled inner city - at five AM. Standing sentry by its entrance, covered in a fine green patina, a statue of Al-Khorezm looked stern and unforgiving. The ninth century Khivan mathematician, whose name Westerners morphed into the word algorithm, his *al-jabr* (algebra) still forms the basis of schoolchildren's nightmares.

Passing through the cavernous mouth of the 'Father's Gate,' an afghanetz wind tore around the monuments and through the maze of deserted, moon-lit alleyways. The minarets keeping silent watch, the stillness of the city made us speak in hushed tones. Not being morning people, the one thing the discomfort of the Alibek had afforded us was the opportunity to see Khiva at dawn.

According to legend, Khiva was founded by Shem, son of Noah. Coming to prominence after the Amu Darya River changed its course away from Konye-Urgench - now across the border in Turkmenistan - Khiva became a state capital under the Uzbek Shaybanids in the late sixteenth century. Prospering as a slave town on the old Silk Road, Khiva's bazaars sold those souls unfortunate enough to be captured on the Kara-Kum (Black Sand) Desert or the Kazakh Steppe.

Considered worse than infidels by the Sunni Turkmen and the Khivans, most of the slaves were Persian Shi'ites. Any Christians or Jews captured were forced to convert to Shi'ite Islam, making them worthy of slavery. Persian girls were particularly popular for harems; Russian men as hard workers were worth up to four camels. As the town changed hands through the next three centuries, its slave market remained the biggest in Central Asia.

With the Khanate crumbling, the city of Khiva finally fell to Tsarist expansionism in 1873, when the munificent and much admired Mohammed Rahim Bahadur was on the throne. A poet-philosopher - pen name *Feruz Khan* (meaning victorious) - Rahim retained his position, but was stripped of his army and expected to pay an unfeasibly large war indemnity. Invited to St. Petersburg along with his progressive prime minister, the Vizier Islom

Hoja, the pair returned inspired. A purely ornamental telephone was soon installed in the citadel, while Hoja set about building Khiva's first hospital, a secular school for both boys and girls and a post office in the hope that a mail service would one day arrive.

Things changed quickly with the death of the Khan. An unredeemed opium addict, Rahim's firstborn was passed over in favour of his second son, the marginally less useless Isfandiyar. Obsessed with his harem and dancing boys, the new Khan left the administration of his demesne to the Vizier, which worked well until Tsar Nicolai summoned the Khan and his retinue to St. Petersburg.

Unfamiliar with virtuous female company, at the official reception Isfandiyar propositioned the Tsarina, before heading to a brothel and contracting syphilis. Scandalised, the Tsar refused to appear in official portraits commemorating the occasion. Returning to his Khanate, Isfandiyar's physician prescribed sleeping with forty virgins to be the cure for his disease. Anxious lest his own daughter should become infected, Islom Hoja quarantined the Khan, making an unrelenting enemy.

Resolving to rid himself of the meddling Vizier, Isfandiyar sought allies, finding them in the shape of an arch-conservative Turkmen warrior called Junaid and the mullahs, themselves threatened by Hoja's modernizing reforms. A scheme was devised; ordered to the palace, it was arranged that the Vizier be robbed and murdered by "bandits" en route. Covering his tracks, the Khan then had his co-conspirators executed, but Junaid escaped to assassinate Isfandiyar shortly thereafter, thus completing the circle.

With the death of the Khan, Junaid arranged to have Isfandiyar's senile uncle, Said Abdullah placed upon the throne as a puppet. Against a backdrop of escalating tribal uprisings and an early example of regional conflict over diminishing water supplies, sixteen months later the city was overrun by Nationalists and Bolsheviks. Abdullah abdicated, ending his days in a Moscow prison hospital. For the next decade, Junaid repeatedly attempted to take back Khiva, but his forays were repulsed.

Exiled by the Bolsheviks, the would-be heirs to the throne returned for a visit after independence. Speaking only Russian and Ukrainian, they strolled around in jeans and miniskirts, taking snapshots of this mysterious and alien land that might have been theirs.

Today, Khiva has a reputation of being a museum under open skies. Beautifully preserved, yet devoid of life, it has a ghostly feel, present yet absent, as if reluctant to rise from its long slumber and face past glories it can never hope to regain.

Boiler Room Blues#2

It was a little after six thirty when the first rays of sunlight began to filter through, illuminating domes and dappling the homogeneous mud walls in golden shades. With a dribbling, toothy grin, Khiva's lone camel, Katya was waking from her sand dune dreams. On the main drag, the ground was being watered in a futile shot at holding down the dust through another windswept, sun-baked day. Stalls adorned with tourist tat appeared, traders dressed in velvet tracksuits laying out their wares. Given the thin trickle of visitors, the cotton bags, furry black afro-like sheepskin hats – *telpeks* - and papier-mâché puppets resembling a Khivan Punch and Judy would largely remain unsold. Not as easily accessible as Samarkand and Bukhara, Khiva had a frontier feel. The coach parties didn't come here.

Soon enough, the *chaikhanas* (teahouses) began to open. Cobalt blue porcelain tea sets patterned with cotton flower motifs clinking; the age-old ritual of steam rising from *piyolas* – small bowls - filled the morning air. Mare's tail clouds drifting high above its squat, round base, behind the principle thoroughfare stood the unfinished Kalta Minor Minaret, its glazed turquoise tiles glimmering.

Commissioned in 1851, Khan Abu al-Ghazi Muhammad Amin Bahadur planned to outstrip his rivals by building a tower so tall it would dwarf the Kalon Minaret in Bukhara, allowing him to spy on his foes some four hundred kilometres away across the Kyzyl-Kum Desert. With Khiva being famed at the time as a land of no mercy where men's heads were lopped off onto hotplates so onlookers could enjoy watching them sizzle, the architect fled in fear of his life. Some say he found out he was to be executed upon the completion of the project - so he couldn't be contracted by the Bukharans to erect a taller one – so he jumped from the dumpy minaret, turning into a bird and soaring away. Upon the Khan's death in 1855, his construction crews also vanished, leaving only this ungainly stump.

Perambulating the back alleys in search of a particular guesthouse we were never going to find, we chanced upon the Zafarbek Hotel and were led by a matronly Russian woman into the manager's office. Weighing in at a good 150 kilos, the manager, Usman was the archetype of an old Khan from a fading sepia photograph. He was also, it transpired, an extremely slick *biznizman*, but in our current sleep deprived state anything had to be an improvement.

Back at the Alibek, our departure was met with much wailing and gnashing of teeth. Ideally, we'd have slipped away quietly, but there was the small matter of retrieving our passports and receiving the infamous registration slips. A residue of Soviet bureaucracy, registration formalities still haunted Uzbekistan. All tourists had to be able to prove where they'd stayed for every night of their journey, and the bribe-hungry militsiya could ask to see these tiny scraps at any point. Holding onto tourist's papers for as long as possible, enterprising hoteliers had also found a way to use this red tape to their advantage, muddying the waters of checking out.

In an effort to spare the feelings of the Alibek staff, we offered up all manner of excuses we'd concocted over our morning choy. It was some time before Dilshod emerged, grimacing as he handed our documents over.

'Hah! I am afraid your room had been taken,' Usman greeted us an hour later as we lugged our bags up to the front of the Zafarbek. 'I can show you another room,' he added, smirking as he scratched at his salt and pepper beard, 'but a little more expensive.'

Donkeys and Disco Balls

Compared to other places we'd visited, changing money was a cloak and dagger affair in Khiva. It took an hour of enquiries before a long-faced man in a shapeless pinstripe suit made his approach. Muttering as his eyes bounced from side to side, he ushered us into a nook in the crenelated city walls. Passing us his phone, monosyllabic conversations followed, a succession of equally poor rates being offered.

Back on the main drag, our queries were met with whispers between traders who were all shifty sidelong glances. Eventually, a woman with a mane of raven hair and a sweet if suspicious smile beckoned us to follow her. Depositing us in the gloomy Oq-Masjid Mosque, converted into a storage space stacked with carpets and cluttered art prints, she disappeared with our dollars. When she finally returned, laden with bags of banknotes, she displayed the uniformly dexterous cypher skills. If counting money were an Olympic sport, the Uzbeks would take a clean sweep of the medals.

Our new room at the Zafarbek contained a single bed, the breakfast we'd painstakingly negotiated only made available after Stan engaged in a prolonged shouting match with Usman. When the promised food arrived, it consisted of an undercooked egg, teeth crumbling lepyoshka and melted slurry in shiny wrappers best described as cheap chocolate rubbed in gravel. The saving grace of the Zafarbek was smiley Svetlana, a pretty ethnic Tatar twenty-something employee who seemed incapable of anything other than grinning and giggling in a shy, yet saucy manner. Carrying our drinks tray, she tripped, sending the silver choy set clattering to earth, which educed a tittering fit and a crimson blush.

Part of our purpose in town was to visit the Khiva Silk Carpet Workshop, a UNESCO launched enterprise where silk *kilims* - hand-woven tapestry rugs - are produced at a rate of one centimetre per day. In the cool, rattan shaded courtyard of the converted madrassa, dark-eyed women pored over their exacting work with a loving precision. Sharp twine grasped between their slender fingers, boxes of natural dyes from zok to indigo, madder root to ishkor ash were spread at their feet. Wispy and cocoon-like, balls of silk lay on plates, the finished articles hanging from the walls.

Thrilled to meet the manager, Madrim, whom he'd read about, Stan bought a carmine red piece measuring forty centimetres square, the largest he could afford. His dinky new hundred euro kilim tucked under his arm, Stan bowed to one and all, but unfortunately misjudged the height of the door frame as he made to leave. Smashing his head, he pirouetted, staggering backwards with limbs forked, ending up in a crumpled heap on the floor.

Behind the workshop, swathed in wooden scaffolding stood Khiva's holiest site, the Pahlavon Mahmud Mausoleum. Known by Khivans as *Palvan Pir* -the Strongman Saint - Mahmud was part wrestler, part poet and part-time furrier. The patron saint of Khiva, today barren women and hopeful newlyweds make offerings of *borsok* (miniature fried doughnuts) at his tomb as part of a fertility ritual.

With Stan still rubbing his head in a semi-concussed state, we clambering up a decaying section of the oft reconstructed city walls. Gaps in the craggy ramparts revealed glimpses of the new town, flat, unpeopled and nondescript. In the distance, a disused Ferris wheel poked through the low tree line, rusting leisurely against a cloudless sky. Spotting us scrabbling down by the southern 'Stone Gate,' an ingratitude of grubby children proceeded to prod us, giving Stan the opportunity to offload the biros he'd been carrying for just such an occasion.

South of the Ichon-Qala, fields of spindly, water hungry cotton took over. Knowing better than to venture too close to the Turkmen border, instead, we headed north. For some time now I'd been living on a diet of cheese spread, *non* bread and out of date crisps, with the occasional undercooked egg thrown in for good measure. There were only two places to eat in the old town, but I'd read about a fish restaurant in the village of Ogahiy, three and a half kilometres north-east. It having been a long while since I'd seen a fish, the lure proved too great to resist.

The heat of the day having begun to abate, we set out at four PM through the eastern 'Strongman's Gate,' passing the only working mosque in Khiva. Parked outside, a mobile pivo trailer - a ginormous wooden beer barrel on wheels – was daubed with a childlike painting of a frosty pint beneath a palm tree. Flowing from the mosque's entrance, a small band of men who'd found prayer to be thirsty work set about making use of the advantageous location of this pitch.

Aside from this, the streets were empty; granite and mossy bronze statues of long forgotten heroes outnumbering the populace. In the main park of the Dichon-Qala - the new town - the cars of the Ferris wheel rocked gently from side to side. Topped with loudspeakers, a broken silver and square Soviet era clock protruded through a spider's web of power lines. Forever fixed at noon, it gleamed like a window into a functional futuristic past.

Farther from town on the road to Urgench, a smattering of buses, Daewoos and Ladas belched a thick black miasma. Bored soldiers stood erect at intersections, eyeing us from beneath their peaked caps. On side streets rarely bothered by traffic, sheep grazed on tufts of brown grass. By the verge of a sprawling cotton plantation, we passed a braying donkey with two young boys hanging lovingly from its neck.

'It's an Uzbek proverb that a man's first wife is his donkey,' Stan told me.

I started to ask him why, but his knowing smile made me realise I didn't need to.

Out of our element in the hamlet of Ogahiy, we were received with stupefaction by disbelieving locals. Like something that had fallen from a Christmas cracker, we had a short-lived novelty value. By this juncture, two hours into our walk, it was abundantly clear we were never going to find the restaurant - if it even existed - and that asking for directions was a non-starter. With the long, starlit night descending, we managed to thumb a lift back to Khiva. A cool kid wearing shades despite the twilight, our driver was eager to talk, but the language barrier meant that confirming our nationality was about the extent of our interaction. Pulling up outside the Ichon-Qala, he raised the palm of his hand, spurning my offer of a fee for his troubles.

'Friend,' he said.

Having failed in our Ogahiy mission, the same two dinner options remained. It was either the Khorezm Art Restaurant or the Khelvak, located on the grounds of its namesake hotel, which was superior in all ways except for the service. Idling into the courtyard, we were joined by Richard from Calcutta, who'd first spotted us in Bukhara and was best described, as Stan put it, as 'most peculiar.'

As we lounged on a tapchan laden with thick kurpachas, the traditional 'caravan' songs drifting from the crackling speakers were rudely interrupted by a jolting, accordion-based muzak cover of "New York, New York." Coming from out of nowhere, this served to add sauce to the random meat floating in the vegetarian dish I'd ordered.

A return to the previous musical regime restoring a sense of harmony, Richard espoused his admiration of Lady Diana and the British Royal family, of whom, much to his bewilderment, I told him I was not a fan.

'I don't understand it. I just don't understand it,' he railed, wagging a long index finger at me. 'What is not to love? I tell you, the British leaving was the worst thing that ever happened to India. Oh yes.'

Having picked at the bones of his greasy dish, Stan was looking green-gilled, but I was getting into the absurdity of the conversation. His imploring eyes drilling holes into me, however, I was persuaded that it was time to leave.

Saying farewell to Richard, we head into the black wall of night, my constant note-taking meaning that I was utterly reliant on Stan to inform me of any upcoming apertures in the road, which were both deep and frequent. Vaulting across an open sewer, we approached our last port of call, the Ekvator *diskoteka*.

Built in 1912 as the Nasrullahboy Madrassa, the Ekvator was shrouded in such darkness I presumed it to be closed. As if triggering a tripwire, however, the moment we stumbled over the threshold a very un-Islamic cross on the ceiling was illuminated in flashing orange lights and disco balls began to spin. Reverberating eerily down the chill stone corridors, dance-pop began to boom. Neon stairs led to a DJ booth covered in holographic stickers which spelt out 'God is a DJ.' Apart from us and the chain-smoking barman, the place was completely deserted.

CHAPTER 7

The Road Less Travelled

The charge of taksi drivers milling about the northern 'Bukhara Gate' weren't shy about stealing fares. Pulling at each other's shirts, their coriaceous faces reddened as they tussled over our luggage. Their confrontation simmering down, by and by the men returning to skulking and kicking at stones.

Funnelling power from overhead cables, Skoda trolleybuses whirred along the road to Urgench, donkey carts, cabs and three-wheeled vans overloaded with ripe, vine green watermelons vying for the remaining space. Passing the turnoff to Qoshkopir, traffic slowed to take in a Daewoo Damas van, which lay on its side like a dead dog in the sun.

Changing cars in Urgench, the provincial capital of the Khorezm Region, we wedged ourselves in with a band of locals. Geometric patterns and cotton motifs adorned the apartment blocks of the city, a Soviet Orientalism designed to marry local tradition and functionality. In a sealed-off government compound, a granite statue of a horse reared up. They enjoyed their heroic equestrian statues. A truly multipurpose animal, they liked to ride it, drink its milk and eat it too.

Nearing the edge of the urban sprawl, we crossed the still, shimmering Amu Darya River. Known to the Ancient Greeks as the Oxus, the once mighty river has been drained to feed Uzbekistan's thirsty cotton crop. Passing a Lada factory, the road gave way to bulky trucks, tractors and cotton pickers. With the militsiya emerging from what had appeared to be the shells of abandoned buildings, a tinge of fear was noticeable in the eyes of our driver and passengers every time we hit a stop sign. Leaving Khorezm Province behind though, even these *kontrol'no tojka* disappeared and there was nothing but a desert that didn't even look like sand, more the ceaseless grey residue from a quarry.

A three-hour journey brought us to the rubble-strewn outskirts of Nukus, wasteland capital of the "autonomous" Republic of Karakalpakstan. Once a thriving agricultural centre, Karakalpakstan is now one of the sickest places on Earth. Respiratory illness, typhoid, tuberculosis and oesophageal cancers are rife, birth defects and infant mortality rates amongst the highest in the world. The deliberate destruction of the Aral Sea for irrigation purposes has caused toxic dust storms so vast they are visible from space, ravaging a half a million kilometre square area. Spreading nitrates and carcinogens, these storms used to hit once every five years, but now come ten times a year.

Farther north, beyond ships lying stranded in the manmade desert, Vozrozhdeniya - Rebirth Island - contains the ruins of a Soviet biological weapons facility immortalised in the game 'Call of Duty.' Covered in telegraph poles set one and a half kilometres apart, sensors on the island's testing range measured the effects of smallpox, brucellosis and bubonic plague on monkeys, sheep and donkeys. Hundreds of tons of anthrax were buried here over the decades and covered only in bleach as a decontaminant. Vacated in haste upon the collapse of the Soviet Union, Rebirth Island was rejoined to the mainland in 2001 due to the Aral Sea's falling water levels. Its anthrax canisters purportedly decontaminated by the US as a payoff for support in the so-called 'war on terror,' today the island is an eerie expanse of smashed test tubes and Petri dishes, its radioactive scraps fought over by smugglers.

An ancient culture, the Karakalpak people were renowned for ignoring Soviet dogma, but look where that had gotten them. It brought to mind a quote from the closest thing to a Karakalpakstan Tourism Website:

'Just think of the excitement of visiting a country that most people have never even heard of? One that is even listed in that wonderfully exotic travel guide *No Holiday: 80 Places You Don't Want to Visit.*'

Nukus

A chunky three storey structure painted in pale oyster, the Hotel Nukus was a cesspit, but in the mind's eye of the proprietor, it was first-rate. All available funds having been spent on the foyer, an elaborate mix of pillars, balustrades and faux marble flooring, first impressions were decent enough. One only had to venture onto the stairwell, however, where a cleaner was lifelessly mopping the threadbare carpet as she dragged on the lipstick smeared butt of a cigarette, to be reminded that first impressions can be misleading.

His passengers the least of his concern, our first hour in the city had been spent on the taksi driver puttering around picking up groceries and dropping in on friends, every cabbie's prerogative. Belatedly deposited outside of the Hotel Rahnamo – whose website bizarrely promised that the room rates included medical cover - we cross-referenced our maps. Lugging our bags in circles around the block bringing us no closer to our goal, if the Rahnamo was there it was wearing a cloak of invisibility.

The familiar sound of dry retching echoing through the unlit hallways, the cleaner showed us to our room. Locking the door behind us - the only way to keep it on its hinges - we tossed our luggage onto the beds. Above the window frame, the broken air-con unit oozed a thick brown substance onto the stained wallpaper.

Their menus identical, there were only two places to eat in town. Its concealed entrance like a portal to some extraneous Gentlemen's Club, the closer of the two was the Sheraton, which for all its polished wine glasses, ribbons and bows failed to live up to its illustrious namesake. The English language menu did offer three different variations of lard and tongue though, as well as some interesting other options, such as the 'Hush Beef's Legs Rise.' Ordering the 'Scam Bled Omelette' I settled into the faux leather booth, where mosquitoes proceeded to make a meal out of me.

Outside, the sun blazing through a sky layered in deepening hues of blue, the air lacked the moisture necessary for clouds to form. Liberally sprinkled around the vacuity of the town, buildings with pumice grey satellite dishes plastered to their roofs were bestrewn with splintered glass and Soviet attempts at Timurid motifs. Knots of unemployed men huddled together, loitering on street corners. In the distinctly unamusing Amusement Park, where a solitary Ferris wheel stood eroded and unmoving, a wedding was taking place. The sullen bride lifting the hem of her ballooning gown, the party posed for a photograph beneath a statue of famed Karakalpak poet A'jiniyaz Uli, immortalised toying listlessly with a two-stringed *dambura*.

In search of ever-elusive moneychangers, we headed to the bustling Markaziy Bazaar, where stoic traders wearing grave expressions endeavoured to sell whatever they could lay their hands on. Old before their time, women with swollen bellies and clumps of hair missing peddled the cheapest brands of loose cigarettes from buckled wooden trays. Empty bottles of vodka at their sides, men with wonky skullcaps lay passed out in the shade of tin shacks. Normally a sign of wealth, here the gold teeth of the younger women were a marker of endemic malnutrition, which coupled with a lack of calcium meant that teeth fell like snow, especially during pregnancy. In Karakalpakstan, it was gold teeth or gums.

Yet it was in this shutdown ecosystem, where the highest rates of tuberculosis on the planet offered a fertile testing ground for new research into respiratory illness, that a remarkable collection of art had survived precisely because of its inhospitable location. Risking denouncement as an 'enemy of the people,' obsessive Ukrainian-born painter, archaeologist and art collector, Igor Savitsky spirited away thousands of avant-garde pieces banned in the Soviet Union. In this farthest-flung corner of the former empire, the lesser seen State Art Museum of the Republic of Karakalpakstan houses works by a forgotten generation. A mishmash of styles and influences far removed from the purportedly uplifting romanticism which Socialist realism had permitted, many of the artists displayed here met with an unsavoury end.

Featuring dazzling, geometric scenes of everyday Central Asian life, the oil paintings of Aleksandr Volkov were awash with colour. When the campaign against free-thinking artists began in the USSR following an edict from Stalin, his Cubo-Futurist vision saw Volkov labelled a bourgeois reactionary. Fired from his posts, he lost everything. Over the course of the next three years, all of Volkov's works were removed from the leading Russian galleries. Up until his death in 1957, upon orders from Moscow, he was isolated from any contact with artists, critics or art lovers. To anyone who wanted to meet Volkov, they declared that the painter was too ill to see them. Still, in many ways Volkov was one of the lucky ones, for at least he avoided the gulags.

A fusion of Dada and Cubism, a piece entitled *On His Knees* is most likely the sole surviving work by Lev Galperin, a well-travelled painter and sculptor from Odessa. No longer permitted to leave the Motherland after returning in 1921, he eked out a meagre existence working to order on bas-reliefs. His paintings adjudged to be counter-revolutionary, he was arrested on Christmas Day of 1934 and sentenced to five years hard labour. During his trial, Galperin dared to voice his scepticism regarding the Soviet system and the state of art in the union. His death certificate simply reads, 'Cause of death: execution by shooting.'

A series of sketches by Nadezhda Borovaya show what conditions in the gulags were like. When her husband was executed in 1938, Borovaya was sent to the Temnikov Camp, where she spent the next seven years secretly recording and smuggling out scenes of everyday life. With dazzling bravado, Savitsky procured government funding to purchase these drawings by persuading party officials they were depictions of Nazi concentration camps.

On the upper floor, a swathe of the museum was dedicated to a visit from Uzbek despot, Islam Karimov. Focusing on his affection for a folk-art yurt, in a set of photographs the grinning President was surrounded by an entourage of bodyguards and toadies. Even in the desert of forbidden art, the authorities were watching.

Yurtbashi

His dead black eyes trailing you, President Karimov scowled down from towering billboards in abandoned construction sites. In this remotest of backwaters, it took three hours to locate the town's sole internet hub, yet elegant clay tennis courts abounded. The President's elder daughter liked tennis.

Born in Samarkand in 1938, Islam Abduganievich Karimov was known to Uzbeks by the nickname "Big Papa" or in whispered quips as "Yurtbashi," head of the yurt-dwellers. Being the most sedentary of the Central Asian people, many Uzbeks tend to look down on nomads. Little is known about Karimov's childhood. It's said his father was an Uzbek, whilst his mother was an ethnic Tajik, but it isn't even public knowledge how his parents died.

Raised in an orphanage, young Islam studied economics and engineering. Joining the Communist Party, he ascended through the ranks, becoming First Secretary of the Uzbek Soviet Socialist Republic in 1989, when his predecessor was fired for failing to quell an outbreak of ethnic violence in the Fergana Valley. When independence came, Karimov's transition to President was seamless. 'If you elect me tomorrow,' he told voters on the eve of 1991's rigged election, 'then I need the right to dissolve parliament. Then I would have the final say.' True to his word, Karimov duly replaced the legislature with a more compliant body. He ruled with an iron fist for the next quarter of a century.

A wily operator, testy and ruthless, Karimov used the 'war on terror' to his advantage. Branding his critics 'Islamic extremists,' in 2005 a demonstration in the city of Andijan over the arrest of "radical" local businessmen ended with government troops opening fire on the crowd. Official figures put the death toll at 187, but the true body count is believed to number well over a thousand. A diplomatic spat post-Andijan soon swept under the rug, US government observations on the state of the Uzbek economy have since used quotes from Karimov's books. 'Pressuring him, especially publically,' Ambassador Richard Norland warned Washington, 'could cost us transit [rights for Afghanistan].'

Executed, expatriated or locked away in mental institutions, the Uzbek opposition are a hapless bunch. Godfather of the dissenters, the conservative and religious Mohammed Solih's pronouncements since escaping to Turkey have largely focused on 'isolating gays and other sick people from the society.' From her exile in Berlin, journalist Galima Bukharbaeva, founder of the excellent *Uznews.net* - one of the only portals for independent news about Uzbekistan - has found herself having to defend attacks from Solih's aficionados, which have included posting images of her head photoshopped onto pornographic images. As of December 2014, *Uznews* has ceased to exist, the names of its contributors having been disclosed following a government hack.

As his health deteriorated, Karimov cut an increasingly isolated figure. In a rare interview dated November 2014, Karimov's grandson, Islam Jr. told the BBC, 'I tried to teach him how to use internet but my grandmother told me "are you crazy? What if he reads the internet and he knows everything?"'

Whilst fawning hagiographers let it be known that 'for his outstanding contribution to creation of a sovereign state based on democratic laws... Islam Karimov has been awarded the title of the Hero of Uzbekistan,' with no heir apparent, behind the scenes a battle to succeed him was raging. Seemingly oblivious, his failing health meaning he was rarely seen on the campaign trial, in March 2015 Karimov secured an unconstitutional fourth term in office, purportedly winning the election with over ninety percent of the vote.

The Devil Wears Khaki

Back at the Hotel Nukus, the door to our room was jammed shut, entry only possible with the aid of the cleaner's locksmith skills.

'Ugh,' she moaned, making no effort to hide her exasperation.

Snatching the key from my grasp and glaring as if we were imbeciles, she opened the door with consummate ease, a stale stench hitting us as it fell ajar.

Eager to wash away the dust from our travails, I ventured into the bathroom, where a scourge of mosquitoes was swarming in the stagnant tua-let bowl. A sobering realisation dawning upon me, moments later I emerged from the trickling shower, shrieking in dismay as I rummaged through my bags.

Hampered by queue jumpers and a reluctance to serve us, we'd spent an hour and a half that morning in the capacious warehouse that was the Uzbekistan Airways Booking Office. Attempting to explain that we wanted to change the date of our flights, I'd thought back to Cholpon Ata, scratching out a calendar and a diagram involving the sun and the moon in my notebook. Shocked that we'd succeeded without even having to pay a fee or a bribe, however, I'd left one of my pair of identical books behind.

An overwhelming sense of relief washing over me when Stan returned from the airline office with my journal - retrieved from a bemused clerk by pointing repeatedly at its twin - I gleefully dragged him out in search of a bar. It was evening, a cool stillness settling over the dark, deserted streets by the time we reached our first point of call, the Sheraton's sister restaurant, Neo. Its dimly lit interior rigid and uncomfortable, the lavatories featured a framed photograph of a turd rocketing from a goat's arse.

Ready for a change of scenery after a two-hour dose of the video channel whilst we waited for a plate of soggy French fries, we ventured towards the main drag. Empty save for two slurring middle-aged men huddled around the dying embers of a shashlyk grill, a single option presented itself. Settling on a rickety bench, we were illuminated by the dysfunctional flickering of a fridge in which a lone bottle of UzCarlsberg stood. It was probably the last bottle of UzCarlsberg in the world, the company, like so many others, having been forced out of the country by an amalgam of the mafia and the Uzbek Prosecutor's Office.

Galumphing along the uneven pavement, a pair of khaki-clad militsiyamen paused by the bars insect eaten lattice fence. A new government agency tasked with tackling a plague of termites born of the Aral Sea's destruction was failing, anything wooden left hollow and brittle.

With the arrival of these gun wielding parasites, the atmosphere changed immediately. Conversation becoming stilted, the barmaid's smile turned to a wary grimace as she clicked the radio off. Having stumbled upon the only two tourists in town, the soldiers blocked the pitch-dark track to the back-alley toilet. Bellowing brusquely and thrusting their bodies into our paths when we tried to pass, they indicated that we should pay them for using this hole in the ground. It may have started as a joke, but if so it was quickly turning sour.

Making their fretful excuses, the establishment's other patrons soon fled from the fleecing. Ushered inside to a secluded booth by the barkeep, in less than a minute the militsiya were glowering over us, all porn moustaches and frying pan caps, cheeks puffed out as they roared.

'Go! Go! *Zakriytiy*! Close!' the flustered barmaid pleaded with us, waving her arms hysterically.

It was not even ten PM.

Distracted by the yelping from a dog fight in the street, the militsiya briefly turned their backs, emitting a menacing chortle at this heady cocktail of their power and this casual violence. Nodding towards them, but never taking her eyes from them, the barmaid stuck out her tongue, pulling a monstrous face whilst using her index fingers to indicate horns.

'The devil wears khaki,' I whispered as we scuttled away into the night.

CHAPTER 8

The Wasteland of the Soviet Dream

The compère span a cumbrous wheel on a bingo based Russian game show blasting from the TV in the dingy basement dining room of the Hotel Nukus. Kicking out a slender leg like a can-can dancer, his make-up plastered, peroxide blonde assistant looked thoroughly bored. Checking out, we hauled our gear around, unsure how to reach our destination. It was only eight AM, but the heat was already increasing rapidly, shade a rare commodity in the thinly spread city centre.

Cutting past guards outside the Council of Ministers building, we were fortunate enough to run into a chirpy chap called Rustam from the Karakalpak Tourism Board, who set us straight. Thus, after being hustled for nine thousand som for a short cab ride, we were ready to board the bus to Moynaq, a place which Savitsky described as the 'wasteland of the Soviet dream.'

As we wedged ourselves into the last two available seats, a barefoot souse boarded, blood from the cuts on his stroke slackened face dripping onto his blue plaid suit. Steadying himself with some difficulty, he swayed about at the stationary bus, spittle flying from his mouth as he shouted at the assembled passengers. Even the driver ignored him. With all the seats occupied, child-sized plastic stools began to appear, the narrow aisle filling with hefty women. The drunk was not to be deterred, though. Clambering over the gangway-dwellers, his ripe form landed on top of me, but he left empty-handed.

Waiting to pull away, sulky children wailed in the laps of their mothers. Wizened old *somsa* wallahs climbed aboard, hawking pastries and packets of sunflower seeds. Overflowing sacks of ripe capsicums and mammoth watermelons were loaded until every last inch of space was accounted for. With the stereo cranked up and all and sundry bawling breathlessly, finally we were underway. Now the obligatory phone passing could begin.

We made it twenty metres before screeching to a halt at traffic lights, allowing yet more people to board. Squealing with glee as their friends embarked, passengers eyes shone as they mouthed joyful greetings, offering each other identical hunks of sacred lepyoshka. The men sat behind us were getting jollier too. Their warm, sticky bottles of hooch rolling around the floor, occasionally they'd tread on my laptop in their attempts to retrieve a wayward tipple.

I stared out the window past the gauzy curtain. Up until the late nineties, the area between Nukus and the town of Kungrad was still cotton fields, now it was a blighted expanse. It was into this salinized void we'd stop to let people off, with nothing but arid earth in sight. Still farther west across the roadless Aral Sea Basin lay the notorious Jaslyk Prison, where opponents of the President "disappeared" and were reportedly boiled to death.

Rattling on towards the halfway point of Kungrad - locally known as Qong'irot - our boisterous backseat boys were becoming increasingly unpopular. Their constantly getting the driver to stop for beer snacks and piss breaks wearing thin, a babushka turned to voice her disapproval, the grey hairs issuing from her chin catching the sun.

Yet whilst they lost their tempers easily, the Karakalpaks were also quick to forgive. Hence, it wasn't long after the Kungrad wallahs had stampeded onto the bus, all elbows in faces as they shouted about their somsas, that the passengers were happily sharing their goodies.

Beyond Kungrad, the road deteriorated into a collection of adjoining potholes surrounded by the forty thousand kilometre manmade sand-salt Ak-Kum, the white desert. Kicking their slippers off - perfectly acceptable outdoor wear – the old ladies and the backseat boys snored their way through the last three hours of the journey.

In Search of the Oybek

Unable to make our desired destination understood, we disembarked beneath a boundless sky on the outskirts of the dustbowl ghost town of Moynaq. It was fifty degrees Celsius in the shade, except there was no shade to be had. Dogs barking heatedly, shoeless children circled us, wanting to shake our sweaty, luggage encumbered hands.

'Ullo, ullo,' a dark-skinned child with a goitre the size of a pomegranate squawked excitedly.

Blanched tumbleweeds danced idly across the town's single road as we ploughed onwards. Stopping to ask the few people we chanced upon the location of the gastnitsa, most just stared back blankly, those that did respond invariably pointing in opposing directions. The way throughout Asia, it was often better to give a misleading answer than to offer no information at all.

Burnt and dehydrated, we'd been walking for an hour and three-quarters when I tripped on a rock, my bags coming down on top of me. Prostrate upon the ground with grit in my mouth, I was about ready to wilt, when like a mirage a purple ZAZ-966 appeared, sparks flying from its exhaust as it scraped along the asphalt. From this vision of a vehicle, a rotund, Weeble-like man emerged, and then another, and another, until there before us stood seven men, gigantic in girth, if not height.

And they spoke English.

'My name is Big Rashid,' the first introduced himself. 'These are my brothers: Gennadiy, Viktor, Yuri, Lavr, Arkhip and Adolf.'
'I'm Stephen and this is my brother Stan,' I said, clasping his outstretched hand. 'We're looking for the hotel,' I explained as he hauled me upright.
'Da, the Oybek,' Rashid nodded knowingly. 'Come,' he added, taking pity on us after scrutinising my dishevelled state.

The nine of us somehow ramming ourselves into his car, I perched upon Adolf's lap with my head wedged between the front seats.

'We've been looking for ages, but nobody knows where the hotel is,' I wheezed, craning my neck to avoid being hit by the gearstick.
'But why would anyone in Moynaq know?' Rashid snickered. 'They will never stay there.'

It was a valid point.

'But there's no sign for the hotel,' Stan protested from his writhen position in the footwell.
'Ha,' Big Rashid scoffed. 'In Oz'bekiston you must pay extra to have sign.'

Rashid and his brothers, it transpired, were ethnic Russians from Kyzylorda in Kazakhstan. I asked what they were doing in Moynaq, but my query met with stony silence, it was obviously a question too far.
   Minutes later, we parked outside a long, nondescript edifice, literally bursting out of the car as its doors swung open. From behind a tall iron fence, a mongrel growled its welcome, drooling as it bore its teeth.

'Oybek, go,' Rashid said, motioning for us to enter the compound.

Lining up to wave us goodbye, the seven siblings cast imposing shadows in the late afternoon sun.

The Edge of the World

The Oybek had seen better days; it couldn't have always been this bad. I later discovered that the *Karakalpak.com* website carried a picture of the hotel abaft a burnt-out bus beneath the caption, "Unfortunately the Oybek is the only hotel in town." It was unfortunate indeed, the building resembling nothing so much as a derelict prison.

The boss was a hirsute, barrel-chested ethnic Russian decked in flip-flops, spandex bun huggers and a sweat-stained string vest. Gruffly indicating for his mother-in-law to mop the squalid ceiling, his armpits smelt of mutton grease. Our presence an imposition, we waited an hour before being led up the stairwell, where a barrage of naked wires exploded from a fuse box with a peeling hazard sticker. Spattered with dead flies, the remaining shards of glass in the landing window looked out across the wilderness. Coated in urine, the shared bathroom had no light and no water, running or otherwise. Apart from that, it wasn't so bad.

There being nowhere to eat in town, our host begrudgingly asked if we wanted dinner, to which I hesitantly enquired if a vegetarian meal would be a problem.

'Ve-ge... humpf,' he snorted. 'I checking. Problema. *Mozhet byt,* maybe.'

I wasn't convinced he'd understood.

'Is there a shop?' I asked, contingency planning.

He stuck his arm through the glassless window, pointing towards a garage down the street which was steadfastly sealed.

'Shop,' he barked.

Heading out to bang on the metal shutter, the darkened garage opened to reveal its treasures. There were three warm beers, two dusty half-full packets of cigarettes and a box of mouldy tomatoes.

We'd come to Moynaq to visit the Aral Sea, or rather the ship graveyard where the sea used to be. Draining of the Aral dates back to the Civil War in the US, when finding his supply of American cotton under threat, the

Russian Tsar decided to use the sea's tributaries to irrigate Central Asia - Uzbekistan in particular - to create a cotton bowl. As early as 1908, the geographer and climatologist A.I. Voekov referred to the Aral as 'a mistake of nature,' a refrain the Soviets would later come to embrace wholeheartedly in their hunger for the white gold. Each bale of cotton soaking up 1.8 million litres of water, the sea's trunks were siphoned off in leaky pipes which rarely reached their destinations, the Aral shrinking to one-tenth its size between 1960 and 2007.

At its peak, Moynaq was home to sixty thousand people, mostly fishermen and their extended families, the Aral producing up to thirty percent of the Soviet catch and saving Russia from widespread famine in the 1920s. Accessible only by air and ferry well into the seventies, the town also served as a popular beach resort for bureaucrats, its airport hosting fifty flights a day. By the eighties, though, tourism had dried up. Digging channels through the sand in pursuit of the diminishing sea, Moynaq's fishermen discarded their ships where they became grounded. The sea's major source, the Amu Darya River no longer reaching its historic terminus, a local saying goes: 'When God loved us, he gave us the Amu Darya, when he ceased to love us, he sent us Russian engineers.'

Today, the town's population number less than two thousand, the remnants of the sea almost two hundred kilometres away across the manmade desert from which a billion tonnes of salt and dust are blown into the atmosphere every year. A spate of NGO interest which followed the collapse of the Soviet Union led to another saying: 'If every scientist and journalist who visited the Aral Sea brought with them a bucket of water, the sea would be filled again.' Unable to overcome corruption endemic throughout the region, most NGO's have long since given up on the Uzbek portion of the Aral. As the last of the so-called Large Aral Sea quietly dies, the people of Moynaq have found themselves left to their fate.

Atop a bluff behind the hotel stood a concrete monument to the disappeared inland sea, a line of ships laid out on the former seabed below. Once we'd escaped a rabble of Kazakh tourists who followed us, convinced we spoke Russian, but were simply refusing to engage with them, the sheer scale of the sand-salt desert was stupefying. The hulks on the seabed played out their lingering demise, all rust and graffiti with only the buzzing of insects to break the still. Huge dragonflies patrolling the exsiccated tract which offered nothing but loss and decay, the extent of the tragedy was immediately palpable.

Striped sunlight spilling through the skeletal ribs of their hulls, sun-baked trawlers lay slowly oxidizing. Animated by history, these inert objects took on an ethereal vitality in opposition to the overwhelming sense of desolation surrounding them. Thorny grey and fuchsia pink thistles destined to become tumbleweeds shook as brackish gusts whipped across the vast emptiness once so teeming with life. With the sea gone, the region was subject to searing summers and freezing winters, five hundred species of bird, two hundred mammals, a hundred types of fish and countless insects unique to the region all now extinct.

At dusk, children came out to play on the jagged boats, devising games with sticks and discarded cans, serrated metal and broken glass peeking through the sand around them. With the sun setting behind the promontory, an aurora pink light fell across the desert, a chill wind whistling through the ship cemetery, itself an extension of the other-worldliness which pervaded the whole town.

Back at the hotel, with nightfall the regular power cuts became more conspicuous. At dinner, we sat around the bare, candlelit table in awkward silence, the old woman and her daughter dishing up *manty*, ravioli style dumplings in random juice to be soaked up with lepyoshka. For the "vegetarian" version, they'd simply fished out the larger lumps of mystery meat. It was the thought that counted.

'Is there any way to order a taksi for tomorrow morning?' Stan asked our host; flights from Nukus being two a day, ten minutes apart, if we missed the bus, we'd miss our plane.

'Niet!' he shouted, a rush of air billowing through his walrus moustache.

Our room being the only one occupied, the pitch-dark floor took on an eerie aspect. The night abandoned to packs of wild dogs, vehicles passed at a rate of less than one an hour. With no light pollution, the stars glistened with a rare lustre. It was just us, the dogs, the family bickering and grandma belching at the edge of the world.

Celebrity

A crowd had gathered early at the Moynaq Bazaar, women in loose dendritic print dresses worn over trousers haggling over slabs of meat. Boys suffering from hyperpigmentation unloaded wilting vegetables from the backs of trucks. Either still drunk from the night before or starting early, old men with Doc Brown hair blundered about in raggedy pinstripe suits, jabbering animatedly at us. In addition to the ubiquitous skullcap, they also liked their flat caps and threadbare Panama hats. Their hair shorn by clippers set to the same length, a smattering of younger men in short sleeve shirts and jogging bottoms marked a generational shift.

An hour late, we boarded the bus for our last long journey of this leg of the trip. There was never a sense of hurry, timetables serving only as a rough guide. The somsa wallahs were out in force this morning, those that couldn't fit on the vehicle contenting themselves with steadily pounding on the windows. Getting right up in the passengers faces with their wares, if those that were patrolling the aisle got any closer, they'd have been force feeding us. It was inconceivable that you didn't want their baked goods. With a collective look of disbelief that we hadn't purchased anything, the somsa women jumped from the moving bus, leaving that familiar lingering aroma of meat pie farts.

With my knees in my eye sockets and someone else's knees in my back, mosquitoes feasted on my feet, which I could neither move nor reach. Pomegranate spraying wildly from overexcited children's juice cartons, Stan clung tightly to his Khivan rug. In front of us, in the row of seats opposite a woman so obese she took up two spaces sat with her hooded eyes trained upon us. Not content with openly gaping, she pulled out her mobile, resting it on one of her flab rolls and filming us through the reverse camera. Our pseudo-celebrity lasted for the entire journey.

Approaching our destination, the only radio station in Karakalpakstan, Nukus FM fizzled into life on the stereo, the wafer-thin voice of Uzbekistan's biggest star, the President's daughter Googoosha seeping through. In addition to her music, the corruption scandal embroiled ex-UN envoy and self-styled 'Princess of Uzbekistan,' Gulnara Karimova also ran numerous businesses and charities, was a filmmaker, poet, fashion and jewellery designer and cosmetics and perfume mogul.

'From her desire for self-expression came her poems. From her poems came the music. Meet Googoosha.....poet, mezzo soprano, designer and exotic Uzbekistan beauty,' read her since removed official website. 'A robber baron... a greedy, power-hungry individual who uses her father to crush business people or anyone else who stands in her way... She remains the single most hated person in the country,' asserts a leaked US diplomatic cable.

Googoosha's mellifluous duet with Gerard Depardieu in which he reads one of her poems - his idea she insisted in one of her regular Twitter outbursts - was playing.

'The sky is quiet, the sky is keeping silent,' the opportunistic French actor drawled, as an ominous hush fell over the vehicle.

CHAPTER 9

Toshkent - Stone City

W ell into the 1990s all flights in Central Asia had been undertaken by Aeroflot planes, usually the notoriously incident prone Tupolev Tu-154. Abandoned where they stood upon the collapse of the USSR, these aircraft formed the backbone of some eight hundred new carriers spawned by the fifteen Post-Soviet nations. There were no seat belts or safety procedures on many of these "Babyflots;" none of that was going to help if things took a turn for the worse. Pouring themselves and the passengers a calming shot of vodka before take-off, stewardesses would dole out double measures for the former tractor drivers ordered to pilot them.

Fortunately, times had changed. Our flight passing without incident, we funnelled into the shuttle bus. The babushka behind me may have been stooped and frail when she wanted a seat, but as soon as the doors opened at the terminal building, she ploughed straight through us, knocking me to the ground.

Hanging back from the scrummage at the carousel, it was nearing midnight by the time we forced our packs into the Chevrolet Matiz, securing its boot with a bungee cord. On a break from university, our driver, the gastnitsa proprietor's son Jamshed, was keen to discuss the latest footballing intrigues at Chelsea. In line with everybody else in Asia, he couldn't begin to comprehend why anyone would support Tottenham.

'We were born into it,' I explained. 'It's hereditary.'
'Ha,' he quipped, 'like disease.'

We cruised through the empty streets of the sprawling Uzbek capital, Tashkent, translated as 'Stone City.' Stopping at a supermarket for provisions, it was a long time since I'd seen a store so large. Having checked into our room at the Mirzo Guesthouse, however, I discovered that the product marked as hummus which I'd bought was still off.

Early next morning, the sullen hotelier Mirzo banged upon our door, thrusting a plate of anaemic eggs in my face. Leaving this offering behind, we set out for the sprawling Chorsu Bazaar in search of moneychangers.

Vibrant and colourful, almost everything under the sun was to be found beneath the bazaars shady green dome or in its oozing offshoots. Wicker baskets in all imaginable shapes and sizes commanded a whole section, as did knickers, candies, potatoes and dill. Filling an upper tier with a pungent earthy aroma, spices took up an entire floor.

'Who buys all these seasonings when there are so few dishes?' I asked as the umpteenth trader waved stigmas of saffron in my face.

Stan just shrugged.

'Does anybody even use saffron?' I grumbled.

Even by my standards, I was getting cranky. My right foot being naturally attracted to shards of glass, hobbling around with plantar fibromatosis, cold sweats and the brown lightning was starting to take its toll.

With Stan traipsing back to the B&B to ask about changing money, I stopped for choy in an alleyway where scattered syringes lay masked by dust. My stomach churning, the smoke rising from bricks of charcoal beneath the metal teapot stung my eyes. Sure enough, when Stan returned the first thing we ran across upon leaving the chaikhana was a gaggle of moneychangers lounging upon thrones built of banknotes.

'Change dollar money? Change euro dollar money?' they cried.

Telephone and power cables ran thick through the etiolated sky. Wrought iron flowers and lampposts lining the wide boulevards, reams of Daewoo minivans chugged past. Missing their intended targets, elaborate sprinkler systems kept the pavements wet and slippery. Although extravagant use of water is a sin under Islamic law, arid Central Asia has the heaviest water usage in the world.

Ducking into the metro, we were immediately accosted by suspicious guards who examined our passports and rifled through our belongings. Metro stations and underpasses were the preserve of the saucepan hatted militsiya. Satisfied at length that we weren't terrorists, we were allowed to buy two plastic tokens and disappear down the escalator.

Considered a military installation, it is illegal to take photographs in the Tashkent Metro. A popular misconception states that stations double as nuclear bomb shelters, but in reality quite what martial purpose any of them could serve is difficult to imagine. The pity is that if there's one thing in Tashkent you'd want to take pictures of, then it would be the metro.

Opened in 1977, each station is distinct, many seeming to belong to a bygone age. From amaranthine latticework to heroic Soviet realist murals, art deco to desert fantasia, the metro has it all. Mustaqillik Maydoni features imposing Doric columns carved out of marble from the Kyzyl-Kum Desert, chandeliers illuminating stars on its floor which reference Ulugbek, the astrologer-King. In Bodomzor Station, lamps sprout from the ground like outsized toadstools, casting a warm orange glow over ceramic images of bread and chillies. Ming Orik, 'Thousand Apricots' does as the name would suggest, as does Pakhtakor, adorned with ornate cotton mosaics further highlighted by bronze sconce lamps, lending a fin-de-siècle quality.

Dedicated to Soviet space exploration and looking like the set of an eighties sci-fi movie, a retro vision of an imagined future, Kosmonavtlar Metro is the pick of the bunch. Lights playing on its reflective metallic surfaces, blue and turquoise geometric forms glow celestially. Glistening algae green pillars lead through a ceiling of irradiated escape hatches. Cosmonauts peer through porthole windows, the taut permed Valentina Tereshkova - the first woman in space - looking as iron and stern as Margaret Thatcher in her pressurised suit.

Staring from the train window wondering what each new stop would bring, my reverie was interrupted by a young man seated opposite who finally gave in to his inquisitive urges.

'Excuse... *Amerikanskiy?*' he asked, blushing profusely.

It transpired that the shy teenager was a student of history at the Mirzo Ulugbek National University. Saying our goodbyes, as we emerged back into the harsh daylight, I wondered how one can study history in a land where the past is both defined and reinvented by the whims of a single man.

Little Timur's City

We cut past the sunken bowl of the Pakhtakor Markaziy Stadium, its oblique floodlights craning inwards. Ponderous quadratic constructions stretching as far as the eye could see, Modern Brezhnevian architecture lined the streets around Gagarin Maydoni Park. Reflecting the dazzling sun, the monolithic Cabinet of Ministers gaudy gold windows looked like nothing so much as local dental work.

A huge earthquake which struck in 1966, killing 300,000 people and levelling the city had left Tashkent largely devoid of sights, a meandering mass without a centre. Cut adrift across a highway at the parks northern periphery, the deserted Earthquake Memorial glorified those who'd helped to rebuild the city. A square, uber-muscular Superman and woman in a state of semi-undress rose high above the symbolically cracked pavement, taking a giant step forward. The Kremlin's announcement that they'd invited these largely Russian 'volunteers' to stay and occupy the apartments they'd erected led to the Tashkent race riots of 1969, the crowd turning on Russian bystanders following a football match between Pakhtakor and a guest team from the Motherland.

Ordered by Karimov to be constructed in every city worth the appellation, the usual cheerless monuments filled the park: the wall of fallen heroes, the eternal flame and the bronze Crying Mother Monument commemorating the half million Uzbeks who'd perished in the Great Patriotic War against *Gitler*. Dissected by a lone bridge, across the emerald Anhor Canal laid the *'Oily' Majlis* - as the Uzbek government's website spelt it - the Senate building. Ringed by fidgety, heavily armed guards, its handpicked deputies meet only a few times a year to rubberstamp the President's decisions.

Money had certainly been spent on the new Tashkent, but with not a paving stone out of place, it felt somewhat illusory. Legions of uniformed women decked in pink and white hats swept the spotless streets with nothing to clear but the odd fallen leaf. Beneath an arch topped with talismanic silver pelicans, coquettish schoolgirls waded in the pools fronting Mustaqillik Maydoni - Independence Square - formerly Lenin Square. Gangs of leering teenage boys in fake logoed jackets hovered under the watchful eye of the militsiya. There were no old people in the inner city. Everyone wore toned down colours. All shoes were sensible, trousers and skirts black, shirts and blouses plain and collared. And in this intensely homogeneous city there was, it seemed, no noise, no excitement and no joy. In this monoculture carven from Karimov's vision, the last thing you wanted was to stand out.

Formerly Karl Marx Street, the Broadway - popularly known as 'Shashlyk Street' - contained unvarying arcades and *kafes*, each with white tables and chairs and a menu consisting of the same five dishes: beef shashlyk, chicken shashlyk, mutton shashlyk, liver shashlyk and plov. Hawkers sold tacky souvenirs from blankets around which people ambled disinterestedly. Street artists etched out caricatures or copies of popular classics such as the *Mona Lisa* or paintings from C. M. Coolidge's *Dogs Playing Poker* series.

An avenue of chinar trees under which aksakals would sit playing chess had lined the Broadway until a few years ago, when one day without warning Karimov had the trees cut down, leaving only the searing sun. Officials claim that the roots of this foreign flora were dangerous, but rumours persist that the trees were felled because they offered cover to plotters planning attacks on the government. Mounted upon his rearing steed, at the acme of the walkway, a statue of Timur – a favourite of low-budget TV costume dramas - had replaced Karl Marx. In a tiny gesture of defiance, an unknown assailant had chiselled the cock off his horse.

Yet despite the reconstruction, the hulking architecture and the ever-present militsiya, Tashkent remained a leafy city filled with fountains, flowers and fountains cast in the shape of flowers. Searching for the music we'd heard in Bukhara, in a shop to the south of the city we came across myriad different types of Karimov pictures for sale, casting him as a renaissance man. There was Karimov the diplomat with George Dubya Bush, Karimov the athlete - a leftover from a failed campaign to host the Olympics - and Karimov the iron man saluting his generals.

The dictator, who calls himself 'Little Timur,' once sponsored a genealogical scheme to trace his descent from Timur, ironic seeing as Tamerlane was a historic foe of the Uzbek people. Gazing at the portraits, with the country having known no other leader, I wondered who would triumph in the inevitable power struggle which would follow Karimov's death. Would the Uzbeks really accept Gulnara as their President? Analyst's opinions varied at this juncture. By the time we returned in 2014, however, my musings had become moot. Her business interests dismantled, the former 'Princess of Uzbekistan' languished under house arrest. The shutters had come down on Googoosha's empire.

The streets swiftly darkening, I was brought back to earth by a mad-eyed adolescent poking me in the ribs.

'Dollar! Dollar!' he screeched.

Escaping his laboured pursuit, we spent our last night in a self-styled Irish theme pub, sipping on vodka which tasted like a cool mountain stream. Derived from the word *voda*, Russian for water, the etymology of vodka comes from 'little water.'

The clock at its entrance approaching midnight, the militsiya converged upon us as we descended into the metro aiming to catch the last tube. Fishing out my papers, I readied my bag for inspection; but they just wanted to help us get home.

Crunching up the gravel alleyway, the sound of music grew louder. Back at the guesthouse, an all-night party was taking place, its booming doof shaking the walls.

'*Svahdbah,*' Mirzo greeted us, raising a glass and cracking his first smile of our stay.
'Wedding,' his son translated.

Departures: Tashkent

The Passport Control Officer scrutinised his komp'yuter screen for some time. Finally allowed through, I noted through the open door at the back of his cubicle that he'd actually been playing spider solitaire.

In a departure lounge which was little more than a motley collection of plastic chairs, people loitered in corners. Having decided that the smoking ban was rubbish and should be flouted, they pressed cigarettes to their lips. In the cosy bathroom, men stood at sinks, finger blocking one nostril whilst they shot dribbles of dusty snot from the other. Given their aversion to public nose blowing, this was the case in most restrooms.

Killing time, we ventured into the only shop, a glass fronted unit where cartoonish ceramics were piled high next to a single and singularly bad brand of vodka, all priced at a four-times mark-up. It was here that the true value of the currency was hammered home, for when I approached the counter, wallet bulging with banknotes I wanted to offload, the salesgirl raised her hand dismissively.

'No accept Uzbek som,' she growled.

PART **II**

CHAPTER 10

To Bishkek and Beyond

I spent ten dreary months back in London with only a cheap porcelain of a babushka on a donkey carrying a swaddled baby, a pocketful of low-value banknotes, scribbled outlines and photographs to remind me. Central Asia felt like a lifetime ago. With the British economy in tatters, it took a clinical trial for me to raise the money to return to the region. Thirteen days into my internment in the disinfectant suffused ward, the moody cleaner suddenly became my pal. Spotting a guidebook on my bedside table, a flash of recognition darted across his russet brown eyes.

'This is where I play as a boy,' he said, pointing at a picture of the Shrine of Hazrat Ali in Mazar-I-Sharif, Afghanistan.

After fleeing the Taliban, Zahir told me, he'd arrived in England via Ashgabat, Turkmenistan. The conflict having scattered his relatives, his brother now lived in Dushanbe, Tajikistan, and his mother and father in Almaty, Kazakhstan. After seven years of drudgery supporting his extended family, he hoped to finally go back to Central Asia in the spring and set up a car dealership with his sibling.

Discarding his mop and bucket, Zahir perched on the edge of my bed as I clicked through a few of my photographs.

'Ah, I have been Uzbekistan,' he murmured wistfully. 'They have the best plov. So good.'

A week later, I met Stan in a pub in North London. Looking to set off in three months' time, I pored over route maps and clicked through pictures of key sights in an effort to convince him to come.

'Fuck it,' he said, his enthusiasm amplified after a bellyful of frosty pints. 'Let's go in two weeks!'

My passport being full, which I hadn't realised, I rang the UK Passport Agency in a befuddled flap early next morning. The first fast track appointment available - double the price for the privilege - was almost a week away. There simply wasn't time. We had to have the Uzbek visa before we could even apply for the Turkmen visa. The Uzbek visa would take seven days and the Turkmen visa, processed in Ashgabat, three weeks to procure.

'No problem,' they told me during my fifth phone call to the Embassy of Turkmenistan; 'apply for visa here and pick up in Bishkek.'

Which would have been just dandy, except it turned out they didn't have a mission in Bishkek. Still, collecting it in Dushanbe sounded promising.

I'd read on the internet that I could acquire the visa for Tajikistan in Bishkek - 'just look for the oversized yurt, its right by it,' - a helpful soul had written on a forum.

The notoriously difficult to obtain Turkmen visa worried me, though, especially after we'd bought the flights out of Ashgabat necessitous to our applications.

Following my careful removal of an old visa sticker to make space in my passport, Stan went down to the Embassy of Uzbekistan.

'Niet,' the woman behind the counter told him, 'not take seven days, take seven working days. That nine days total *normal'ny*, but now ten days because holiday. Unless you pay fast fee,' she added, 'this charge extra fifty percent.'

Ten days later, we entered the foyer of the Embassy of Turkmenistan. A marble palace in miniature with plentiful Presidential portraits and carmine red rugs hanging from the walls, it was a foretaste of things to come. Eyeing us suspiciously, the bushy-browed young clerk straightened his clingy grey suit and indicated for us to sit.

'Why you want to come to my country?' he asked.

His opening gambit more an accusation than a question, his words echoed through the empty hallways. I'd heard it before. It was never a good sign when consular staff couldn't understand why anyone could possibly want to visit.

'We will email you decision in three weeks, yes or no,' he concluded, emphasis falling on the 'no.'

Nervous and excited as always before a trip, back in the pub we mulled over our plans and preparations. Stepping outside after a few, we ran into a friendly drunk.

'Ullo, my name is San and I love UK,' he greeted us, offering moist, overly long handshakes. 'I am refugee, da, but now I stay UK. I love Britain, is great country!'

'Where are you from?' Stan asked him.

'Oz'bekiston,' he answered, 'but now I stay UK.'

'Ha, we're going to Uzbekistan for the second time,' I told him. 'We leave in two days.'

'Huh? But why?' he slurred incredulously.

'It's very beautiful,' I replied straightforwardly, not really wanting to get into it.

'Ha! Beautiful? Beautiful for visit, maybe, but Karimov is crazy man. UK is best country,' he gushed.

'But why are you here? Why are you a refugee?' I enquired repeatedly, only to receive the same response.

'I love UK. Karimov is crazy man. I love you guys and UK.'

Leaning in to hug us, San stumbled, his chin audibly cracking as it struck my shoulder. Lurching backwards into a metal dustbin, he sat amidst the garbage chuckling for a while, before dusting himself off and careening away down the street.

'Karimov is crazy man,' we could hear him bawling as he tottered into the night.

Back inside we clinked our whiskey tumblers together.

'To Bishkek and beyond,' I offered as a toast.

Return to the Kyrgyz Republic

Our arrival at Manas International Airport again met with wild applause, perhaps it was the relief of landing safely, or maybe the passengers were just relieved to be released from the confines of the plane. Certainly, we were all glad to be free of the beardy guy who'd boarded in Istanbul and spent the entire journey shouting.

'*Aye a namana!*' he shrieked at the top of his voice; whatever that meant.

Exiting the Airbus, the inebriated Turk tried to pick a fight with a man he kept smacking in the face with his luggage. His only crime pushing the offending bag away, the potential opponent looked concerned, but the Turk's inability to stand unaided put pay to his brawling instincts.

I'd made a reservation and arranged an airport pick-up with the Sakura Guesthouse, who'd emailed back to offer the following sage advice;

'Look for the middle-aged Russian man.'

That didn't narrow it down much.

Sure enough, though, there was the taksi driver – who'd later attempt to double charge us for the ride - holding a sign which read 'Mister SteEva.'

With our luggage in tow this time - along with a blonde girl called Eva Fruge from Grenoble in the French Alps - we drove towards the city, the honeycomb sun lifting over ripening fields and glistening on the distant, snow-capped Ala-Too Mountains.

'Militsiya,' our portly driver snarled with undisguised disdain as we passed a baton-waving traffic cop in a capacious saucepan hat.

It was good to be back.

Speeding through vaguely familiar suburbs, we drew to a halt on a dirt track and were led through a rusted garage door. Told to sit in the Sakura Guesthouse's freezing garden whilst our driver whisked Eva to her room, we waited and waited. Surveying the modest grounds over pilfered cups of warming instant kofe, the advertised swimming pool, it transpired, was a four by two-metre waterless hole with splintered planks lain across it. Through the chill morning air, from beyond the compound the early morning sound of car horns and dogs barking soon began to rise, unlike the proprietor.

The Gold Scandal

With the lady of the house put out by my attempts to rouse her, we headed into the city centre in urgent need of shade and som. Entering the OJSC Bank on Togolok Moldo, we met a Danish couple, Henrik and Hettie from Copenhagen, who'd just returned from Lake Issyk-Köl. A series of demonstrations against the Kumtor gold mine - located on the southern shore - having spread as far as Cholpon Ata, the Russian and Kazakh tourists had all gone home.

'There was nobody there,' Hettie explained, furrowed lines carved into her gaunt face. 'We stayed right on the lakefront, but the beach was totally empty.'

'Empty,' Henrik echoed. 'The locals, they were all very worried.'

Coupled with these protests, incidents of bubonic plague in the oblast hadn't helped orchestrate a late season rush.

It is reasonably common knowledge that Kyrgyzstan has no money, but not as widely understood why this is the case. The first President of the independent Kyrgyz Republic was Askar Akaev, a short, bald, obscure scientist whose furious coal black eyebrows threatened to join forces. Commonly referred to by the American press during the Clinton years as the 'Kennedy of Central Asia,' he proved less popular with Russian President Yeltsin, who famously once played out a tune on his skull with a set of wooden spoons. An unlikely candidate propelled to power as a figurehead, Akaev's ascension masked an elaborate game of realpolitik which he navigated astutely, refusing to align himself with any particular party or ideology.

The removal of Soviet subsidies and the dissolution of the social safety net hitting the country hard, Akaev managed to steer a relatively calm path through troubled times. A programme of denationalization created high hopes in the West that Kyrgyzstan could become an 'island of democracy,' a leading light for reform in the region. The fact that these mass privatisations turned out to be appropriations, ensuring those who supported the President were rewarded with ex-Communist properties and businesses was largely glossed over.

Akaev's downfall began with the arrival of Boris Birshtein. Originally a Lithuanian Jew, Birshtein's long criminal record meant that he changed his citizenship almost as often as his underwear. Arriving in the newly independent, opportunity-rich country, the by now Canadian financier persuaded Akaev he could help him make Kyrgyzstan the 'Switzerland of Central Asia.' Appointed Chair of the Presidential Committee for Reconstruction and Development, his office faced the President's, affording him unfettered access.

There were sixteen tonnes of gold in the Kyrgyz Republic's vaults when the Soviet Union collapsed, Birshtein's role to attract investors by using these reserves as collateral. Wooing Akaev with a lavish, all-expenses-paid trip to meet his shady cronies in the Canadian Government, Birshtein soon had a contract brokered by Skadden Arps for the Cameco Corporation to run the Kumtor gold mine. The head of the Trade Representative Office of Kyrgyzstan in Moscow later recollected a conversation with the former

Minister of Metallurgy of the USSR, V. Durasov warning him that 'those are people without scruples.' Deeming the agreement 'not in the nation's interests,' the Kyrgyz Parliament have been fighting to annul it ever since.

In November 1991, Birshtein flew out to the remote mine with Canadian Trade Minister Monte Kwinter and the first Prime Minister of independent Kyrgyzstan, Nasirdin Isanov, a vocal opponent of Birshtein and his scheming. Their flight back to Bishkek purportedly grounded by fog, they set out to return with a police escort via the Jalalabad-Osh road, but were involved in a collision still shrouded in mystery. With Birshtein and Kwinter emerging unscathed, Isanov 'moaning and groaning and holding his head' was taken to a nearby hospital where he died, much to the surprise of Kwinter.

'A strong, robust man in his early forties,' the Canadian Trade Minister latterly recalled, 'his injuries definitely did not appear to be life-threatening.'

Shortly after the "accident," fourteen of Kyrgyzstan's sixteen tonnes of gold "disappeared" on private jets belonging to Birshtein and a supporter, who just so happened to have been appointed the new Prime Minister. Only escaping impeachment through the dissolution of parliament, Akaev's days were numbered.

Russian newspaper *Izvestiya* subsequently exposed Birshtein as a secret agent working for both the KGB and Mossad and a gangster involved in economic scandals in Russia and Ukraine. The FBI reported that he'd once hosted an organised crime summit in Tel Aviv attended by top mafioso including Semyon Mogilevich, 'the brainy don,' described as 'the most dangerous mobster in the world.' The case of the gold scandal is still open at the Kyrgyz Prosecutor's Office. Only a single banker has ever been indicted.

Flags and Parades

Emerging from the gloomy confines of the bank, we said our goodbyes to Henrik and Hettie. Ready to embark upon our primary mission in Bishkek

- the procurement of Tajik visas - my attempts to hail a taksi were thwarted by vehicles having to detour around a staggerer. His sandals flying into the air, the sot tumbled backwards with a roar, falling into an arik which a young mother had just finished helping her toddler relieve herself in. Drainage ditches were popular toilets, especially for children. Pulling up her little girl's panties, the woman paid little heed to this cataleptic fellow upon his newfound pillow of poo.

Eventually finding a cab driver who knew roughly where the embassy was, we set out towards the southern suburbs in search of the 'oversized yurt.' Beyond the crawling traffic lay the highway to Kyrgyzstan's second city of Osh, a road so mountainous no buses could traverse it.

Entering the mission, Stan distracted the clerk whilst I peeled out my old Kazakh visa, making space for the Tajik one. Upon collecting our passports the next afternoon, however, it transpired that including the Gorno-Badakhshan Autonomous Oblast entry permit, the visa had taken up two pages; instead of making the best use of the spots I'd made available, they'd inexplicably put the large sticker on top of my Kyrgyz entry stamp. Trouble lay ahead.

Unable to see where we were through the throng of bodies on the trolley-bus back downtown, we disembarked before the centre. Strolling through crumbling blocks, we passed a shop called Babushka Incorporated, planted amidst a row of shed-like wooden outlets. Its air-con unit chugging madly, men loitered outside a bar no more than three metres wide, its tin walls draped in PVC banners adorned with colossal pivos.

Emerging into Dubovy Park, I noted that the grounds had been upgraded with a series of busts. At the rear of the park, a disturbed young mind had etched colourful chalk outlines of characters on the pavement. 'Warface' brandished a gun and a meat cleaver, whilst 'Stalker' resembled the Tin Man from *The Wizard of Oz*, but with restless, grabby hands.

At the postern of the White House, a military parade was taking place, blue-bereted militsiya marching to a refrain pumped from loudspeakers that sounded like the theme from *The Great Escape*. Eager to assist in blocking the roads, a police car sped by, its siren dying with a sorrowful, low 'brrrphfff' as it hit the back of a traffic jam. A couple rattled past on a tandem bicycle, all gleeful grins as they tried the newest craze to sweep through Bishkek. Lounging on the grass, a group of Russians with deep-set eyes passed a bottle of Vivat vodka between them, appraising the scene with a characteristic blend of disinterest and condescension. Beyond the military minions, the displaced statue of Lenin stood with an arm outstretched in invocation, as if dreaming that this was his parade.

We stopped for dinner at Edgar's, where the menus highlights included pizza topped with rabbit, carrots and sour cream, and a house salad comprised of rice, tomato, banana and liver of codfish. For beer snacks, there was the evergreen pickles and lard. Seeing that we weren't going to order anything beyond ice tea, the staff refused to unlock the toilets, settling for charging us double for the drinks because they were 'big glasses.'

As dusk fell over Chuy Prospektesi, I noted that the disconcertingly extensive array of punch bags had already been set up. The Kyrgyz really liked to hit things. *Kurut* - dried yoghurt and salt sweets - had now made it to the capital, and Shoro had competition in the shape of Tah. Vendors of the rival beverages scowling at each other as they packed their wares away for the night, the Shoro wars had begun.

With the fountains set to dance in Ala-Too Square, the parade was drawing to a conclusion, soldiers whooping and cheering as they released helium-filled balloons carrying a gargantuan national ensign. A source of much contention, the Kyrgyz flag, scarlet with a sunburst yellow tunduk, fluttered as it barely lifted into the dusky sky. A parliamentary motion was underway to change the flag, too redolent of both Soviet times and recent conflicts. 'Why is it not blue sky, but blood that is seen through the tunduk?' a member of the flag-changing commission had asked. The answer, most probably, was that there was an abundance of leftover cloth dyed in Soviet red.

Nothing much having changed at Pele, including the videos, we headed back to the Sakura. Guests working their way through tall plastic tumblers filled with Angry Squirrel vodka - the bottle branded with an indignant squirrel protecting its nuts - a party was in full swing. Someone had even

dug out speakers for the obligatory doof. Sitting in the poky garden were
Eva and her parents, François and Sylvana, who'd just arrived from a meditation retreat in India. Stan and I having footed Eva's share of the cab fare
from the airport, François was irate about the driver's attempt to charge her
again.

> 'We will get to the bottom of this. We will clear this up!' he fumed, the
> skin stretched tight across his flushed face.
> 'Don't worry about it, its par for the course,' I said, trying to defuse the
> situation.
> '*Non!*' Sylvana chipped in, waving her arms, her razor short ginger hair
> emphasizing her emaciated appearance.
> 'It's only five dollars,' Stan reasoned.
> 'That's not the point,' François gnarled, his jaw movements appear-
> ing to begin where his high cheekbones ended. 'Nobody cheats my
> daughter!'

The door to the main house creaking open, the hotelier emerged. Shaking a
hand free from an overlong dressing gown sleeve, she pointed at a laminated
sign requesting silence after eleven PM.

> 'I throw you all out in the morning,' she hissed crossly, yet ever so qui-
> etly at the assembled wayfaring rabble. 'People try to sleep.'
> 'Nobody try to sleep,' a booming Italian guest retorted. 'We all out
> here partying.'

This was true, although I had some sympathy for the beleaguered proprietor's plight.

She needn't have bothered. Blessed with a muezzin determined to set a
new world record for the longest call to prayer, at quarter past three in the
morning the speakers at the local mosque emitted a shrill cry which set the
dogs to howling. All hope of slumber lost, we lay awake watching skull-
capped true believers flock past our window.

Lenin's Love-In

Situated behind the Manas plinth, balbals dating back to the sixth century - carved stone figures used as burial markers - and an open air gallery of kitschy horse paintings led to the State Historical Museum. The basement and top floors dedicated to folk traditions, the requisite yurt took pride of place. Its entrance guarded by life-sized statues of stallions covered in blood red felt, their pupil-less black eyes had a touch of the devil.

Flat and romanticised locket shaped frescos on the ceiling continued the theme of equestrian love, fields of poppies thrown in for good measure. Their oculus encrusted and rotten, glass cabinets were stuffed with snow leopards and other taxidermied animals of an unknown genus. Giant ladles on display for the larger than average vat of kumis, surly looking mannequins handled the apparatus after which Bishkek was named.

Emblazoned with Soviet banners, the central floor featured stern, faux-bronze reliefs of the huddled masses and limbless soldiers enduring in a state of disrepair. Ginormous revolutionary red ensigns and panpipe-like poles representing bolts of lightning surrounded an installation depicting the storming of the Winter Palace. Grisly photocopied photographs of skull totems were pinned to a wall, the ceiling mural of a sky aflame, conscripts impaled and widows weeping. Eyes bulging with fear, brave comrades stared down rows of the imperialist's cannons in scenes reminiscent of the biblical depths of hell.

All chiselled features and jutting chin, effigies of Lenin struck poses somewhere between prophet and superhero. Resembling something from the X-Men comics, in an imposing sculpture set in an alcove on the stairwell, Lenin and his cohorts strode purposefully forward. Despite the attempt at pomp and ceremony, however, the whole affair was suffused with a sense of melancholy. Soldier's hands and guns sellotaped back together, even Lenin had needed his arm taping up. Secured under glass, mixed in with this paraphernalia were personal items which had belonged to some of the eighty-five killed in the revolution of 2010, included a tracksuit, pyjamas, children's socks, a bottle of cologne and a chipped mug.

Emerging from a wall around the next corner, Marx and his trusty financier sidekick Engels were trailed by loyal apostles. Greatcoats and old wooden
muskets slowly rotting in display cases at their feet, models of tractors and railway engines that had once represented the vanguard of technology now looked
clunky and archaic. Not playing out as it was supposed to, history had derailed.

Around the corner at the Frunze Museum, with bored attendants in each
room tailing us, it seemed we were the first visitors for a while. Handsome in a
weathered way, a glint in his clear eyes, Mikhail Frunze rose through the ranks
to command the Southern and Eastern Fronts during the Russian Civil War,
defeating Kolchak's White Army at Omsk before subduing Bukhara and Khiva.
Having learnt from the master, portraits depicted him delivering speeches with
an outstretched arm, putting on his best impersonation of Lenin. By 1924,
though, suffering from ulceration, a photo of Frunze showed his cropped grey
hair receding and brow prematurely furrowed. The revolution had taken its toll.
A supporter of Stalin's rival Zinoviev, when forced to undergo routine surgery by
Uncle Joe in 1925, he "mysteriously" died of chloroform anaesthetic poisoning.

Interrupting the homage to locally born Frunze, a random array of Stalin
paraphernalia had muscled its way into the exhibits. Whilst the Georgians
had toppled the Kremlin Highlander's statue in his hometown of Gori, his
likeness lingered here. A poorly executed depiction of him had even found
its way onto a rug, the moustache right at least, his most distinguishing feature bar his raging, homicidal paranoia.

Before the exit stood the evocative thatched hut of Frunze's boyhood,
purportedly transported to the museum brick by brick. Beneath its low ceiling, a musty odour permeated the assembled artefacts. The bassinet, rocking
horse and guitar gripped by a deathly still, the clocks upon the whitewashed
walls had long since stopped.

Manas

Hailing a taksi out of Bishkek, we set out for the airport at five AM. The
highway bisecting amber wheat fields, just beyond a caucus of crows lying

inexplicably dead in the road, thirty kilometres west of the city we passed the US Manas Air Base. Black olive tents peeking from beyond a perimeter fence, lines of corrugated barracks painted in straw beige stretched out behind them.

A contentious issue and weapon for political point-scoring, for over a decade this cash cow had offered avenues of corruption to the Kyrgyz elites. When the logistical hub to support the war in Afghanistan first opened in 2001, the public response was initially positive. Spinning the deal to lease the site as economically beneficial, President Akaev promised there would be new jobs. Trying to get married off to an American soldier could also prove lucrative, he all but added.

Home to an array of aircraft and some three thousand US personnel at its peak, 2002 proved to be the honeymoon year, servicemen and their girls shopping in town amidst a climate of great local expectation.

'I think it's fair to say there will be a long-term presence here well beyond the end of hostilities,' US Air Force Colonel Billy Montgomery commented.

Realising that its post-9/11 stance had been too conciliatory and the old enemy planned to stay in its backyard, the Russians retaliated by opening their own Kant (Sugar) Air Base, twenty kilometres east of the city.

'Our base is here forever,' General Mikhailov, the head of the Russian Air Force stated; and rent free at that.

Within a relatively short space of time, it became abundantly clear that the supposed benefits of the American garrison would never materialise. With fuel companies owned by oligarchs and all food and water flown in, only contractors willing to grease palms could get work. A trough for the President's cronies, Manas quickly became a symbol of nepotism. The public mood had already soured long before US Private Zachary Hatfield escaped punishment for shooting dead an ethnic Russian delivery driver in 2006.

Never satisfactorily explained, the soldier's claims of self-defence simply didn't add up.

Whilst publically politicking that Manas should close, Russia continued to amass huge profits from its contracts to supply fuel to the base. Returning from Moscow in 2009 with a financial aid package worth over two billion US dollars, Kyrgyz President Bakiev further muddied the waters of this Cold War in miniature by serving an eviction notice on the Americans. Thinking he could play the two superpowers against each other whilst also courting China, this publicity stunt he never intended to follow through on backfired. Bakiev had overplayed his hand. The fact that his son Maxim, later arrested in Britain, had embezzled three hundred million dollars of Russian aid didn't help. This was in addition to the vast sums he effectively stole from Russian tax collectors through money-laundering and the 'grey-import' mechanisms of the state-controlled Asia Universal Bank.

On the 7th of April 2010, the Bakiev house of cards came crashing down. With demonstrators attempting to storm the White House being mown down by snipers on its roof, an off-duty taksi driver jumped the wrought-iron fence, stole an armoured personnel carrier with a roof-mounted machine gun and found an Afghan War veteran buddy happy to return fire. Called in to put down the uprising, cadets from the police academy received conflicting orders and dithered, some changing into civilian clothes and deserting. Bakiev and his entourage fled Bishkek post-haste. For the second time in five years, protestors took selfies with the President's personal effects before rampaging through the city on a looting spree.

Initially fleeing to his southern clan base and the erstwhile supporters he'd long forgotten, when attempting to deliver a speech in Osh, Bakiev was pelted with rocks. Shortly thereafter, offered safe haven in the dictators' club of Belarus, he left the country for good. Trading tit-for-tat allegations that each side had been behind the revolution, the Russians and Americans both had their reasons for privately approving of it.

Pulling up at the barriers outside the Manas International Airport, I noticed a handful of Kyrgyz eyeballing rows of gravestone grey US McChord military transit planes which lay docked and baking on the tarmac. Some having brought cameras and packed lunches, it was a day out, fun for all the family. Ushered through security, we made our way past the bulky transport carriers, their leaden monotony broken only by the tiny stars and stripes daubed upon their tailfins.

With American military involvement in Afghanistan tapering off, throughout 2013 the Kyrgyz authorities continued to avow that the Manas base would be decommissioned. Despite initially viewing President Atambayev's statements regarding termination of their lease as mere gambits on the path to negotiations, US efforts to persuade the government to let them stay - which included intensive training courses for the nation's Special Forces - proved to no avail. As Kyrgyzstan is inexorably drawn back into Russia's orbit, it is likely that closure of the base was a prerequisite to membership of President 'Ostrich legs' Putin's Eurasian Customs Union. The third most remittance-based economy in the world, one-fifth of the Kyrgyz labour force works abroad, almost exclusively in Russia, affording their former master great sway over the minnow republic.

With the base formally closing in February 2014, Kyrgyzstan will have to do without roughly three hundred and fifty million dollars a year in contracts, airport fees and fuel purchases paid for through shady off-shore companies on behalf of the US Department of Defence. In addition, local authorities will have to forgo the sixty million dollars in rent that Washington paid annually, about three percent of Bishkek's budget.

CHAPTER 11

Welcome to Osh

With the child seated behind me feverishly punching the back of my chair, I leafed through an in-flight magazine article entitled '*Understanding Kyrgyzstan*,' which offered such pearls of wisdom as 'In Kyrgyzstan the cassette recorders are still happy to be in using.' Crossing a patchwork of fields, as we left Bishkek behind the land below became remote and uninhabitable. Passing low over snow-capped peaks, the plane ploughed through turbulent skies.

Emerging from the clouds above the lush green Ferghana Valley, the light outside was blinding. Hamlets dotted along the banks of an aureate river, fires snaked along a distant mountain range. A sprawl of silos and Soviet apartment blocks signalling the outskirts of ancient Osh, we landed to no applause, which surprised me seeing as this route had suffered a crash-landing less than eighteen months earlier.

My portly neighbour refusing to budge, I began to wonder if he'd become wedged in his seat. Quite some time after all the other passengers had disembarked, though, with a superhuman effort, he shifted his buttocks. I needn't have worried; the airside transfer bus wasn't going anywhere. When it did move, it detoured around the farthest flung taxiways before depositing us back where we'd started.

Inside the dimly lit terminal of the Osh International Airport, we glanced around looking for a baggage carousel, quickly realising that there wasn't one. Twenty minutes later, an overloaded truck pulled up, but taking one look at the eager faces of the assembled crowd, the driver sped off. Another twenty minutes passed before he returned with a disgruntled looking underling, who climbed the swollen mountain of luggage and began tossing accoutrements from the back. A hubbub erupting as people tussled over look-alike items, we decided to take a step back and wait for the commotion to subside.

Exiting the airport with John, an English guy we'd been chatting to, it became clear why everyone had been in such a hurry.

'Well come to Osh! I am Guljigit,' a hackman rasped syllabically, striding up and rubbing his hands.
'He says the last marshrutka just left,' John - who spoke a little Russian - translated. 'He says he wants 250 som. That's really fucking expensive! I told him we'd pay 150 tops.'

It becoming apparent that the airport cabbies were a cartel and our man was in charge, with neither side willing to budge, a stand-off developed. Following us to the bus stop, where we confirmed that the last marshrutka had indeed departed, Guljigit tried to persuade us that his asking price was fair.

'He says it's the normal rate,' John sighed, the other drivers crowding round and nodding vigorously in agreement with the boss, who with his palms pressed to his mouth was busy miming.
'He says he needs the money to eat,' John explained.

A very, very big boy, he certainly hadn't been going hungry.

With the light failing and all hope of us finding any sustenance fading fast, by this point I'd have been ready to pay more than the 250 som - about five US dollars - he'd asked for, but another forty minutes passed before Stan and John reluctantly admitted defeat.

Secure in his victory, we'd barely left the grounds of the airport before Guljigit informed us that he'd be making a stop.

'I Muslim,' he boomed. 'I must pray.'

Underway again half an hour later, I elucidated upon our destination.

'We're going to the Osh Guesthouse,' I said, handing over a map and pointing out its location.

My nagging suspicion that our driver had taken Osh Guesthouse to mean any guesthouse in Osh proved all too true. Pulling up at an isolated hotel in fog swathed woodlands, he sauntered off attempting to claim a commission. Compounding his disappointment at the loss of a finder's fee, we proceeded to have him circle the city, stopping to ask directions of equally clueless pedestrians. Some four hours after the flight had landed, we were still none the wiser as to the whereabouts of the accommodation we'd booked.

When we finally found the place, I rather wished we hadn't. Located down an alley past a rank smelling armada of dumpsters, the Osh Guesthouse was on the top floor of a decaying block. The stairwell scattered with broken glass, the gastnitsa was actually a converted flat run by a surly bunch of devout Islamists in keffiyeh headgear and floor-length white thobes. There was one toilet and shower for all the overheated guests and the staff, but the toilet didn't flush and the shower didn't shower. Plastered all over the paper-thin walls were lists of rules: 'Remove shoes here, No drink, Close doors, Turn lights off, Observe curfew,' although a group of travellers having recently been robbed and beaten, this last directive was perhaps fair enough. Osh, it transpired, barely smiled in the daytime, let alone at night. Glancing through the front door, John resolved to make alternate arrangements.

Paying no heed to the curfew, in the kafe across the main road - the only place left open - we ordered food and decompressed. Laughing in a manly, excessively loud manner, locals mingled with khaki-clad militsiya. One hand firmly upon the machine guns that hung at their sides, their gaze rarely shifted from us.

Osh Bazaar

'Why you so late?' the irate night doorman barked.

Clambering over the bodies of the proprietor's snoring buddies, we sheepishly made our way to our closet-like quarters. If the rules weren't going to trip you up, the faithful passed-out on the parlour floor would.

Our room baking hot, there was no option but to leave the juddering pedestal fan on, the problem being that the only socket left its lead trailing across my face. The coiled bedsprings jabbing at my ribs; sleep wasn't going to happen. Just before six AM, the sun emerged from behind the tower opposite, blasting through the window.

We walked towards the centre; the dated buildings squarer and greyer than in Bishkek, hexagonal windows, pylons, masts and satellite dishes adorned them. A mural on the side of one six-storey block featured MIG fighter planes, the building next to it, in stark contrast, decorated with ginormous Care Bears. A serpent wrapped around a challis was a repeated motif on the fences of housing estates, a nod to Samanid philosopher-physician Abu Ali ibn Sina, who used venom as a remedy. First published in 1025, his *Qanun* stood as the standard medical textbook in Europe from its translation into Latin in the twelfth century through to the 1650s.

Obviously poorer and far less developed than the distant capital, Kyrgyzstan's second city felt like a different country. With hardly any foreigners in evidence, a more fervent religiosity was immediately apparent. Headscarves found in great abundance, men sported taqiyah caps and luxuriant beards.

Cutting through Zaina Betinova Street, signs in Cyrillic beckoned us towards Ош city centre, old women begging from the roadside setting their grandchildren to chase after us. Wedding season may not have been started in the capital yet, but in Osh it was in full swing. Rows of bridal shops doing a roaring trade, dressed dummies stretched in long white lines.

A solitary Shoro vendor snoozing under her umbrella marked the periphery of the Jayma Bazaar, Central Asia's biggest outdoor market and lifeblood of the city. It was eight AM and tempers were fraying already. Traffic at a standstill, floral gowned traders waved stick brooms, threatening to batter a stubborn taksi driver who'd parked in front of their stalls. At carts overflowing with non bread, shoppers tossed their purchases into plastic buckets or

Morrisons carrier bags, anomalous given the setting. Kalpak-clad old men in rubber boots and greatcoats picked through piles of ripe watermelons. The once fecund soil of the Fergana Valley producing an array of fruit and vegetables, whole rows of the bazaar were dedicated to onions, others to stubby, wide yellow carrots.

During Tsarist times, three million acres of the Fergana Valley were under cultivation. Largely focused on food crops, a million acres was also given over to permanent forest, from which the authorities distributed up to 200,000 trees to inhabitants of the province free of charge each year. The Soviet era saw the valley unequally divided between the new republics in favour of the Uzbeks, the forests destroyed and food production forcibly abandoned in favour of lucrative cotton. Although a balance of crops is slowly returning, evidence suggests that the land is now exhausted, poisoned by pesticides.

In the covered area of the bazaar, bored men in striped shirts, socks and sandals followed their wives obediently through the maze. Flannel jogging bottoms, paisley and leopard skin prints hung on display, chintzy Wayne Rooney t-shirts leaving the footballer looking more like Shrek than ever. A grist of flies covered piles of bloodied meat on the ground, crystal candies glistening like geological finds. Unable to resist any longer, I bought myself a handful of kurut balls, the popular super salty rock hard dried yoghurt snack.

Given the region's propensity to explode into ethnic violence, gun-wielding security forces were visible and hands on here. In their mishmash uniforms and lapel pins, they watched over every nook and cranny with itchy trigger fingers. Lesser spotted ethnic Uzbeks were easily identified - they may have been nervous, but they still liked their bling - the Kyrgyz dress sense conservative by comparison.

Following the ouster of President Bakiev in the Second Kyrgyz Revolution of June 2010, a wave of anti-Uzbek sentiment swept through the Osh Oblast. In episodes redolent of Nazi Germany's *Kristallnacht*, Uzbek houses were daubed in white paint with 'Uz,' singling them out for marauders. Their neighbourhoods destroyed in five days of unremitting bloodshed, the Uzbek government launched a brief troop incursion into Kyrgyzstan, before opening its border to a wave of 100,000 refugees. Impossible to verify, estimates of the dead and displaced vary, with between two hundred and two thousand killed and up to 200,000, mostly women, children and the elderly displaced. Of those that fled across the border, the majority now live in tent camps, pulling water from thinly spread wells.

Solomon's Throne

Located on the banks of the Ak-Buura (White Camel) River, Osh's equivalent to Bishkek's Panfilov Park offered an assortment of tarpaulin topped karaoke booths and a rifle range. At a game involving the use of a rubber mallet to clobber a comedically grotesque bulls head with golf balls for eyes, the swag man scowled at my photography.

A Ferris wheel dominating the park, the Sunday afternoon constitutional saw the town in full swing. The grey fairground rides enlivened by children's excited squeals, machinery clanged as parents looked on with toothy grins. Greetings being offered, everyone appeared to know everyone. Finding shady spots, teenage boys slurping on ice creams waded in the chalky blue river, little crakes flying low around them and swooping at the water's surface. On the far bank, a group of men occupied in dislodging a metal girder from the river's edge for purposes unknown were finally victorious, releasing a hearty roar.

On the scrub slope leading back to the main drag - "For Sale" signs in its cobweb coated windows - a discarded Aeroflot Yak-40 plane which had once served as a video salon seemed to be slowly sliding towards the river. Farther uphill, fountains were spraying the algae-ridden concrete, a sombre notice discouraging against the temptation to cool oneself with the warning of a two thousand som fine.

Above Lenin Street, a glistening three storey aluminium drainage cistern and aborted building projects dotted the hillside to the west of town. If Osh was as historic as it is said - locals claim the city to be older than Rome – there were very few signs of it.

Hoping that the heat would soon abate, we walked towards the view-point Solomon's Throne, the barren crag overshadowing the city where Mohammed is said to once have prayed. On the slippery, narrow incline, the elderly were causing bottlenecks, a babushka panting and laughing with her family as she repeatedly fell flat on her arse. Despite being considered idolatrous, a remnant of Central Asia's pre-Islamic past, cloth ribbons of invocation hung from wishing trees. At the summit, a small shrine originally constructed by Babur - founder of the Mongol Empire, a descendant of Timur and Jenghiz Khan - had been rebuilt after twice being destroyed, first by an earthquake and then by the Soviets. Superstition holds that would-be mothers who ascend to *Dom Babura* and slither down a crack in the holy rock will give birth to healthy babies.

Situated on the southern slope of the bluff, the call to prayer drifted up from Kyrgyzstan's largest mosque, holding a capacity of twenty thousand people. Newly built with funds from Saudi Wahhabis, it had recently been inaugurated by President Atambayev, who, like other regional leaders before him, had been wooed by promises of Saudi money.

Sunni supremacists wishing to revert to the seventh-century ways of Mohammed, Wahhabi missionaries first arrived in Central Asia in 1912, setting up cells in Tashkent and the Fergana Valley. Declaring holy war not only on the West, but also on other Muslims, the Wahhabis labelled all who disagreed with them heretics. Having suffered lean times under the Communists, now they were back and loaded with oil money. Of the Osama Bin Laden school of thought, their goal is to destroy secularism and create a region-wide caliphate based on Sharia law, this despite the fact there has never been an Islamic state in Central Asia.

Amongst the Wahhabi's affiliates are the Islamic Movement of Uzbekistan, formed in the early nineties by Tohirijon Yuldashev, a twenty-four-year-old college drop-out, and Juma Namangani, an ex-Soviet paratrooper turned train robber. Raising funds by kidnapping Japanese geologists and American mountaineers, in 2000 the IMU briefly took Osh, holding its mayor for ransom and coming within striking distance of its goal of seizing Tashkent.

With the IMU largely absorbed into the Afghan Taliban, ignored warnings of the impending 9/11 attacks on America are said to have emanated from Yuldashev, who like Namangani, has since been killed. Looking to engage those alienated by state-appointed imams, who as a recent recruit noted, offer only 'prayers for a bigger cotton harvest and instructions for how to go to the bathroom properly,' the IMU are currently calling for a jihad in Southern Kyrgyzstan. With the IMU largely absorbed into Afghanistan and Pakistan, in June of 2014, after swearing allegiance to ISIS, the organisation claimed responsibility for the attack on Jinnah International Airport in Karachi, Pakistan, which left 36 dead. There are currently upwards of two thousand ISIS recruits from Central Asia, with the movement's hierarchy focused on recruiting more disaffected Uzbeks.

Descending Solomon's Throne with the muezzin's *adhān* still ringing in our ears, we passed the same old lady we'd overtaken during our ascent. Her rosy cheeks puffed out as she sat wheezing, she was still no nearer the summit. Sun-baked and having a moment, back at the base I was providing amusement, first by mistakenly going into the ladies tua-let and then falling in a ditch. Sitting in a shady café, a middle-aged woman enjoyed my misfortune so much that she choked on her bread, lumps of mushy non flying from her nose.

Endgame

In the Jayma Bazaar earlier that day, we'd run into Eva, last seen knocking at our door in Bishkek to hand over the disputed cab fare. The Fruges, it transpired, had managed to arrange onward transport to Sary Tash and asked if we'd like to share the ride. Having scratched our names and itinerary on the noticeboard in the Osh Guesthouse some days ago, paying a deposit for the privilege but hearing nothing, we jumped at the chance. Back at the guesthouse, however, the owner, Daniyar was less than pleased.

We met the French family to iron out the details over dinner at the California Café. The only Western-style eatery in town, its dishes named after Hollywood stars of the nineties, I picked at a plate of Sandra Bullock as Stan wrestled with an undercooked Arnold Schwarzenegger. One of the endless power cuts kicking in, the staff laid their heads upon table tops in the semi-darkness, watching condensation run down bottles of ketchup filled an entire refrigerator. Ensuring a sugar rush for teetotallers with a sweet tooth, everything in Osh came covered in a blanket of ketchup.

The lights fizzling back on, the kettle resuming its juddering, as lumbering through the entrance and beckoning for us to follow him outside, there was Daniyar's trusty sidekick, Nurlan. A guilty blush upon his globose face, he passed me a phone, his apoplectic boss on the other end of the line.

'You put deposit, you cannot change mind,' Daniyar carped. 'You go Sary Tash, there is no transport; you never leave Sary Tash. You stupid! Cannot change mind, is not fair. Not fair!'

It seemed pretty clear - despite their days of inaction - that we weren't going to get a refund.

Ambling back to the gastnitsa to deal with the situation, we passed Osh's sole nightclub, where pudgy, crew cut militsiyamen in starchy shirts sat nursing drinks. Despite its name, Club Angar hadn't really gotten angry yet, more slurry and morose. There was still time, though.

Skirting the estate playground, its swings removed and the metal frame redesignated as a washing line, we trudged up the stairs with an increasing sense of foreboding. Fortunately, Daniyar had calmed down a little, even reimbursing a token amount of our money.

'I know how this works,' he said, playing the big man in front of his buddies, the living room so crowded that we could barely squeeze into it. 'I do this bizniz long time. I give you som, you say nice things,' he almost smiled; either that or he was suffering from a bout of indigestion.

Not eager to stick around, we slipped out to the café opposite. When we returned at ten thirty PM, the drowsy night-porter reluctantly prised open the door.

'Why you so late?' he demanded.

CHAPTER 12

To the Trans-Alai

Climbing over Nurlan and escaping unnoticed, we met the Fruges at six AM. Our vehicle arriving early, with barely time to procure supplies for the journey, I grabbed a box of biscuits and a few bags of out of date dill flavoured crisps. I never saw a packet of crisps in the entire country that wasn't past its sell-by date, the farther from the capital one travelled, the longer ago the expiry date.

Beginning in the Kyrgyz second city, the Pamir Highway - the second highest international road in the world - runs the length of Tajikistan and down through Southern Uzbekistan before terminating in Mazar-I-Sharif, Afghanistan. An ancient Silk Road route in use for millennia, paving of the *Pamirsky Trakt* was completed in 1934, enabling the Soviets to move troops and supplies more freely through one of their remotest outposts.

With the outskirts of Osh receding behind us, following the valley and the rippling Marshypan River, low within its banks at the height of summer, the M41 cut through rolling hills. In scattered settlements, whitebeards sat chatting in disused bus stops designed to resemble kalpaks, their freshly washed rugs laid out on the scarcely used bitumen to dry. Villages became yurt camps, horses roaming freely and blocking the road in this nation which boasts more steeds than cars. The Osh weekenders having gone home, a cluster of yurts stood empty at Chyrchyk Pass, herds of animals mingling as they grazed.

Ascending through lush pastures, the oppressive heat began to dissipate, rocky outcrops framing the long bridge to the tiny Alay District capital of Gulcha, where three tributaries joined to form the Kurshab River. Beyond the gap town of Gulcha, signs in the shade of towering escarpments delivered warnings about landslides. Horses were replaced by hardy donkeys with ruddy cheeked infants in woolly hats perched upon them, cotton saddlebags swinging at their sides. Infrequent domiciles grew grimier, old Volga GAZ the preferred mode of transport at three thousand metres plus. From beyond iron red ridges shaped by erosion, glacial peaks began to peer.

We drove past imposing precipices, striated lines of colour revealing the age of the rock. Toiling diligently on hairpin turns, Chinese road crews in hard hats balanced upon flimsy wooden scaffolds leading to the Taldyk Pass at 3,615 metres. Their work slow progress, they'd been at it for a number of years. A few hundred metres above them, a squat white obelisk marking the pinnacle was guarded by a lone mastiff, barking furiously as we rumbled past.

Descending to the desolate settlement of Sary Tash, the majestic Trans-Alai Mountain Range demarcating the border with Tajikistan was thrown into sharp relief. A windswept hamlet where the three main roads to Osh, Tajikistan and Kashgar in China converge, its location has led Sary Tash to become a major stopover on the heroin highway, along which ninety tonnes of AIP (Afghani, Iranian and Pakistani heroin) is shipped every year.

As we alighted a little woozy from the altitude, a line of elders on a wooden bench inspected us with a mild curiosity. Their ribs protruding, sickly looking cows and mules foraged around power pylons on the stony ground. Insignificant against a backdrop of foothills, a man on crutches in a greatcoat shuffled past, his breath visible in the dappled late afternoon sun. In a village where temperatures dropped to minus forty-five degrees Celsius in the winter, even the Ladas wore blankets.

Flanked by a group of children, their faces caked in mud, François, Stan and I went in search of lodgings whilst the women hung back at the car. Despite signs advertising hotels, we were met with reticence and collective shaking of heads. Whether there was no accommodation available or our presence was unwelcome remained unclear.

Abandoning the futile search, we headed onto Sary Moghul, part of 37,000 acres which had been leased to the arable land starved Tajik govern-ment up until 2004. Passing huge white radar stations, like giant golf balls adrift in the grassland, wild yellow flowers lined the roadside, a solitary eagle following us, soaring high above the car.

Njebre's House

Maroon rugs adorned the floor and walls of our whitewashed room, the rough and ready rafters running across the ceiling formed from gnarled halves of tree trunks. All broad smiles, bushy haired Abdish and his mother Njebre at the Sary Moghul Community Based Tourism Homestay had been most welcoming, seeming genuinely pleased to see us. Ushering us inside, button-nosed Njebre - wearing a shapeless waistcoat over her dress despite the heat - laid out a spread of non, choy, kurut, apricot jam and apples, which we feasted upon until the flies ultimately won. Kazakhstan may have had the largest apples in the world, the mighty if unfashionable Aport, but its neighbour had the smallest, the tiny fruit barely the size of a plum.

As we strolled through the village, greetings were hollered from atop of hay bales and roofs where dung bricks were being piled for use as winter fuel. The lustrous eyes of children peered with interest from compounds. Its engine fairly screaming, having unsuccessfully attempted to back his mud-spattered Lada Zhiguli out of a ditch, a man stood wistfully stroking his chin-muffler beard. Roosters crowed as they strut from the path of a convoy of Kama3 trucks, a hundred kalpak-clad aksakals on the open backs headed for a meeting taking place in the middle of a field.

At an elevation of over three thousand metres, everything in Sary Moghul had a homemade feel, the wonky, mismatched cupolas on the mosque fashioned from what appeared to be upturned milk urns. In the bazaar - a collection of twelve low-roofed huts and a converted cargo container - sheets of plastic served as windows. In one shop, a grinning old man in a dopy was busy stuffing two bottles of arak, which the babushka in charge had pulled from under the counter, down his trousers. Clearly well practiced in this intricate manoeuvre, the bottles slid snuggly into his rubber boots.

'When the Russians left they took their vodka with them, so the Kyrgyz tried to brew their own,' François commented, brushing wisps of thin, mousy blonde hair from his forehead. 'But vodka being, how you say, like trademarked, yes, they needed to come up with a new name for it, so they called it arak.'

I didn't know at the time if this were true or not – it turned out it wasn't - but never one to pass up on a new experience, I thought we'd better give it a try.

So with dust in our eyes and our drinks crunching between our teeth, we sat on the concrete steps outside Njebre's house watching the sunset over the pink Trans-Alai Mountains. The anise drink tart and harsh, I shuddered as I swallowed.

'Just as well we didn't buy the kumis,' François laughed. 'It's fermented with horse urine, you know. The stronger it is, the more piss it contains.'

This assertion also proving to be false, it seemed he'd taken too much of Sacha Baron Cohen's *Borat* at face value. A difficult place to pin down, a mist of misinformation and conjecture has a tendency to hover over Central Asia.

At the side of the house, a group of overexcited infants were chasing a pink balloon Eva had given them across a recently ploughed field. Among them were fair-skinned, blonde haired youngsters some say are the descend-ants of the armies of Alexander the Great, others tracing their lineage to the Scythian hordes.

A diverse collection of oft-warring tribes, the Scythians worshipped the sun and their horses. United in the face of a common enemy, mounted Scythian warriors repeatedly thwarted the advances of Alexander the Great; the first recorded use of what were effectively mobile guerrilla units against conventional forces. Finally defeated at the Battle of Jaxartes in 329BC after being cornered in a fixed location, with no written language of their own, scattered petroglyphs tell the story of the Scythians, a people who have dis-appeared as an ethnic entity.

Disturbed by the children's cries as they raced past it, the family's umber donkey set to braying, an occurrence so regular you could set your watch by it. Approaching the beast, Eva held out her hand with a mind to pet it, but springing to its hooves, it came at her, head bowed like a charging bull.

'*Merde*,' she cried, sending water canisters flying as she fled.

Hitting the end of its rope tether just seconds before reaching her, the jennet whinnied and set to rolling on its back in the dust, soon disappearing in a cloud of its own making.

Kyrgyz folk music emanating from a cassette player, the lilting twang of the *komuz* - a fretless stringed instrument comparable to the lute - flowed from the house. Smoke rose from pipes protruding through corrugated tin roofs in the foothills of the majestic Pik Lenin. Carrying a bucketful of vegetables, hunched over and struggling to mount the three steps to her door, Njebre beamed at us as she faltered past in her all weather neoprene boots. Exchanging a few whispered phrases, François and his wife, a nurse who spoke scant English, nodded knowingly.

'It's Parkinson's,' François sighed. 'Sylvana has seen it many times before. I'm going to write down the names of medicines they need, but I don't know if they can buy them in Kyrgyzstan, even if they could afford them.'

Kissing Njebre's hands as a sign of respect, a knot of relatives arrived. Family was everything here. Among the latecomers was Almas, an English Language student who, having heard there were native speakers in town, wanted to practice. Wearing the headscarf Njebre had proudly dressed her in, the bright blue eyed Eva had been cajoled into giving him a lesson, but the shy Almas was taciturn about forming sentences of his own.

'Yes, I know this,' he said, tugging nervously at his fledgling tash and syllabically repeating the words she read from his textbook.
'Good, your English is very good,' Eva coaxed, 'but what is it you want to do?'

'I want to be guide,' Almas replied, turning to spit over his left shoulder and leave a loogie on the rug which nobody paid any attention to.

A Kyrgyz superstition holds that two angels live behind each individual, a white angel upon one's right shoulder and a black angel on the left. When a person spits over their left shoulder, it forces the dark angel back, preventing it from destroying one's plans.

The stringy snot still lingering on the carpet, having spotted my camera, initially wary teenage members of the clan were eager to have their pictures taken. I dutifully took a series of snapshots, their subjects blushing and giggling as they viewed their digital portraits. That the region was cut off by snowdrifts for months at a time, electricity patchy at best and all water drawn from wells was told in their prematurely cockled faces. Only eighteen, despite her striking beauty, Abdish's daughter looked over a decade beyond her years.

With the moon ascended and the stars shimmering brightly, outside a tranquil hush had descended. Even the donkey having stopped braying, the loudest sound was the transistor station for Sary Moghul, buzzing like some Sci-fi automation. Aside from this, there was nothing to be heard but the gentle trickling of a stream and fleeting bursts of late evening birdsong.

Pik Lenin

Part of the Trans-Alai Range marking the border between Kyrgyzstan and Tajikistan, 7,134 metre Pik Lenin, the second highest mountain in both countries, looked remarkably accessible from the homestay. Sitting on the patio steps, feeling as if I could almost touch the looming mountain, I'd dreamily opined as to how far away it actually was.

'Ten kilometres?' I'd ventured.
'Maybe fifteen,' Stan mused, squinting into the distance. 'It's always farther than it looks.'

Setting out early next morning hoping to reach the foothills, we resolved to find out.

In the centre of the village, men were employed in making repairs to roofs and digging drainage ditches ahead of the long freeze. A toothless old swain playing catch with his granddaughters stopped us to shake our hands enthusiastically, asking me to take a photo of the thrilled young girls.

We crossed a clear brook on a rickety wooden bridge, women in wellies tarrying from stone-washing their laundry to wave. By far the tallest thing in town, wooden pylons skirted a pasture where weary horses stood motionless. Beyond a crumbling graveyard at the edge of the hamlet, a clay red river added a colour previously absent from the settlement's palette. On islands in the riverbed, flowers sprouted from between olive green rocks, some proud and strong, others like sickly forget-me-nots sapped of pigment by the sun. In a shallow pool, tadpoles circled, metamorphosing towards their first hops.

Across the water, a gulley filled with small, sapphire blue posies gave way to a cracked, inhospitable plain ominously littered with the skulls of sheep. Dust devils ripped through the steep biome, the ground ridden with stag beetles. The village receding from view, power lines stretched into the expanse, dominating the desolate space.

By the time we reached the grassy knolls, which had looked all of twenty minutes away, we'd been walking for two and a half hours. The earth speckled with dandelions, milk thistle and glossy, coal black boulders, from a distance it had appeared as if there were one hillock before the range began. Chased up an incline by a herd of stampeding bulls, however, it became apparent that the hummocks stretched for klicks, each ascent leading to yet another previously obscured.

A further two hours later, with water supplies running low, we settled on a viewpoint, the hazy mountains still looking as far-off as when we'd started out. A preponderance of stacked stone shrines marking this as a place where others had also chosen to turn back, we slumped down upon the stinging crabgrass. The verdant alpine tors rolling on ahead, flies buzzed around us, the strengthening wind buffeting clouds of yellow butterflies. A golden eagle soared above, stalking long-tailed marmots which poked their heads from burrows like whack-a-moles, before scurrying back underground.

With blisters on my blisters beneath the savage sun, we tried to take a shortcut back, following tyre tracks through the void until they disappeared without warning as if the vehicles had been swallowed up. His shirt wrapped around his head, Stan looked like a bearded babushka as he attempted to ford the red river, floundering upon slippery stones hidden below the surface. By this juncture, I was using one of my detachable trouser legs as a hat, the other covering an arm.

Leisurely trotting along the riverbank, a boy upon a mule who doffed his cloth cap was a welcome first sign of civilisation. Finally crawling back to Njebre's to enjoy a last meal of leftover vegetable soup, boiled potatoes and porridge mixed together; we compared our burns with the equally crispy Fruges.

Problema

Staring expectantly towards the horizon through clouds of breath, with the sun yet to rise we waited in the chill morning for our transport. Pacing up and down to keep warm, an hour passed before the driver pulled up, sheepishly reporting a snag which must have been obvious when the ride was negotiated the night before. The four-wheel drive yA3 unable to seat all of us, someone would have to go in the boot. Still, we reasoned, it was the only option available, although despite craving a shower - hot or cold - I was sad to be leaving Sary Moghul.

Our bags tied to the roof rack, hugs and handshakes abounded, even locals we hadn't previously met getting in on the farewell embraces. Pulling away, it wasn't long before the floor was shaking, some Russian doof with a Turkish twist blasting from the stereo. The nodding head dog stuck to the dashboard seemed to be getting into it; either that or it was the condition of the road.

Toddlers selling bottles of gasoline racing after our vehicle, we zigzagged through potholes. The empty M41 deteriorating to become no more than a gravel track, it took an hour to reach the mountain range which had looked so close. The pounding beat deposed by a Kyrgyz comedy duo replete with a laugh track - their timing somehow reminding me of Peter Cook and Dudley Moore – we veered around the first of many broken down trucks. Dwarfed by mountains, yak herds were omnipresent on the *jailoos* - high summer grazing pastures – as we weaved between peaks, the worrying stench of petrol fumes escaping from the engine.

Beside a swing gate barrier blocking the road, four soldiers in fatigues and flip-flops sat listlessly smoking cigarettes at the Bor Döbö border post. Appearing from the sole concrete building, an officer approached, collecting documents and attempting to read our names aloud with limited success. Counting the passports, he scanned the vehicle perplexedly for the fifth passenger.

'Da,' he murmured, clocking Eva scrunched in the boot.

Returning from the confines of the shit-smeared outhouse to hear the guard barking my name, my heart sank. As herders passed freely from state to state on the edelweiss covered mountainside, down below them I had a 'pasport problema.'

Despite Kyrgyzstan being visa free for most Westerners, including British citizens, I still needed an entry stamp in order to exit the country, the same stamp buried beneath my Tajik visa by the embassy staff in Bishkek. My efforts to peel up the Tajik sticker proving futile, to the snarling of dogs yanking at their chains, a bevy of new guards emerged, eager to see what all the fuss was about. Comprised of much squinting, holding my document up to the light and mumbling, a form of pass the passport ensued. Calls to superiors were purportedly made, resulting in a collective shaking of heads, arms folded in gestures that screamed 'though shalt not pass.'

Waiting in the car, Stan and the girls were getting fidgety. After an hour or so of this stand-off, a Tajik guide and his British wards passing in the opposite direction pulled up. Speaking excellent English and Russian, the guide agreed to help, though seeing there was trouble, the British couple avoided me like the plague.

'Just put some money in your passport and hand it back, yes?' François advised. 'Like it says on the dollar, "In God they trust."'

Unruffled, yet somewhat concerned about worsening the situation with the offer of a bribe, I saw little other recourse other than to follow his advice. Ten minutes later, our Tajik aide emerged from the office.

'They say they really want to help you,' he informed me, 'but they don't want to help you for only twenty dollars.'

Having chanced upon this stroke of good fortune, they weren't going to let it slide easily.

Patting his pockets in search of a lighter, a guard emerged from the outhouse with a crumpled cigarette dangling from his lips. Snatching the lighter from my hand, François thrust it at him.

'Take it, it's yours,' he said in Turkish, at which he was proficient.

Accepting the gift, the official gave a thumbs-up and we smiled falsely.

'How you say,' François whispered, 'butter them up.'

Beckoned back into the office, I slid another ten dollars into my passport.

'Pasport problema,' the official mumbled gravely, wrapping his knuckles upon the desk.

Seeing the additional ten dollar bill, the dark clouds lifted from his face. Picking up his rubber stamp, he punched in a backdated entry.

'Pasport, Niet problema,' he said, reversing his decision and tucking the banknotes into his top pocket.

'Shh,' he added, putting a finger to his lips, before ushering me out of the office.

Exiting the room, I noted a poster written in English fastened to the door. 'Corruption,' it read, a large red 'X' drawn through the word.

As we sped away through the gate which had been left open since our Tajik friend and his charges arrived, several of the patrol who'd not been privy to my transaction shook their fists. 'Problema, problema,' they howled, as the tyres propelled grit into their faces.

CHAPTER 13

Tajik Arse

Littered with malachite green rocks, the red soil highway ascended through twenty kilometres of no man's land. Belonging to no nation, there was no upkeep here, our car labouring through ever widening glacial runoffs. Giving the engine a rest, we paused by a cluster of abandoned, shed-like dormitory buildings at the 4,282 metre Kyzyl-Art Pass. On a bicycle far too big for him, a solitary boy pedalled in circles, his feet failing to reach the ground when he stopped to accept a bonbon Eva offered him.

Passing a statue of a Marco Polo Sheep, we climbed a final peak before descending to the Tajik border. A windswept outpost, with its flimsy padlock disregarded, the open gate to Tajikistan swung in the stiff breeze. Amongst the scattered detritus were two windowless, cylindrical metal tubes which doubled as soldier's lodgings, stacks of wood and bricks preventing them from rolling away down the mountainside. In putrid lime and yellow uniforms, the guards were a motley bunch, all unwashed and unshaven. Saucepan caps at askew angles, adjusting their puffy jackets, they eventually turned their attention to us.

'Angliya? *Français?*' they chorused.
'Angliya,' I replied.
'Français,' François responded.
'Tajik?' Eva asked of them.
'Niet,' a conscript answered definitively, 'Pamiri. Welcome to Gorno-Badakhshan.'

A self-governing region within Tajikistan, despite covering forty-five percent of the land mass, the Gorno-Badakhshan Autonomous Oblast contains only

three percent of the Tajik populace. Having hitched their wagon to the losing side - the Islamic Party and the leftist's alliance of convenience - during
the civil war, the Pamiris have faced neglect, privation and persecution ever
since. Receiving next to nothing by way of government support, throughout
the nineties only humanitarian aid saved the Pamiris from mass starvation.
The region still suffers from crippling poverty and an economic exodus of
those in search of gainful employment.

From the Passport Control Office, we inched our way to the Regional
Permit Office, an alloy cube outside of which sentinels were standing over
a solar panel which lay in pieces upon the ground. Poring over an instruc-
tion manual which resembled something from Ikea, they scratched their
heads. Those that weren't involved hovered lethargically, more intent on
handing out flyers for friend's guesthouses in Murgab than expediting our
progress.

'*Vrahch*? Doktor? Who is your doktor?' a remarkably clean cut young
officer demanded, bustling up to our yA3 with a previously unseen
sense of urgency.

One of the soldiers needing a course of injections, by sheer chance we
had a nurse on board. So with Sylvana whisked away and François in
her wake, the rest of us waited outside, Eva occupying herself by pet-
ting two drooling, starving looking dogs I wouldn't have touched with an
extremely long stick. Wondering if the white patches on the earth were
saline deposits, Stan crouched on all fours and licked the ground; a peculiar sight. Emitting a sound like a cow trying to sneeze, apparently it didn't
taste good.

His eye caught by the map I was holding, a recruit with a beard which
sprouted in bunches approached. You could smell him as he ran a blackened
fingernail across the page.

'Tajikistan good?' he asked.
'Da,' we nodded, despite not having set foot in the country yet.

Half an hour later, Sylvana and François emerged from the permit office.

'Ha ha,' Sylvana chortled, as she clambered into her seat. 'We 'aven't even crossed ze border yet, and I 'ave already seen Tajik arse!'

Offering loud thanks, a beaming posse crowded round, waving us on our way as we finally entered Gorno-Badakhshan.

By January 2014, all borders between Kyrgyzstan and Tajikistan would be shut indefinitely to Kyrgyz and Tajik citizens following clashes over a bypass road in disputed territory. Whilst both sides blame the other, what's clear is that mortars were fired and both armies suffered casualties. With only half of the 971-kilometre border between the two countries delimited, conflict is likely to escalate as population numbers along the frontier increase.

Furious Fruge and the Black Lake

Skirting the border with China's conflict-ridden Xinjiang Province, the Pamir Highway followed a snaking barbed wire fence for hundreds of kilometres. Across the barren Mars-scape, the Chinese government were busy busing in Han settlers in order to outnumber and dominate the local Uyghur populace. Where wooden struts had been stolen, parts of the fence sagged. Unattended gates left open, tyre tracks told of illegal transit.

I later spoke with journalist Joshua Kucera.

'There's a widespread belief in Gorno-Badakhshan that the President's daughter controls the shipping across this border,' he told me. 'It's no doubt pretty lucrative. Many Tajiks believe that the government's interest in regaining control in Gorno-Badakhshan has to do with gaining control of smuggling routes. From the Pamiri's perspective, though, they see the central government as trying to eliminate their cultural and religious identity.'

As the international boundary between the two theoretically autonomous regions drooped to our left, in the front of the vehicle François was brushing up on his Tajik.

'Dushanbe, Seyshembe, Sharshembe, Beishembe, Juma, Ishembe, Jekshembe,' he chirped, reciting the days of the week.
'Knub, da!' our driver encouraged him.

Passing marooned trucks, a lifeless, monotonal vista led us to the village of Karakul. The mountains of the Pamir Knot encircling it, the moment the freezing Karakul Lake came into view, Tanacetum gracile and tiny mauve flowers began to push through the parched waste. We stopped to take photographs, my vision blurry in the crisp air at an elevation of over four thousand metres. Marching toward the barbed wire barrier, Stan set off in an attempt to illegally cross into China, Eva undertaking an unsuccessful stab at sprinting at altitude.

Checking his watch before rolling down to Karakul, our driver started back-pedalling about tarrying in the village.

'What's the problem?' I asked François. 'We negotiated that we were going to stop here.'
'Why are you asking me?' he shouted, his face an incandescent crimson, arms flapping like a hatchling; 'I don't speak Tajik!'

Unbeknownst to me at the time, despite having invited us to stay at his chateau in the French Alps the evening before, this was the last time François would ever speak to us.

With our driver pulling over at a checkpoint, whilst conscripts attempted to wrest a living wage from him, I took my chance, vaulting from the car and heading into the remote, inhospitable hamlet. An abject place that lacked colour, beneath high, fluffy clouds, even the beiges and pastel blues were tinged with grey. Leaning power pylons dwarfed a ramshackle, rugged collection of mud-brick dwellings. A ghostly air of desolation permeating the settlement, clumps of plaster falling from shacks added to growing piles of rubble. Rusted gates fallen from their hinges, buildings without roofs crumbled beside a stripped playground. Its metal requisitioned, the remains of a climbing frame laid collapsed and mangled.

Disintegrating boulders led down to a low ring of grass and salty deposits surrounding the lifeless lake. Dominated by mountains and covered in a constant shroud of haze, the highest lake in Central Asia is locally known as 'Big Black' for its hue when frozen over throughout the bulk of the year. Created by a huge meteor some ten million years ago, the lake was eerie and still, its deep waters mirroring the mountains.

The ground spattered with the skulls of sheep and ibex, a downed fence lay coiled and snagging at my ankles as it twisted from the shoreline back to the checkpoint. Above the town, an ominous, imposing former Soviet garrison which had once housed two hundred soldiers lingered in a state of terminal decline, windows boarded up and slates missing. Nearing the road, with altitude sickness kicking in, I heaved and staggered, nearly tripping over a dead fox cub in which flies were starting to take an interest.

'*Americano?*' an old woman with two wary toddlers hiding behind her stocky legs emerged to call after me.
'Angliya,' I replied.
'Ah, *Brit-an-nya*,' she muttered knowingly, seeming to be satisfied and smiling broadly as she waddled off.

These were the only people I saw in Karakul, everyone else presumably grazing flocks in the high pastures or gone to look for work.

The most remittance-based economy in the world, forty-seven percent of Tajikistan's GDP is sent in by the 800,000 Tajiks working abroad, largely in Russia. Both a boon and a curse for the authorities, whilst this mass migration removes those seen as unemployed malcontents, it's also a source of embarrassment to the extent that official figures are no longer released.

Humiliated and extorted by border guards, these ex-pats are easy targets for the Russian police and are often subjected to attacks by neo-fascist groups. Living in dormitory blocks overseen by gangmasters on the plains of Siberia, many die on the job, but they couldn't survive back home. The poorest of the post-Soviet Republics, forty-seven percent of the Tajik population live in poverty, subsisting on less than two US dollars a day.

An expert in organised crime and corruption in post-Soviet Eurasia, Alexander Kupatadze later told me that other Tajik ex-pats are 'heavily involved' in smuggling. 'According to Kyrgyz Drug Control Agency officials,' he said, 'the leader of the Tajik diaspora has been laundering money by purchasing real estate and restaurants in Egypt and Dubai, as well as investing in agriculture in Austria.'

Lecturer in Central Asian Studies at the University of Glasgow, Luca Anceschi spoke about yet another facet of the situation.

'The fact that these people tend to settle leads to wider issues,' he explained. 'Now Russia has become more aggressive [and] started to change their understanding of citizenship, they could become an even more permanent part of the Russian state. This is something which could be detrimental in the longer term, a brain drain if you will, or a loss of manpower.'

Mumbling something about the militsiya, with many kilometres left to cover our driver was in no mood to wait whilst I pondered the finer points. The wheels screeching as we made a sharp exit, Karakul quickly receded behind us.

The earth alongside the highway turned to red hematite, the taller peaks of the Muzkol Range striped in black and a glistening, brilliant white. Rising through the majestic Ak-Baital 'White Horse Pass' at 4,655 metres, the four-wheel drive rattled as it struggled, our driver failing to inspire confidence as he leant out the window to check on an offending tyre.

Passing the first vehicle we'd seen in over four hours, derelicts began to appear, golden marmots scurrying across the road or squelching as we flattened their corpses further still. Stopping to use an outhouse, the caved in *tyanet* amounted to no more than split wooden beams across a shallow pit and a few bricks behind which to hide one's blushes.

Descending through the troposphere, the Chinese fence disappeared; a strip of vegetation along the fringe of a glacial runoff marking a return to the jailoo. Passing Chechetkin, the first inhabited settlement for a long time, our driver had just pulled over in an attempt to rustle up return fares when the fury of Papa Fruge kicked in.

'*Où allons-nous…* Where shall we stay in Murgab?' I heard Sylvana ask, his response being to smash the guidebook from his wife's hands.

A torrent of expletives followed, only some of which I clocked what with them being in French. Sticking his fingers up at the driver repeatedly in a wildly exaggerated manner, François screamed all the way to Murgab. The thirteen and a half hour journey had been both amazing and awful in its bone-shaking longevity, but coming during the final stretch, this was all too much.

Entering the outskirts of Murgab, I have rarely been so glad to arrive anywhere. That the driver didn't know the place Stan and I had hoped to room couldn't have mattered less. Disembarking, I tried to make small talk to placate François, but his face was filled with thunder.

'It is better you don't speak to my father,' Eva whispered, pulling me aside. 'When he's like this he's mean. He has a problem,' she added, making the universal sign for crazy.

We checked into the Pamir Hotel. When Eva returned moments later, handing over a piece of luggage Stan had forgotten in our eagerness to escape, she said nothing, looking sheepish as she slinked away. We'd never see the Fruges again.

Yaks and Yaoli's#1

Meaning 'River of the Birds,' Murgab was a pallid town where even the few tufts of grass which crept from the unyielding earth were taupe. In this windswept, low-rise community of wonky domiciles with misset windows, the Pamir Hotel was the only modern building. Originally constructed for a visit by President Rahmon and his cortege, it had recently been recycled into a guesthouse, a single coat of handprint besmirched bice green paint barely concealing the cold concrete beneath.

Sputtering between surges and brownouts, *electrisifi* illuminated the hotel in fits and starts. Things were significantly better than a few years previously, however, when the ethnically Tajik and Kyrgyz halves of town - never on the best of terms - had shared the supply, taking turns on alternate days.

Provided for the benefit of his guests, the hotel manager's pride and joy were a collection of plastic Yaoli sandals which sat in neat rows on two wooden shoe racks by the entrance. It seemed to cause him great pain if he spotted a lodger not wearing them. When we stepped into the hall donning our own footwear, it appeared as if his heart would surely break.

There being nowhere else open in town, we made our way to the hotel dining room, where my attempts to order food were only moderately successful.

'No meet? No understand,' the attendant sighed, rolling her sharp black eyes.

On the flickering TV screen, music came courtesy of a rotund, fifty-some-thing Tajik woman sitting in a field of yellow flowers, rocking from side to side as she crooned dolorously. It was reasonably soothing after so much dance-pop. As the bard finished her lamentation, the waitress slammed down my bowl of 'lamp soup,' chunks of some unfortunate creature doing the backstroke in it. With roads impassable throughout the long winter, no reliable refrigeration and no crops growing even at the height of summer, renouncing meat made no sense here.

A painted blue sign by the highway outside the hotel highlighted Murgab's remoteness, its closest neighbouring settlement of note 233 kilometres away, back in Sary Tash, Kyrgyzstan. The biggest town in the Eastern Pamirs by a distance, Murgab's population numbered less than four thousand. Complete with a couple of paved roads, it was a place of some substance compared to Karakul, yet it was still possible to shuffle from one end of town to the other in twenty minutes.

On the streets of Murgab, piles of scrap metal sat waiting for Chinese trucks. Jagged and twisted chassis formed temporary playgrounds for the town's youngsters, who scuttled breathlessly between them. Beside the stripped shell of a bus, what looked like a steam engine seemed absurdly out of place. With the lowest level of car ownership in Central Asia, the Pamirs were a repository of vehicles disowned by the rest of the world. Despite bearing a striking resemblance to a child's bootee, the police's Lada Niva's were luxury items compared to the old Yugo and Moskvitch models which puttered about town.

We meandered down to the Tourist Office, where, having heard a rumour about a landslide, the sole member of staff was unsure if the road to Khorog was traversable.

'I would check for you,' she said apologetically, 'but phone lines all down. I think is best you find driver at bazaar.'

In different shapes, sizes and states of disrepair, Murgab Bazaar consisted of a mishmash of cargo containers with doors and windows roughly hewn into them. Dallying around these metal husks with nothing to do, bored soldiers eyed women in long, flowing *kurta* dresses and thick *shalvar* trousers. Velvet a favoured material, many wore reds, pinks and mauves with embroidered trims. *Rusari* headscarves wrapped above their noses like surgical masks offering protection from the grit carried on gusts of wind, the women of Murgab also wore a smattering of mascara and eyeliner. Exchanging greetings, they picked through the meagre array of clothes, oils, fruits, vegetables and meats on offer. When we located the moneychanger at an emporium specializing in onions, noodles and long since expired snickers, our man counted out a handful of Tajik somoni banknotes whilst trying to interest us in his finest socks and toilet paper.

Finding a café, I endeavoured to explain that we'd like eggs by flapping my arms and clucking, before miming pulling something from my butt.

'Da,' the old girl nodded, '*kooreetso, yightsoh.*'

I got eggs with my chicken at least.

Yaks and Yaoli's#2

Away from the bazaar, stray dogs outnumbered people. Urine trickled down pylons propped up by the whitewashed walls of compounds, some of which boasted satellite dishes. A sea of power cables and a vast blue sky stretched towards the bird free river and a small mosque with two stumpy minarets at the bottom of the valley. Humbled beneath lofty Chinese peaks, the masjid clung proudly to its austere little slice of heaven.

In the winding alleys of the Kyrgyz part of town, firm handshakes and slow motion cheek kissing were taking place. The thin air filled with dust, a gasoline odour lingered, even the locals ambling at this altitude. Their track-suits tops and bottoms mismatched, boys in baseball caps called out greetings, waving excitedly at us. More circumspect, middle-aged men preferred a uniform of cotton slacks, woolly jumpers and suit jackets, the elder generation in kalpaks, greatcoats, rubber boots and reflective aviator sunglasses.

Crossing the divide between the two parts of town, cool grey stones placed high on the mountainside spelt out 'Welcome Our Hazirimam,' referencing a visit by the Pamiri's self-proclaimed spiritual leader and benefactor, the Aga Khan. Whilst the majority of Tajiks are Sunni Muslims living in a secular dictatorship, the Pamiris are almost exclusively Shia of the Ishmaelite Sect.

Entering the Tajik half of town, visible swathes of powdery particles swirled around a sudden glut of flags, sloganeering taking hold. Photoshopped into a construction site, the hard-hat wearing President Rahmon pointed out his people's path to progress from a water damaged poster. Backed by the Tajik flag - red, white and green with a golden crown and stars - a plaster cast Lenin postulated from the centre of a needlessly wide boulevard. A towering billboard featured a well-groomed protagonist declaring abstention to be the way forward. '*Het!*' he exclaimed, declining the offer of a shot of vodka. Circling the Lenin statue addled, some on the streets hadn't heeded his advice.

Although it contained the region's administrative buildings, the Tajik side of town was a more ramshackle affair. Gone were the satellite dishes; replaced by sheets of metal ridden with bullet holes which had been recycled as building materials. By mildewed lumps of cardboard set across myriad glassless windows, old ladies struggled to draw water from charitably donated hand pumps. In one of the most water-rich countries in the world, forty-one percent of the population don't have access to clean drinking water.

Despite animal sheds standing empty, the scent of faeces filled the streets. With most working age men abroad or in the jailoo fattening up their yaks and sheep for the eight-month winter which lay ahead, those left in town that weren't decked in khakis were employed in driving taksis or fixing numerous broken-down trucks. Their features more sculpted than their Kyrgyz counterparts, elders in flat caps waddled by, taking their evening constitutional.

Next to the town's garrison, an eroded relief formed the backdrop to the simple column, star and wreath of a Soviet memorial to the Great Patriotic War. On a second wall, children's paintings paid tribute to civic-minded soldiers. On a hoarding obscuring a dilapidated building next door, a stern, officious President Rahmon was represented by an image from his younger, though no more handsome days.

My nose blocked with clotted blood and dust, struggling to breathe we headed back to the hotel. Sitting on the steps in our Yaoli's later that night, shooting stars cascaded across the pinpricked sky of a town which didn't have much, but had stars to spare.

To Khorog with Bob

Wearing the same jeans and shell suit top as the day before, our driver, Sharms turned up in his silver minivan at six forty-five AM as arranged;

which proved to be utterly pointless. With no need to start the engine, he rolled back downhill to the bazaar and the long wait began. It was a bright, clear morning. A few men pushing their cars along, women collected water from wells, children playfully lobbing stones at each other. Aside from that, the streets were empty, containers at the bazaar chained shut.

His skin fried a crispy shade of brown from the UV radiation at altitude, Sharms raised a bristling, expressive eyebrow, attempting to explain that we were holding out for just one more person.

'St. Eve,' he said, holding up a single finger.

Throwing his arm towards the highway, he made the whooshing sound of motion.

As the sun lifted, a surfeit of taksis began to congregate. Each arriving automobile eyed hopefully by expectant passengers, their drivers disembarked to air-kiss comrades before settling in for a well-earned nap. Every hour or so, we'd circle the town before coasting back to the bazaar with little sign of progress.

Shaking our fluffy dice, Russian electro blasted from a scratched disc in the stereo, locals leaning across to turn the volume down whenever Sharms stepped out to smoke, which happened frequently. If the CD was skipping in the parking lot, there was no hope on the road. Knocking his short peaked cap off each time he climbed back in, Sharms soon set the dice to bouncing once more.

With rumours circulating about a hitchhiker that might be headed in our direction, I set out to find him. Wary about Stan's ability to hold up our transport should more punters by some miracle arrive, I hit the incline to the main drag at a brisk pace. Wheezing as I neared the peak, I introduced myself to an Australian, his head wrapped in a Crayola yellow bandana which proceeded to hang down past his derrière.

'G'day, I'm Bob. How ya going?' he greeted me, his face set in a broad smile.

Enquiring as to his destination, I panted something about the situation.

'Aw, shit yeah,' he replied to my suggestion that he snag our last seat.

With the long-legged foreigners ensconced in the rear, luggage piled on top of us, the diminutive Tajiks stretched out lazily in the remainder of the vehicle. After two more stops, we were on our way, grinding to a halt just a kilometre out of town at the first militsiya checkpoint, where a tortuous queue of Chinese juggernauts were impatiently waiting to pass in the opposite direction. It wasn't long before a truck ran us off the road and into a ditch, Sharms shaking his fist at the billowing vapours left by its long departed driver.

In a landscape devoid of landmarks, *Chatyr Tash* - Tent Rock - counted as a significant site. Visible from a great distance, it was chiefly remarkable for its perfectly square shape and for simply being there. Eighty kilometres elapsed before we passed a building, mouldering stone and mud with a yurt beside it, a rather hopeful sign indicated it to be a 'Hotel.' Alongside this lodging, dirty white sheep were attempting to graze on the brush, large clumps of anomalous, afro-esque fuzzy black fur sprouting from their sides like fully formed telpeks.

'Pamiri evolution,' Bob commented.

Reaching a plateau of colossal boulders, dark, moody clouds hovered, scattered yurts and lean-to's taking isolated living to a new level. On this, supposedly the most fertile plain in the region stood Alichur, a semi-deserted encampment of icy nothingness.

With the rest of our party entering a shack for a meal of yak stew, Stan and I wandered through the village. Desolate, forlorn and eye-shrivellingly bright, it was the bleakest place yet. Desiccating everything in its path, a cold wind whipped through the streets. The uniform blue and white single storey dwellings barely standing, pylons with downed cables emitted a creaking sound. Transfixed by our presence, a few shy children 'ullo'd' us, a puppy repeatedly untying our shoelaces with its keen teeth.

Still, there were places to stay, though you'd have to be desperate to break up the journey to do so. Trading on the region's historic past, the Marco Polo Gastnitsa had saved its biggest lashing of paint to proclaim its star attraction, 'BATHROOM' in bold letters. It was the only hotel in town to have one.

Name checking distant Khorog and Dushanbe, ear bursting Bollywood pop Tajik style exploded onto the stereo as we pulled away. Tabla rhythms filled out with resonant ruhbabs, flutes, emotive vocals and a choral backing built through a dervish of time changes without pausing for air.

'Geez, that sorta sounds pretty good,' said Bob, and so it did; but as the tempo slowed so did the car, the furrowed unsealed road continuing through low, cinereous mist.

My knuckles already bloodied from clinging onto the grab handle as we bounced along, decelerating was bad news, for it meant the highway was going to get even worse.

Continuing largely off-road where the surface was marginally better, we passed Taapokakty. Declared a town by a road sign, like so many others settlements it was nothing more than a drove of sheep and a collection of four buildings, only one of which was still habitable.

Cattle grazing on the scant sward above the compact ice, we skirted salt flats which stretched to the filmy blue Tuz Kul and Sassyk Kul - 'Salt Lake' and 'Stinking Lake' - though not quite close enough to smell if the latter's name rang true. Climbing through the cloud line over the lunar landscape of the Koi-Tezek Pass at 4,272 metres, in the back we had no choice between open or closed windows, which left agape let in a glacial blast. The fellow in front losing control of his cigarette, it flew backwards at pace straight into my eye. Seeing him turn, I thought it was in response to my yelp, but digging about on the floor, he picked up the butt and carried on smoking.

The temperature rising abruptly as we descended towards the town of Jelandy, we overtook twenty-eight wheeler Chinese HGV's on hairpin turns in the driving rain. By a remote silhouette statue of a Marco Polo sheep,

Sharms reversed for his fares to take in the rare sight of fish, like outsized tadpoles in a trickling stream, some even taking photos on their phones.

Feeding a sweeping valley of scarlet flowers, the rolling whitewater of the Gunt River reintroduced colour to the panorama. There were even trees; stark, blighted little things, but trees nonetheless. No sooner had we reached the river, though, than we hit the landslide referred to at the Murgab Tourist Office. The torrent having washed the bridge clean away, trucks were queuing back for over two kilometres. A group of men busy trying to push a jalopy over a temporary dirt track on the side of the mountain, Stan stopped to give them a hand, but it just kept sliding back down, eliciting cries as they dived from its path. Exiting our minivan, the passengers scrambled around the landslip, enabling Sharms to gain just enough traction to navigate his way across.

Swerving around mangy dogs laying nonchalantly in the road licking their balls, we were soon beyond the heaving K22 Chinese truck stop, where vehicles from Xinjiang congregate on the modern-day Silk Road. An hour later, emerging from beneath sections of concrete overhang which protect the highway from avalanches, Khorog came into view.

CHAPTER 14

Last Year's War Zone

Unceremoniously dumped at the bazaar despite earlier assurances to the contrary, we were greeted by a military salute from a man walking a pack of twenty Alsatians without leashes. A lush reeled in front of a backfiring LuAZ 969, the car renowned for killing its occupants through carbon monoxide poisoning. Khorog smelt of dung and vodka. Boasting a variety of racing Ladas with tinted windows and a single working traffic light, with a population just shy of thirty thousand, the capital of Gorno-Badakhshan felt like a thriving metropolis after our recent peregrinations.

Khorog is where the dry steppe meets the alpine tundra. White insect collars painted at their slim feet, an abundance of twenty-metre-tall poplar trees shot from the sandy soil. In the City Park, what looked like spores fell constantly. Men stood on rocks pole line fishing at the Gunt River's edge, the wooden buildings on the hillside opposite resembling picture perfect Swiss chalets.

By the entrance to the park, men were busy quaffing *bogka* and hugging. It was the weekend; there was nothing better to do. Flashing red fairy lights wrapped around their steering wheels, boys danced to banging music on the backs of pickup trucks. Christmas lights sparkled all over town. Although it was the end of June in a Muslim state, a giant cut-out of a luxuriantly white bearded Ded Moroz - Father Frost, the Russian Santa Claus - and his helper, the snow maiden Snegurochka adorned the wall in a *Mafo3an* (shop). Like Karimov before him, looking to control perceived foreign influence in his country, Rahmon had banned all things Christmas from state TV; but nobody watched the government channel anyway.

Out of toilet paper and feeling an impending bowel movement, Bob entered Santa's grotto.

'Aw mate, fuck, how am I gonna explain this one?' he ruminated, finger to his lips.

In response to Bob's little shit dance, something like a charade of explosive diarrhoea, the bemused, blank-faced proprietor offered him a bag of shash-lyk flavoured crisps.

We hiked past pine trees up a steep track towards the hillside Pamir Lodge, lovely to stay at, nigh on impossible to find. Along the way, buildings had been freshly plastered, all signs of last year's conflict vanquished except for where the bullet holes were too high to reach. Certain that we must be near the guesthouse, at each new turn locals shook their heads, chuckling as they sent us back along the trail. They'd seen it all before.

The only Central Asian country to have descended into civil war following the dissolution of the Soviet Union, Tajik independence was reluctantly declared in September 1991, only for conflict to erupt less than seven months later. Rigging elections, First Secretary of the Communist Party of Tajikistan, Rahmon Nabiyev armed pro-government militias to uphold his takeover. In response, a rag-tag opposition of unlikely bedfellows: democrats, drug-runners, separatists and Islamists backed by Al-Qaeda, obtained weapons from jihadis in Afghanistan.

With President Nabiyev toppled in a coup d'état, the Russians and Uzbeks continued to arm the old guard with a new face, Emomali Rahmonov now at the helm. Backed by paramilitaries from his power base in the Kulyab (Swampy Place) District, Rahmonov undertook an ethnic cleansing against his Gharmi and Pamiri adversaries, filling mass graves and razing villages in a campaign which left up to 100,000 dead and over a million displaced.

National Reconciliation Day on November 9th marks the 1997 agreement which officially ended the civil war; the United Tajik Opposition signing a UN-brokered power-sharing agreement the new President had no intention of honouring. On the fifth anniversary of Rahmonov's effective coronation a celebration was held, a procession of limousines entering the palace compound. Dancing girls in various states of undress appearing, the late leader of the Islamist party, Sayid Abdulloh Nuri sidled away, the vodka soaked President taking centre stage.

'Either you will all dance, or I will sing,' he barked at distracted looking Swedish emissaries.

These were not hollow words, for within minutes he was behind the microphone twirling and crooning.

'I am Rahmonov, and I will always be Rahmonov,' he bayed. 'I don't care whether you like it or not.'

He wasn't Rahmonov for long, though, shortly dropping the 'ov' from his name for being 'too Soviet.' Neither an academic nor a bureaucrat, Rahmon had gone from being the boss of a collective farm to running the country, but his manner remained the same. Promoting inept functionaries from his hometown of Dangara to key government posts, as the Tajik intelligentsia complained, the village had come to the city.

The Pamir Lodge

Nestled against the bare grey precipice, the basic facilities on offer at the Pamir Lodge included a lukewarm hand wash from a bucket in the family toilet at the owner, Zubaida's discretion. Bleating as it circled, the tethered buck goat tied itself ever tighter to a tree in annoyance at its female companion's freedom to roam the yard. The men of the premises, meanwhile, had been engaged in digging a pit which seemed as if it might reach the centre of the earth, presumably for burying flotsam. As they downed their shovels for the night, though, a sudden storm rolled in from the Hindu Kush, transforming their work into a murky swimming pool.

Listening to torrential rain pound on the corrugated tin roof, we had a nightcap on the veranda, Bob removing his bandana to reveal a shiny bald head where I'd presumed his flowing surfer locks to be.

'There used to be some hair, yeah, but I'm like getting fuckin' old now mate,' he hollered over the drumming of the downpour. 'Twice now on this trip, I've been told I look like Richard Branson. I guess I can see some resemblance; like in the nose, the eyes. Just imagine him without the hair and the face fungus, eh? I don't mind being compared to him, I guess, but I reckon he wouldn't like being compared to me.'

His whole adult life spent traveling or saving for the next trip, Bob had stacked shelves in a Brisbane supermarket for the last two decades when he wasn't on the road. Now fifty, he was contemplating whether this ten-month journey would be his last big adventure. It set me to wondering if I'd travel indefinitely.

'There are so many things I wish I'd seen,' were the last words of the great-aunt who helped raise me.

I didn't want it to end with regrets.

Delivering me from my fleeting melancholy, an English couple touring the Pamirs by bicycle for their honeymoon emerged from their sodden tent to join us beneath sturdier shelter. The girl, Danielle having damaged her spine when run off the road, they'd been stuck in Khorog for sixteen days now.

Killing time whilst waiting for his Iranian visa, the doyen of the establishment skittered up. Introducing himself as Christian from Newcastle, New South Wales, he took great pains to describe himself not as an Australian, but a far superior Novocastrian. For the next hour, he rambled on about his love of the Kazakh people, which felt anomalous given that he hated just about every other nationality - including his own - with a passion.

'The bloody Kyrgyz, nothing but moneygrubbers,' he snarled, scrunching up his crow's feet. 'And don't even get me started on the Tajiks.'

I had no intention of doing so.

Shaking off Christian, as the night wore on the alcohol started to flow freely.

'Say yea, would you like to hear my impression of a dog?' the rosy-cheeked Bob asked out of the blue.

His uncanny barking stopping a stray dead in its tracks, it tilted its head in a questioning attitude and stared unblinkingly towards us.

'Ya see, he's thinking "Well where the fuck is it then? 'Cause I know you're not a dog, ya cunt,"' Bob laughed. 'I do a pretty good sheep too.'

We took to comparing passport photos. Whereas Bob was never to be seen without a broad smile - he even wore a toothy grin whilst sleeping - in his passport picture he'd followed the new guidelines and saved his smile for later.

'I took it myself. I reckon it came out alright, though; what'd you reckon?' he asked, thrusting his passport at us.

'Mate, you look like a psychopath,' answered Stan.

'Aw, Yeah? Fuck,' Bob spluttered in disbelief.

With his shaved head, stark bandana tan line and glinting blue eyes bulging from their sockets, I couldn't deny it.

No Flights Today

Emerging from a deep slumber into the crisp morning air, I was greeted by grandma tutting as she unwound the bellicose buck from a tree. A clowder of cute ginger kittens milling about his feet as he chowed down on stale non and jam, Christian swiped at them, eliciting a hiss.

'I bloody hate cats,' he greeted me. 'And another thing, I hate Malaysians too,' he snapped, struggling to spread a chunk of rock hard butter across his bread; 'they're so bloody backwards.'

Unprepared for this encounter, I couldn't begin to fathom how we'd gotten onto the subject of Malaysia.

'I've got a lot of friends in Kuala Lumpur,' I countered, not wanting to get drawn into a conversation with this little Cockroach and his big attitude.
'Oh yeah? Well, I hate the Chinese too,' he railed, his skin drawn tight like a sphincter. 'I hate them the most, they're so bloody rude.'

It was becoming difficult to take this caricature of a man seriously.

'Anyway, guess what I've got?' he probed excitedly, waving his phone in my face.
'A Samsung Galaxy?' I answered disingenuously.
'No, you pommie bastard,' he spat, 'my Iranian visa number came through!'
'Oh, that's great,' I said, though I had a feeling they'd be better off without him.

Escaping Christian the racist traveller, after breakfast we headed down towards town. Every trough on the periphery of Khorog a landfill site strewn with plastic and sewage, insects swarmed around the jetsam. With only her eyes showing against the flies, fumes and dust, a woman sat at the side of the road with bottles and a funnel, offering fuel come rain or shine. Crossing the bridge to the centre, a cleansing took hold, the pavements levelling out, trees perfectly spaced on the litter-free sidewalks. Khaki-clad police guarding the traffic light, girls in Western jeans and spangly tops patrolled this part of town, firmly permed hair framing their Persian meets Southern European features.

In two coloured kurta dresses, flared at the bottom and worn over baggy shalvar trousers like pyjama sets, women in traditional costume were to be found at the bazaar haggling over boxes of a laundry powder called *Paria*. From watermelons to linoleum, carrots to Draino, goods were literally falling off the backs of lorries which doubled as stores. The monobrow, medically known as synophrys, was popular here. For those not fortunate enough to have been born with one, a leafy green herb called *Usma* was on sale. Dried in the sun, ground up and repeatedly applied, it would do the trick, leading to a beautifully plush growth.

Utilising Stan as a beard to zoom past, I snapped pictures of the best stalls, unibrows and the odd drunk passed out on a bench. Even when I wasn't using him as a cover, Stan had a way of skulking into shots, half a bewildered expression or a sunburnt nose appearing in every other frame.

At the edge of town, the cult of Rahmon took hold, the many aspects of the President depicted in endless titanic banners and billboards. Moody Rahmon walked through the mountains before being transformed into a scholar, giving a Nazi-style salute and then pulling disco shapes. He would indeed have been a man for all seasons, except for the fact that the same image of him kept reappearing, just Photoshopped into new situations.

Giving unattended black bulls roaming along the apricot lined highway a wide berth, having made it this far we decided to keep walking to the border with Afghanistan. The odd pimped-out minivan rumbling past, a few kilometres down the road we reached Khorog Airport. Padlocked shut with no flights expected, cows searched out clumps of grass which lifted from cracks in the runway. Children cycled up and down three to a bike, one seated, one on the handlebars and one standing on stunt pegs. At the end of the airstrip, Paria having removed the stigma of hard to shift stains, a line of white sheets was hung out to dry.

Not remotely eager to undertake the nineteen-hour journey to Dushanbe by road, the lack of flights was a dilemma holding us hostage. The Yak-40 passing between mountains with barely enough space to accommodate its wingspan, daily flights were cancelled at the first sign of clouds. Despite being the only route for which Aeroflot would pay its pilots danger money, there had only ever been one confirmed crash, the incident of 1993. Rebels forcing the pilot to attempt the trip to Dushanbe with eighty-one people on board - notwithstanding his protestations that the plane could only hold thirty-two - the aircraft had hurtled straight off the runway and into the Pyanj River, killing seventy-seven. Unconfirmed rumours of a more recent incident involved the Taliban, who having plundered a cache of American weapons near Faizabad decided to test their new anti-aircraft missiles on the first thing which passed overhead.

Where the Gunt River joined the Pyanj, dried poppy husks sprouted from the roadside. Overturned buses lay in the waterway and on its steep banks, cows munching contentedly around them. A suspension bridge sponsored by the Aga Khan reached out to Afghanistan, a joint Tajik/Afghan market taking place upon it every weekend, reuniting families split by the artificially imposed border. Across the becalmed waters, a green and pretty Afghan village lay barely sixty metres away.

Opium Oases

The thoroughfare to the Pamir Botanical Gardens passed through farmland where scarecrows wreathed in sparring pads doubled as punch bags. Speeding vehicles weaved around the asphalt searching for the smoothest part of the crazy paving. Perched upon by tidings of magpies, an array of watchful Rahmon posters saw the great leader's pudgy face coated in trickling white droppings.

Reaching the easternmost outskirts of Khorog, bagman mansions hugged the hillsides in opium oases. Springing from the scree in circles of vegetation proximate to peaks, they offered easy access to the porous border for Afghan mules, plus they could have seen the Tajik police coming an hours climb away. In all likelihood, though, the junta's top brass owned them or were in the pockets of those who did.

Under the terms of a bilateral treaty, until 2005 Russian troops patrolled the bulk of Tajikistan's border with Afghanistan. Since this agreement was ceded by the Tajik authorities on the grounds that it was capable of manning its own frontiers, conditions at border outposts have deteriorated drastically, seizures of heroin halving. With ninety percent of the smack in Europe originating in Afghanistan, circumstantial evidence suggests that senior government ministers provide protection for major traffickers. 'All large-scale smuggling features some involvement of officials,' Dr Kupatadze told me, 'either in the form of protection such as large bribes or direct participation.'

Piqued by international criticism, President Rahmon has levelled counter-allegations of Russian complicity in the heroin trade. 'Why do you think generals lined up in Moscow all the way across Red Square and paid enormous bribes to be assigned here?' he complained to US officials. 'Just so they could do their patriotic duty?'

Decimated by the dissolution of the USSR and the civil war, since the mid-nineties Tajikistan has seen an explosion of heroin, becoming known as a 'narco-state.' In 1997, researchers estimated that half of eighteen to twenty-four-year-olds were employed in the drug trade. As to how high up the criminality goes, in 2000 the Tajik Ambassador to Kazakhstan was arrested in Almaty with eighty-six kilos of heroin in his car. In 2001, the Deputy Minister of the Interior was murdered, the prosecution in the case arguing he'd been assassinated for refusing to pay for a shipment of fifty kilos. A statement released by the UNDP in 2001 estimated that drug money accounted for between thirty and fifty percent of the entire Tajik economy. In the absence of a legitimate economy, perversely the flow of narcotics appears to have kept the country from falling apart. 'The state is really at the intersection of the benefits and detriment which come from corruption,' Dr Anceschi observed. 'On the one hand, having the local administration connected with corruption has its benefits, because it's added a new layer of patronage.'

Of course, the status quo has also served the international community, who needed a stable Tajikistan to ensure flight paths for the so-called 'war on terror' in Afghanistan weren't disrupted. In any case, efforts to restrict trafficking have often backfired, an increase in checkpoints only disadvantaging small time operators and enabling cartels to take control. As Peter Reuter points out, 'there are economies of scale in corruption.'

Interspersed with the chassis of burnt-out buses, at the foot of Khorog's tors sat the ostentatious cars of the 'New Tajiks,' their tinted windows gleaming. The proliferation of flash cars in one of the poorest countries in the world had led to a saying; it was no longer 'how much did it cost?' but 'how many kilos did it cost?'

After numerous false starts in our search for the botanical gardens, an intense, unkempt gatekeeper jumped out at us.

'Gimme somoni!' he demanded, thrusting out his palm.

We had arrived at what we presumed to be the entrance. Even after the gate, unmarked forks in the road made it unclear in which direction we were headed, further into the overgrowth or towards a kingpin's compound.

Ducking power lines, we skirted the bottle strewn graves of former groundskeepers. A cloud of tangerine tipped Lepidoptera drifting over thistles, butterfly collectors were the big money tourists in Khorog, but after last year's conflict, they'd all cancelled their vacations. Ascending the ridge for an unobstructed, vertiginous view of the town, in the distance a hydro-electric power plant hummed. Referencing a visit from the Aga Khan, white stones laid on the steep escarpment spelt out 'Welcome our Hazir Imam Golden Jubilee.' They'd have been sore if the Imam of the Atomic Age wasn't looking out of the right side of the plane when he landed.

On the long, winding way back down, the skies opened, a battery of icy hailstones drenching us to the bone. Half an hour later, we managed to thumb a ride in a number three minibus. Routes one and three were the only buses in Khorog, each with a different single song playing on a loop on the stereo. The conductor holding out a calloused palm, unlike the one, though, the three wasn't free.

Back in the centre, the streets were empty. Headed to our lodgings after a meal of *kurtob* – a surprisingly delicious mixture of yoghurt, tomatoes, herbs and fatir bread, somewhere between cold pasta and pastry – as twilight descended we came across a wedding reception at the Marco Polo Lounge. Pennant streamers lining the streets, it seemed as if the whole town was there. In the main hall, men were riding broomsticks, prancing through the ritual 'horse dance.' Other popular Tajik dances include the 'dance with a jug' and the 'dance with a spoon,' though neither made for the most animated of partners.

Guests leaving the worse for wear, one drove off with no lights on, blocking the road with an awful grinding sound as he slipped out of gear. Sitting there revving frenetically, he stalled the engine, flung open his door and retched onto the bitumen.

The Road to Dushanbe#1

Apart from policemen lovingly buffing their Ladas, at six AM the streets of Khorog were deserted. Leaving town, just beyond the airport conscripted boys in fatigues were busy sweating over a regimen of squat thrusts. Stickman scarecrows springing from the fertile soil, cows grazed on a tied island, the Afghan mountains mirrored in the still Pyanj River at dawn. Watching children headed to school across the water, it was difficult to comprehend the sheer scale of the conflict Afghanistan has suffered.

The flight to Dushanbe a weather-ravaged pipedream, we tagged along in the ride Bob had organised.

'Ya' know the beardy guy at the internet shop?' he asked.

'The place with all the fly paper?' Stan chipped in, every inch of surface space bar the keyboards being taken up with the stuff, dead Diptera piled high upon it.

'Yeah, well it's his cousin; keep it in the family, right? But it's sorta like a really fuckin' good deal,' Bob enthused.

This proved to be true, for handing over three hundred somoni each and loading our bags into the four-wheel drive, we still had room to stretch.

Of a Grecian, Hitchcockian aspect with a prominent Roman nose, our gold-toothed driver, Gafur filled up with petrol. Mobile pressed to his ear and a super-slim cigarette singeing his cracked lips, clumps of smouldering ash fell past the nozzle. He wasn't bothered. Lighting another cigarette from the butt of the preceding one, he fielded endless phone calls. He was obviously a well-liked guy.

In outlying hamlets, men in flat caps with bristling tashes stood waiting by the roadside, though for what it remained unclear. To a two-disc live special of Russian pop - the only CDs Gafur owned - we bounced through their villages on an M road that was no more than a rutted country lane.

'*Spaceeba,* spaceeba, spaceeba, spaceeba,' the songstress caterwauled.

It might well have been Gafur's mum performing karaoke.

Along the Pyanj, muddy rapids settled to still beaches at which one could've been at home with an umbrella and a cocktail. It would've been a pleasant place to have a paddle if you knew where the landmines were.

We crossed the Bartang River, which feeds through Lake Sarez from its source in the Wakhan Valley of Afghanistan. Five hundred metres deep and containing seventeen cubic kilometres of water, Lake Sarez was formed in 1911 when a landslide caused by an earthquake blocked the river's path. With glacial melting causing water levels to rise by eight inches a year, pressure on the natural dam is building.

In this earthquake-prone environment, were the dam to be breached a tidal wave two hundred and fifty metres high moving at five metres per second would kill up to 130,000 in the sparsely populated Tajik flood zone alone. The waters eventually settling in Afghanistan and Uzbekistan, refilling the Southern Aral Sea in the process, it would be the worst natural disaster ever witnessed by humans, and all this in a region where water is destined to become the new gold.

On the banks of this distributary lay the district capital of Rushan, an arenaceous settlement of apricot and poplar trees. Locals walking cows and donkeys on rope leads noticing our otherness, a brief glimmer flashed across their eyes as we sped by, dogs with lolling tongues barking as they chased after the car. On the outskirts of Rushan, the ruins of a Bukharan fortress rose from craggy peaks. One of the last vestiges left by Alim Khan's *beks* (governors) after he fled from Bukhara, Southern Tajikistan is littered with ruined garrisons.

Putting his lot in with the reformers, then switching sides in the face of the mullah's strength, in his final years the last Emir of Bukhara was a leaf in the wind. These were the dark days of mass executions, book burnings and an intellectual exodus from the Khanate. When the ripples from the Bolshevik Revolution reached his kingdom, Alim Khan declared holy war upon the Russians and their reformist allies, the Young Bukharans. Russian gunners initially forced back by frenzied, knife-wielding zealots, tit for tat retributions took place before, in their inevitable victory, the Red Army set about raping, pillaging and murdering their vanquished foes. On September 2nd 1920, soldiers raised the Red Banner from the bombed-out lantern of the Kalon Minaret.

Escaping to the backwater village of Dushanbe, Alim Khan sought international support, but found no backers. With the Bolsheviks advancing, his *Basmachi* (bandit) Army of Islam riven by infighting and his requests for aid having gone unanswered, the last Emir floated across the Pyanj to Afghanistan on a raft made of wood and sheep-gut, never to return to his homeland.

The shadow of our vehicle thrown onto the swirling Pyanj, dwarfed by Chinese juggernauts we reversed to within an inch of precipitous drops. As they rumbled past, the road disappeared, dust clouds drifting in their wake. Aside from the flow of trucks, traffic was barely existent, a fleet of Mercedes with blacked out windows hugely conspicuous on the switchbacks.

With reception lost, even Gafur gave up on his phone and we were alone. Stopping at a bosky garden stand for a lunchtime bowl of plov, a blown-out tank lay on its back in the foamy waters, agriculture flourishing across the border where a series of new mansions were under construction.

Settling up, we were soon swerving through hairpin turns on bilious stomachs towards a district checkpoint, where the smiling guard saw no need to delay us.

'Gift,' he said, handing over a carrier bag filled with tiny apricots and waving us on our way.

The Road to Dushanbe#2

The Gharmi town of Kala-I-Khumb is a nondescript crossroads where the M41 departs from the Pyanj. Beneath arching lampposts, women checked the price tags on flower print one-size-fits-all kurta sets hanging outside a single store. Men sat in the scant shade drinking choy over games of *toguk korgool* – which translates as 'nine dung balls' - each trying to capture his opponent's precious ordure.

Once home to the Basmachi movement, scene of forced relocations during the 1950s, the restive mountains of the central provinces have long been inured to violence. To the north in the Rasht Valley, four United Nations Observers were murdered shortly after the signing of the armistice which officially ended the civil war, leading to a UN withdrawal. Sporadic disturbances still ongoing, at least sixty-four government soldiers were killed in four separate incidents through September and October 2010. With the Gharmi people discriminated against and given little in the way of funding for infrastructure since picking the losing side in the civil war, the authorities claim this area to be a hotbed of drug-runners, IMU members and Taliban forced out of Pakistan and Afghanistan.

Leaving the Pamir Highway for the first time since Osh, beyond Kala-I-Khumb Turkish road crews ensured that the route along the river improved somewhat. Grinding through the village of Punishar, the sloping shores of Afghanistan were only twenty metres away. The 1,300-kilometre border would have been impossible to police, even if the will was there.

Across the Pyanj, earth-coloured buildings melded into the landscape. Niqāb covered women walking protracted distances between villages, vast tracts of land were without power. Powdery clouds rising from a cliff face, a group of elders had stopped to watch a landslide in progress. Skirting the avalanche, two men on a dirt bike gave us an enthusiastic thumbs-up. It was the only vehicle I saw on the Afghan side.

Exiting Gorno-Badakhshan, checkpoints became more frequent.

'Pasport, pasport,' Gafur chimed, disappearing into Cimmerian shacks with our documents.

Pulling off the highway beyond a frontier post, we parked under a waterfall, using it as a carwash. I later found out there were spot fines for driving dirty automobiles in Dushanbe, the police particularly keen on stopping those with Pamiri plates.

Veering away from an unmanned watchtower in the middle of the river, we left the Pyanj behind, climbing through a vista of wheat fields and hay bales. Bright turquoise roller birds emerged from subterranean nests to circle overhead. At the Shurubad Pass, two kontrol posts sat fifty metres apart, bees from apiaries which fanned out across the tawny hills buzzing around them. Traffic jams here amounted to honking until donkeys and goats cleared from the road.

The lumber town of Kulyab contained the first high-rise since Osh, the giant Tojik-Sodirot Bank towering above the thronging bazaar. A surfeit of grandmas propelling rusting rattletraps, I've never seen so many people pushing cars as in Tajikistan. Despite a plethora of amputees lining the wide streets, a grandiose arch showed that Rahmon hadn't forgotten about his home district. At one point, he'd even mooted moving the capital to his birth village of Dangara, but in an utterly impoverished state, this was a step too far even for the great dictator.

Cruising through mottled, undulant yellow fields, militsiya flag-downs appeared in addition to checkpoints. Exhausted, I awoke some time later, Stan and I's heads conjoined in sleep, to see Bob looming over us, grinning as he snapped away.

'Nah, I don't have a thing about photographing guys sleeping,' he chirruped; but it wouldn't be the last time.

I'm not sure how he managed to drive for so long, but as the hours went by Gafur's manoeuvres became more reckless, overtakes on blind summits multiplying. We heaved a collective sigh of relief, therefore, when after fourteen hours we arrived at Lake Nurek. Reception having returned to his mobile, Gafur was happy enough to stop for a while.

Majestic in the peach evening light, the calm, brilliant blue reservoir dotted with earthy red islands was surrounded by a chain of hills. Shadows from a ridge creeping across verdant flora, low clouds sat upon a bluff at the farthest extreme. Exiting the car, we were greeted by children touting trinkets and Snickers bars, but once left in peace, the lakes beauty was breathtaking.

Covering ninety-eight square kilometres, some have claimed that the artificial reservoir is behind an increase in seismic activity in the region. Constructed by the Soviets between 1961 and 1980, the three hundred metre Nurek Dam is the tallest fully operational hydropower station in the world, producing seventy-five percent of Tajikistan's electricity. Swathes of the country remain in darkness, however, the power generated being siphoned off for an aluminium factory from which President Rahmon pockets the proceeds.

Now Rahmon wants to build an even taller dam, the 335 metre Rogun Dam, which would choke the arteries of Uzbekistan's lucrative cotton crop. Vowing to derail the scheme at any cost, Uzbek President Karimov responded by stopping deliveries of natural gas to Tajikistan, warning that the project could spark 'not simply serious confrontation, but even wars.' The chief source of bilateral rancour, Central Asia is a prime contender for a water war.

Leaving Lake Nurek, the 2.2 kilometre long Shar-Shar Tunnel led to a second underground passage sectioned off by barricades. The Tajiks liked their tunnels, but they had a tendency to collapse. North of Dushanbe, the five kilometre Anzob Tunnel, never properly completed, is known as the 'tunnel of death.' With no lighting or ventilation, it's constantly flooded, jets of water springing from the serrated rock surfaces. Thick pollution makes breakdowns potentially fatal, cyclists being forced to sign an injury waiver before entering.

After two short mechanical failures on our hour long detour - wiggling and throttling something under the bonnet did the trick - we hit the town of Dusti, which lived up to its name. Cutting through fields of sunflowers, the road blossomed into a three-lane affair as we neared Dushanbe. Sporadic fruit and veg kiosks lining the kerb, if you felt like blocking the slow lane to shop that was fine. Even if you chose to drive down the highway in the wrong direction, no one was particularly perturbed.

Reaching the city's outskirts, scrunched satellite dishes competed for space on the roofs of tower blocks. Pulling to the side of the street, Gafur indicated a shop.

'*Maga3in*,' he kept repeating, pointing ever more animatedly.

We'd been on the road for sixteen hours, were fried, goggle-eyed, had no idea where we were, and given the extent of my language skills at the time, it was unclear if he wanted us to meet the family or buy them a book.

'Hello, my friends,' a smartly dressed, clean-cut teenage boy ambled over to greet us. 'How are you today?'
'You speak English?' Stan asked him, seeking a remedy to our current quandary.
'Ah,' the boy replied wistfully, tilting his head, 'I do not.'

Whilst Gafur enjoyed his happy reunion, hugging his granddaughter tightly, a host of men emerged from a winter grey block.

'Chelsea, Abramovich, da, da,' they mumbled approvingly upon discovering our nationality.

With the air of proud fathers, they clearly claimed the Russian oligarch as one of their own.

Another hour elapsed before I was handed a phone. A forceful fellow burbling unintelligibly on a terrible line, the only thing I understood was his last statement;

'Paz me someone who English better.'

Whatever was supposed to transpire didn't, for two hours after our arrival in Dushanbe, our luggage was loaded back into Gafur's four wheel drive. Wishing us good luck with warm handshakes, Gafur delivered us to our hotel, which had only been a few hundred metres away all along.

With arms glued and fingers masking taped back on,
Lenin attempts to rouse his disciples, Bishkek State Historical Museum.

A kalpak-clad man inspects Arbuz Melons
at the Jayma Bazaar, Osh.

Through a tangle of intermittent power lines,
Solomon's Throne rises above Osh.

Anyone for karaoke? An abandoned Yak-40 slides towards the Ak-Buura 'White Camel' River, Osh.

Loading Njebre's donkey, Sary Moghul.

Enjoying arak as the sun sets over Pik Lenin; the view from Njebre's house, Sary Moghul.

Leaving Njebre's house at the crack of dawn, Sary Moghul.

After walking for four and a half hours, we still seemed to be no closer to Pik Lenin, Trans-Alai Mountains.

In the absolute middle of nowhere, a boy circles on his outsized bicycle, Kyzyl-Art Pass.

Crumbling Soviet era garrison against a backdrop of Chinese peaks, Karakul.

Created by a meteor ten million years ago, Karakul Lake.

The Ak-Baital 'White Horse' Pass, at an elevation of 4,655 metres

Government abstinence campaign billboard, Murgab.

Children eager to have their photograph taken, Murgab.

Scrap metal dreaming of China, Murgab.

Murgab Bazaar.

Trucks queue at a landslide, Gunt River.

A lone cow grazes by the shell of a bus on the border with Afghanistan.

The mountains of Afghanistan reflected in the Pyanj River.

Moody Rahmon, from the Aspects of Rahmon series, Khorog.

Lake Nurek.

Statue of Rudaki, Dushanbe.

Founder of the Samanid Dynasty, Somoni Monument, Dushanbement, Dushanbe.

The pain of selling non at the Shah Mansur Bazaar, Dushanbe

Timur statue between the severed remains of his Ak-Saray Palace, Shakhrisabz

The ancient Nejameddin Kubra and Sultan Ali Mausoleums lean in as if to finally touch, Konye-Urgench.

Couples leave offerings on Forty Mullahs Hill, Konye-Urgench.

Stan, angry Abdullah and the ladies of the truck stop, Darvaza.

The Gate to Hell, Darvaza

A row of marble towers in Berzengi, Ashgabat

Niyazov's Holy Ruhnama Monument, Ashgabat.

The Arch of Neutrality, Ashgabat; its twelve metre tall golden Niyazov no longer rotates to face the sun

Real world living quarters, Ashgabat.

The Presidential Palace and related buildings in Ashgabat; highly illegal photographic fare.

The world's tallest indoor Ferris wheel at the Alem Entertainment Centre, Ashgabat.
As foreigners, we weren't allowed inside.

CHAPTER 15

Monday Monday

Adusty hamlet when chosen as the capital of the newly created Tajik Soviet Socialist Republic in 1929, Dushanbe, meaning Monday, is named after the day of the week on which the village held its main bazaar. Rechristened Stalinabad, one of up to thirty thousand places which Uncle Joe fashioned after himself, the new capital acquired a national library, a ballet and an opera house. 'Socialist in content, but national in form,' these striking new Constructivist and Neoclassical buildings featured wide arches and imposing Corinthian columns adorned with eight pointed stars. This was the epoch before Soviet architecture became lifeless and pre-fabricated.

Dating from this period, the pastel pink Gastnitsa Vakhsh, where the mujahedeen had holed up during the civil war, was a paradigm of faded grandeur. In the foyer, bullet holes may have been plastered over, but the once rich red rugs had grown dull and threadbare. The light fittings long since failed, above the stairwell a bronze chandelier hung by a single cord. Somehow still intact, on a stained glass window the rigid lines of a peasant warrior and his steed were partially concealed by a sagging polyester valance. A home away from home, a notice at reception let it be known, 'If not pay room ten AM, evicted your room.'

Scowling up at us from behind a barred window where she was engaged in shuffling a pile of papers, the matronly receptionist screamed for the *dezhurnaya*, the lady in charge of our floor.

'Nadja!'

A dizzying whirl of differing sirens and horns filling the airless streets, it was Monday night in Dushanbe, and after our epic journey, it was time for beer. Next door to the hotel, belly dancers beckoned for us to enter the empty Money Exchange Bar, a fatal sounding combination. Obscured by a rolling shashlyk fog, across the square in Ayni Park we found a pivo centre, a rapturous, camp waiter leading us to a table and wiggling his arse provocatively as he piled our packs onto a chair.

'My friends, my name Arif. You are from? Have children?' he asked.
'Angliya. Australia. No children,' we answered in succession.
'No children? Aw, so sorry,' he commiserated, pursing his lips as he shook his head, no doubt wondering what was wrong with us.

The way throughout Asia, it was inconceivable that anyone would make a conscious decision not to procreate.

Tajikistan supposedly having the cheapest beer in the world - and that's after the price doubled in the last two years – the staff were chiefly interested in pushing a bar snack. Smoked and stringy, I later discovered it to be a type of cheese called *chechil*, but at eight times the price of a cold pint of Sim-Sim, it was a battle to keep sending the fibrous dish back.

'Not want?' Arif squealed, looking quite incommoded.

It was futile; no sooner was it removed than a waitress would appear, striding purposefully up and slamming the plate back down on our table.

Having "borrowed" one of Bob's cigarettes, Arif kept tittuping past and helping himself to more, which he proceeded to deliver to the establishment's other patrons. Perhaps this was the price of refusing the sinewy snack. Upon learning that they intended to charge us more than the cost of a drink for each visit to the urinal, however, we decided enough was enough and asked for the check.

Fishing through a fistful of somoni for our change, a single US dollar sat within the Arif's stack of banknotes.

'I keep with my always, for luck,' he explained, seeing our eyes drawn to the anomalous bill.

Lifting his arm, he made a jet engine noise, forming a pillow with his hands and gently resting his head upon them.

'Save for America,' he said; 'America my dream.'

The Artificial City

Three-quarters of a million people inhabit Dushanbe, many from the historically Tajik cities of Samarkand and Bukhara, others drawn in having been displaced by the civil war. In front of the Vakhsh Hotel, where a series of lavish new fountains were being assembled, a guild of persistent beggars hung out, setting their children on passers-by. Those that didn't use their progeny as props, I gifted a handful of differently shaped twenty diram coins. It wasn't easy to give when small change often came in the form of paper clips and chewing gum.

I had imagined that any city named after the day it held its main market had to be dull, but despite its artificiality, Dushanbe held a certain charm. The odd man out in Central Asia by virtue of their Persian ancestry, a statue of Ismail Somoni, founder of the Samanid Dynasty from which the Tajiks claim their cultural heritage took pride of place at the major intersection of Maydoni Dusti (Freedom Square). Flanked by lions, wearing a crown, a cape and holding aloft a sceptre as he gazed over the fume-belching traffic, the holy warrior looked more like a mage. This symbol of nationhood stood on the spot where an angry mob had toppled the largest Lenin statue in the country back in 1991, which was later sold for scrap.

With snow-capped mountains as a backdrop, from the corners of the junction enveloping Somoni, giant LCD screens advertised trashy Western action movies and tawdry Chinese gadgets. Illuminated by the artificial glare, an army of women swept the litter-free plinths around the patina coated colossus feet.

Adjoining the intersection, in Bag-I-Rudaki, the city park named after the ninth century Persian poet, a statue of Rudaki was cast in a similar heroic aspect. Standing with a contemplative mien beneath an arch where the sunlight caught rows of fountains, it was as if Rudaki himself had conjured the watery rainbows. On pathways patterned with hexagons, arrows and abutted squares, men in imitation Fred Perry and Ben Sherman shirts idled on benches, cooled by the fountains welcome spray. Sweltering in drainpipe jeans, the youth suffered for their fashion, their glistening thick black hair swept into Bieber fringes. Emerging from beneath their trousers, effeminate sandals were all the rage, the more glitter and the thinner the straps the better.

Unfit for a feudal King, its façade like a four star Arabic hotel, the Old Presidential Palace had been replaced by the golden dome and Doric columns of the new Palace of Nations. Costing more than the country's annual health budget to construct, it had swallowed up a fair chunk of the park. Behind the new palace at Komsomol Lake, another piece of public land had been chiselled away to accommodate the world's largest teahouse. Emptying the state's coffers of an estimated sixty million US dollars - one percent of the nation's GDP – with such opulence reserved for bigwigs and visiting dignitaries, it was unlikely that the public would ever be allowed inside.

Facing the teahouse stood the Central Republican Stadium, home to football club Istiqlol Dushanbe. Widely seen as heir apparent to his father's throne, the President's twenty-eight-year-old son, Rustam founded the club for which he played as a striker and captained before becoming 'too busy' and hanging up his boots. Now a Major General, head of the Customs Service, the State Agency for Measures Against Corruption and the National Football Federation, it has been alleged that the Istiqlol Dushanbe's winning of the National Super Cup for four of the last five seasons is down to favourable officials and the intimidation of opponents. Bullying is nothing new in Tajik football. In October 2013, having scored twice against his hometown club, striker Ahtam Hamrokulov returned to his apartment to find that disgruntled officials had cut off his water and electricity supplies.

In front of the Palace of Nations, a flagpole stood in its full phallic glory. Built in Dubai at a cost of five million dollars, it was the world's tallest when hoisted, but the ongoing rivalry between members of the dictators' club has since seen it outdone by Saudi Arabia. Emphasising nationhood, from flower pots to sweet wrappers, flags were everywhere in Dushanbe. Running along Prospekt Rudaki, the leafy, pleasant spine of the city, trolleybuses had Tajik flags protruding from every fissure, just in case you forgot where you were.

The elegant Neoclassical architecture fast disappearing, Dushanbe had an illusory, transitory quality. A haven for money laundering, the poorly assembled, characterless new high-rises were more expensive than equivalent buildings in Europe. With the President harbouring pretentions of future stateliness along the lines of the oil-rich Kazakh capital or the desert emirates, whole swathes of the city were construction sites. PVC banners with images of water and poppies - the nation's true wealth - cloaked the immodesty of these slippery erections. Still, the covering canvases would have been advertising hoardings in the West.

Yet in their bright, brave new world, their pockets stuffed with ID cards and official documents, Dushanbe-ites wore troubled expressions, smiles a rare commodity. Blocking the road with whistles to their lips, the portly, self-important militsiya stopped motorists every fifty metres along Rudaki, grimaces and handclasps followed by the ritual presentation of papers and baksheesh.

The Old City

In the lively Shah Mansur Bazaar, the ripe smell of costermonger's apricots and peaches hung thick in the air. Their black hair tied back, women in cheetah and panther print dresses shopped for salami flavoured peanuts and a detergent called Mud. Looking like walking marquees, the bigger ladies wore stripes or explosive tie-dye patterns. Rummaging through pink plastic handbags in the tarpaulin covered walkways, the occasional skinny girl in short shorts turned men's heads.

With money changing hands around them, the destitute begged on the periphery with a quiet desperation. Anguish etched upon the faces of unsuccessful traders, the price of failure was all too apparent. Stopping at a backstreet chaikhana to sit and observe everyday life, I found myself the subject of much gaping. The broom-wielding proprietor beating off a deep fried early drinker who lurched at me, I stared down into my cup, careful not to catch the wrong person's eye.

Away from the bazaar, the back-alleys retained a bygone sense of peace, an old world charm. Emerging at the Haji Yakoub Mosque and Madrassa, a row of shops sold nothing but thobes and *chutsis*, men's black and white skullcaps. Where worshippers spilt onto Rudaki, though, the police stood Argus-eyed. Like all of the Central Asian states, Tajikistan was a Muslim country where it was dangerous to be too devout. In September 2015, clashes over the death in police custody of a man detained for 'wearing his beard long' led to seventeen fatalities.

At night, Dushanbe screeched, overexcited boys roaring rowdily and revving their engines like Formula One drivers at traffic lights along the main drag. Those that stalled were met with howls of derision. Sat directly behind them, by now the police were disinterested; perhaps they'd had enough after baking in the sun soliciting bribes all day.

Farther from the centre, the sunken pavements were not so even. Old pastel buildings lingering in a state of disrepair, piles of refuse were backed up in stagnant drains. With shrieks reverberating through the streets, we walked towards the Soviet era cable car up to Victory Park, but the boarding platform rotted through, its cables hung flaccidly.

Outside of a restaurant on Dusti Khalkho, recalling the golden age before the Russians left, machinery broke down and feudal conditions gradually returned, a tractor stood on a plinth. Failing to live up to the illustrious standards set by its sister café, none of the holy trinity of *Biffburger wif wurst, Surly marinated meat* or *Shashlyk by lamp* made an appearance at the Restaurant Merve. Bob wanting to keep hold of the menu, the usual tug of war broke out, but this time writ large, the waiter displaying a singular determination to reclaim his sheet of laminated card. Throughout the country, the Tajik wouldn't stand for letting you hold onto a menu.

'Jeez,' Bob sighed, the carte du jour ripped from his grasp. 'I only wanted to take a look at the desserts.'

Back at the Vakhsh, staring up at the cracked ceiling, I wondered if this was perhaps the same bed opposition leader Sayid Abdullah Nuri had slept in during the civil war. The mattress told me it was certainly old enough. In 2006, long after the mujahedeen had checked out, a bombing at the Vakhsh had gutted the reception area, killing a curious member of the public who was either inspecting or stealing an unattended bag. Responsibility for the explosion never claimed, it may have simply been a case of wrong place, wrong time.

'Nadja!' I heard the receptionist squeal, stirring me from my reverie.

Whilst engaged in carefully peeling a used Indonesian visa from my passport to make way for the Turkmen one, I noticed the door to our room start rattling. The Vakhsh being renowned for pilfering, the door shook frequently, but this time, it was followed by a knocking.

'I try for wrong room,' the blushing, likely would-be thief dissembled; 'now key broke in lock.'

The Embassy

Having heard nothing about the status of our visa applications, we traipsed to the Turkmen Embassy, finding it closed for reasons unknown. Swatted away from the iron gates by a rangy guard armed with a machine gun, I put repeated long distance calls into the mission in London, only to be told that our bushy-browed friend had 'gone for a walk' and then 'gone to lunch.' It was ten thirty AM in the UK.

With our authorisations eventually emailed through - an hour later I'd even managed to print them - that afternoon we asked the Burberry-clad, blue eyed Russian in the Tourist Information Office for the location of that rare commodity, an ATM that accepted Western bankcards.

'Ah, it's easy,' he laughed. 'Just go up Rudaki until you see farming Rahmon.'

Alighting from a trolleybus half way up the main drag, sure enough, there he was upon an outsized billboard. Fuzzy-edged and badly pasted into the scene, Rahmon in all his hayseed glory stood in a field, caressing a non bread as if it were a babe-in-arms.

It was forty-five degrees, the streets literally melting into imprints of tyres and sandals. The classily named Public Pub reflected in its mirrored panels, a security guard admitted us to the air-conditioned Orienbank. Sliding in card after card, the two men in front of us at the single ATM took turns to withdraw cash from different accounts whilst farting relentlessly. Kindly stepping aside to let us have a turn, they crowded round with piqued interest. Peering over my shoulder as I tapped in my pin, there was no respite from their guttural musicality.

Determined to beat the crowds, at seven AM the following morning we headed back to the mission. Something having made me sick to my stomach, huddled over and trying not to vomit, I boarded trolleybus number one. A carousel of age-related musical chairs on which the elderly and the devout travelled for free, trolleybuses in Dushanbe rarely seemed to go anywhere. Conductors hanging from their doors calling for punters who simply weren't there, when they did eventually move, sparks flew from the pantograph. Climbing onto the roof, child assistants attempted ad hoc fixes with oily spanners when the cables fell to earth, which happened at regular intervals.

As we disembarked on the northern outskirts of the city, a child in a Bayern Munich football shirt with fairy lights, flags and speakers sellotaped to his chopper narrowly missed me. Tajik pop turned up to the max, this was clearly the coolest kid in town, his retinue in tow. Not content with fluffy dice in their cars, a pair of giant dice hung from the front of a mini-mall. A metallic red and yellow *Waypma* kiosk (kebab house), its symbol the infamous golden arches of McDonalds turned upon their head promised 'The best or nothing.' Flies bombinating around a rack of lamb oozing thick, white grease, nothing it was then.

Outside the embassy, amongst the horde in the shadeless street, there was Christian the racist traveller.

'Ah, g'day boys,' he greeted us. 'Where ya' staying then?'

'The Vakhsh,' Stan answered.

'Oh, don't even get me started on the Vakhsh,' Christian grunted, his face contorted in disgust. 'They were rude and ignorant.'

The rude part was true at least.

Inside the tenebrous building, the chain-smoking bureaucrat in charge had a quick temper. Her bloodshot eyes pleading for respite, his put-upon secretary was clearly feeling the strain.

'You must copy colour for your passport,' she translated his yapping.

'But we submitted that in London. They've granted us the visas already,' I pleaded, waving the confirmation letter.

A further fit of snarling from her boss persuaded me that, although they had no idea where one could procure a colour photocopy, we didn't have a choice.

Fortuitously, egressing through the heavy double doors, Christian was still outside, leading us to a copy shop situated in what looked like a bomb shelter beneath a housing estate. We would never have found it otherwise.

'Ah, ya' bloody welcome, boys; good luck,' he said, chewing his vowels in response to our outpouring of gratitude.

Back at the embassy, we rejoined the now swollen queue. With no one coming in or out, the single public bench was overloaded, my head spinning as I crouched down under the scorching sun. Asking how long we'd been waiting, a Gharmi fellow called Dallar with shaggy side swept hair translated to the sympathetic throng that including having been sent away for copies, we'd been there for four hours. Sensing an opportunity, it was at this point I decided I'd had enough, shoving my way through to the front, where miraculously, the security guard stood aside and the gates parted.

From behind the confines of the musty counter, the secretary slipped me a bank transfer docket. We needed to pay at the National Bank of Pakistan, only they didn't know where that was. As we emerged distinctly flustered, to whimpers of exasperation from the masses, the gates slammed shut for the day. It wasn't even noon.

With it becoming apparent that no taksi drivers knew where the bank was, lady luck smiled on us once more, Dallar offering to hop in and give directions. His mother a Turkmen, he'd been at the embassy to apply for dual citizenship.

'How long will that take? How much does it cost?' I asked him.

'Maybe two weeks, maybe two months; maybe never. The cost, they don't know,' he answered forbearingly. 'Maybe I go for job in Turkmenistan,' he continued, raising his voice above the stereo. 'I am frozen chicken importer, yes, but no jobs in Tajikistan; not for Gharmis anyway.'

At the diametrically opposite end of the city, the National Bank of Pakistan must have been in the financial district, for every second outlet was an exchange booth, each with standardized rates on its chalkboard and all equally devoid of business. Of course, the bank was shut, staff sitting about chatting amongst themselves whilst toying wistfully with their phones. When we returned after lunch, it transpired that they'd been more obliging when they could tell you they were closed. The mobile gazing continuing, security guards gossiped, a cleaner in a hijab languidly mopping the checkered floor. Sent to a window to complete our transaction, there was no one behind the counter.

Some hours later, with the police having blocked off Rudaki, we found our trolleybus back to the mission stymied. Flowing from a glass fronted building, dignitaries poured into a fleet of black Beemas and Mercedes most likely stolen off the streets of Germany. Reports in *Bild* claim that two hundred pilfered vehicles have surfaced in Tajikistan, largely in the possession of the President and his entourage. The Tajik government have so far ignored entreaties from the German authorities on the issue.

Stuck in the resulting traffic jam, impotent citizens vacated their cars and headed for the shade of trees. Walking back to the mission, we passed a babushka ascending a pile of trash which had distended during the day. Horse-flies buzzing around her, the mound of garbage now reached half way up a compound wall.

The Turkmen Embassy open for an hour for collections only, queues had dissipated. It seemed not many made it this far.

'*Foto!*' the paunchy functionary demanded, spraying us with spittle as he snatched the precious remittance slip from my hand.
'Photo Angliya,' Stan attempted to explain.
'Uk pah?' he sputtered uncomprehendingly, his eyes bulging.
'Angliya, foto already,' Stan repeated.
'Angliya? Uh!' he grumbled; but with his secretary no longer there to lean upon, there was an underlying sense of resignation.

Leafing interminably through my passport, the envoy found the only available spot, tacky from the used visa I'd peeled out. Running his fingers through his regimented short back and sides, he wiped a sweaty palm on his pressed cotton slacks, reluctantly returning to the offending page. A cloud passed across his stubbled face, but choosing the path of least resistance, he inserted the official sticker and slammed our passports down upon the Formica counter. It had taken three days and cost eighty-five US dollars to obtain a five-day transit visa, but victory was finally ours.

Jiving Rahmon

On our last night in Tajikistan, with Stan laid low suffering from a viral infection I'd kindly passed onto him, I arranged to meet with John, who we'd last seen in Osh. Locating him and his Italian friend Enrico on the steps of the Opera House - built under orders from Stalin as a 'gift' to the

Tajik people - we sauntered over to the bustling Kafe Moskva. Fierce and finger-wagging, a Russian barmaid with a tightly curled perm brought us a round of overpriced, room temperature Baltika, banging the mugs down with such force that I thought they'd shatter.

Mopping up the foamy spill with a wad of toilet paper, John explained how on the drive from Khorog, they'd stopped to pick up an injured man on the side of the highway.

'He was bleeding all over the back seat,' John said. 'It was pretty bad. He told us he'd skidded off the side of the road into the river and his friend hadn't made it, but we wondered if he'd swum across from Afghanistan.'

Attempting to catch the waitress's attention, Enrico raised his hand, but propped against a glass doorway, she just shot daggers at him. Resigned to self-service, Enrico rolled his eyes and set off for the bar.

Continuing his story, it transpired that John had shared transport to Dushanbe with Christian the Novocastrian.

'He's a funny guy,' John chuckled, swiping at the cloud of mosquitoes which were feasting upon us. 'He hates Islam with a passion, so this trip is all about challenging himself. He's a staunch gay rights activist, you see, so he believes that even in a country where it could land you in prison, you should never stay in the closet. His last stop is the UK. It's his Holy Grail; he's on a pilgrimage to Buckingham Palace. He loves the Queen.'

Like Indian Richard who we'd met in Khiva the year before, Christian was an ex-colonial in love with and in search of a lost empire.

Enrico returning with three even warmer beers, the conversation turned to Tajik politics. With Presidential elections due in November, Rahmon was running for an unconstitutional fourth term in office. A UN Elections Observer stationed in Dushanbe, Enrico was amongst the first wave of monitors to arrive, undertaking groundwork in an attempt to ensure that at least the ballot wasn't rigged.

'I dare say Rahmon will get ninety something percent of the vote,' I ventured.

'Maybe eighty percent,' Enrico replied. 'Dictators are catching on. They're more realistic these days.'

Enrico had recently been in Azerbaijan for the parliamentary elections, overseeing a backwater district where a candidate loyal to President Aliyev had won with one hundred and six percent of the vote. He was clearly very popular. Moving with the times, the Azeri authorities had released a mobile app allowing the public to keep track of the election; unfortunately the results were posted the day before the vote.

'It was a valuable experience,' Enrico recounted drily, wiping the dust and steam from his browline glasses, 'even if the Russians had already decided the results. Their observers turned up, shook hands with the appointed victors and left. The main opposition didn't win a single seat.'

'I thought there were protests in Azerbaijan about the time of the Eurovision Song Contest?' I asked.

'Ah yes, they allowed selected demonstrations to take place especially for Eurovision,' he answered. 'It served as a façade of democracy for the watching world.'

A video had recently surfaced of Rahmon at one of his son's weddings - held at a cost of one and a half million US dollars - which had ended in drunken dancing and karaoke. Taking to the floor three sheets to the wind, the President had started twirling and crooning, embarrassed grey cronies soon spinning around him like some nightmarish boy band on a reunion tour. A clip of his antics had become an internet sensation.

'So Rahmon banned *YouTube* from Tajikistan to "prevent the misconduct of the people,"' Enrico finger quoted. 'The site was down for three weeks whilst the President's gofers worked out how to remove the offending material from Tajik cyberspace.'

By September 2013, human rights activist Oynikhol Bobonazarova had been confirmed as the sole genuine opposition candidate for the post of President. In a speech announcing her candidacy she admitted that scared for her safety, her relatives were against her decision to run. They needn't have worried. Within a month government officials had ensured that she couldn't even register, going so far as preventing her from procuring supplies of stationary. Rahmon duly won the November elections, attaining a fourth term in office with just shy of eighty-four percent of the vote. In May 2016, Rahmon secured a landslide in a referendum which effectively made him leader for life.

The Sound of the Tajik Rap Underground

In the gloomy foyer of the Vakhsh Hotel, we said our goodbyes to Bob.

'Well, I hope ya enjoy Turkmekistan,' he twanged cheerily.
'Turkmenistan? Yeah, it should be great,' I said.
'Yeah, I'll prob'ly be off like tomorrow to Penjicunt,' he rasped, tripping on the curled corner of a weathered rug as he eased the still weak Stan's rucksack from his back.
'You mean Penjikent?' I asked.
'Yeah, Penjicunt,' he replied.

After a protracted man-hug, Bob gave us a final thumbs-up, flashing a pearly grin as we departed into the morning light.

Much as my guts disagreed, it was good to be getting back on the road. Catching a numbered jitney freshly spurned by a disgruntled looking elder on account of the driver and his co-pilot's choice in music, we cut past a trolleybus as its cables clattered to earth. With rap blasting from the stereo, our chauffeurs were chancing their arms.

Having had their music effectively outlawed as 'unpatriotic,' Tajikistan's once politically minded community of rappers has seen a schism. Since 2014, rap has been banned from buses, minicabs, public spaces, state TV and radio; the few private stations refusing to play it for fear of losing their license. Performers whose music is 'alien to national and universal human values,' as the Mayor of the Tajik capital Dushanbe put it, are also barred from holding concerts, the authorities refusing to issue the necessary permits. Whilst many have fled the country complaining of persecution, others have found a way around the media blackout: praise the president! So parading in front of Dushanbe's phallic flagpole, stars such as Boron now rap about how President Rahmon is 'God's shadow [in] paradise on Earth.'

I spoke with David Lewis, Senior Lecturer at the University of Exeter, as to why free speech is seen as such a threat.

'Although dissenting voices might not seem to have much support, they undermine the model of a highly controlling, but popular regime that President Rahmon has developed,' he said. 'Even a few voices disturb the self-image that the political leadership has developed, and the government is concerned that criticism can quickly develop into wider political opposition. Most alternative voices end up in emigration, one way or another. The regime has been very active in pursuing dissenting voices both at home and abroad. It has tried to use Interpol to track and detain political opponents and radical Islamist activists alike. There have been credible allegations of violence against émigrés, and cases of forced returns and imprisonment of Tajiks in Russia.'

Born in the Tajik city of Khorog, rapper Dorob YANs family was forced to flee the country after the civil war of 1992.

'My father was a rebel and he fought for the people, so he began to receive threats from the government,' YANs told me. 'I lived in Kyrgyzstan until 2005, and then I moved to Russia, where rap has amassed a huge listenership.'

Falling afoul of the security services in Moscow, YANs was apprehended after releasing a track criticising the Tajik President, entitled "Do Not Be Silent."

Politicians with full stomachs,
Never get tired of the money in their bank accounts.
Meanwhile, the people remain silent and believe,
That one day the feast will come to their streets.
I am the son of this city and of this poor country,
And who, if not we will be able to escape this darkness?
We are surrounded by construction, hotels and boutiques,
While our homes have no water or electricity, and all without reason.
Why do our people have to be slaves in a foreign country?
My motherland gently weeps and waits, waits,
To be liberated by its people."

'The people who detained me were employees of the Tajik law enforcement agencies together with the Russian authorities,' YANs said. 'They detained me three times. With the third detention they began to threaten me: that they would put me away for a long time, that I would never have any chance to be free again, that I should not have put out the track "Do Not Be Silent," and also that they could just eliminate me - i.e. have me murdered - and that's not even all the threats. At the same time, they wanted to open a criminal case against me and have me extradited. When they released me they said, "We're not saying goodbye." They blocked my pages on social networks. I began receiving threatening phone calls, both from Russian phone numbers and Tajik ones. I realized that I had to lay low for some time and I flew to Kyrgyzstan.'

I spoke with rapper S.O.R - resident in Dushanbe - about the problems inherent in being a musician in Tajikistan. Having raised the money to make his first record by carrying sacks of cement around a market, he spoke not just about the politics, but also the economic dimension.

'I've been doing music for about 15 years,' he said, 'but from the beginning it was very difficult as there was no studio. In music, especially with rap, it's impossible to live, impossible to earn money. Old school rappers aren't making music anymore, the reason being so that they can live. You have to work because there are hungry people in the house. It's very important that there's an alternative scene, but unfortunately, no one will say that and no one supports rap artists, including the Ministry of Culture. The 2000s was a different time; that was the time of real underground rap.'

With freedom of expression and youth movements under fire, an oppressive air hangs over the streets of Dushanbe. There's little to engage young people. Blocking the road with whistles to their lips, by day the militsiya stop motorists every fifty metres along the main drag, grimaces followed by the presentation of bribes. By night, the city screeches, boy-racers rowdily revving their engines. In a country with extremely narrow perceptions of what's considered a good job, for many a career as a musician is a choice that falls beyond the pale. In this climate, some rappers have taken to pleasing the powers that be.

Outfitted in the national colours, posturing as they dance around heritage sites, the video for 'Tajikistan' by Adaba, Mr. Skap and Sam Salamov plays out like a tourist board advert, celebrating everything from the national airline to the Tajik football team. Interspersed with shots of the president, the track asks listeners to raise the flag and celebrate independence, achieved with 'God's' – aka Rahmon's - help.

Taking this logic a step further, the video for Boron's 'Dear Motherland,' sees the rapper inspired by the words of the president, 'leader of the Nation, Grandpa Emomali.' The platitudes clearly worked; in April 2016 Boron's track becoming the first rap video featured on state TV for over two years.

'In Tajikistan, there's a big industry of festivals, where people celebrate holidays, birthdays, and weddings together,' an NGO source who wished to remain anonymous told me. 'These artists that sing about "sun" and "God" etc, they simply want to be invited to these events. Government officials may well organise these festivities and if they invite a singer they'd like to listen to a "proper song," if you know what I mean. I think those singers are just following an economic perspective; they simply want to get a job.'

Currently blacklisted from entering his homeland, YANs remains a firm believer in the power of music to effect change.

'Without the youth, there's no future,' he told me. 'The government doesn't pay attention to them and this is their mistake, the effects of which will be felt later. Out of boredom, many have already gone off to fight in Syria, but don't even know what they're going to be fighting for. 'I'll continue to make political tracks to address the Government of Tajikistan. When my father was 92 years old, he defended his people. Now it's our time. But our fathers had to protect their people's interests with guns, while today we only need a pen and paper.'

Talco Powder

Offering up every last remaining somoni to the swarm of long distance cabbies at the Zarnisar Bazaar transit hub, once it became clear that we had nothing more to give, we were on our way.

Ensconced in the rear seat, I was shortly festooned with a baby, as to the sound of Ace of Base's 'All that she wants,' we ploughed through a haze of neglected roadworks.

'It'll be nice to see an actual road again in Uzbekistan,' I leant forward to say to Stan.

Little did I know.

Decked in a black and white polka dot headscarf with silver sequins like beady eyes, my middle-aged neighbour chuntered at a steady pace, browbeating the young driver. Whilst I'd never seen a female driver in Central

Asia, women were often firmly behind the wheel. Breaking out in a cackling fit, she repeatedly tapped me on the shoulder, tears streaming down her face. Either there was a joke I was supposed to get, or I was the butt of.

We ground past obsolete marshrutka stops spattered with hammer and sickle reliefs and a final billboard featuring Rahmon in a poppy field sniffing the sweet red flowers. Whilst it might not have been the image he wished to present to the West, it was a more realistic representation at least.

Beneath a plethora of electrical pylons, fields of sickly black grapes and rice paddies poisoned by fluorine powder led to the President's walled off aluminium factory, its chimneys rising like red and white striped rockets. All of its ore imported, the Talco plant near the border at Tursanzade is the world's third-largest aluminium smelter, using thirty-nine percent of the country's power.

Referring to the company as a 'cash cow' for the regime, in a leaked cable from 2008, then US Ambassador Tracey Jacobsen opined that 'the people of Tajikistan effectively subsidize Talco by living without adequate health services, education or electricity.' Next to none of the income from the 'technically state-owned Tajik Aluminium Company' has ever found its way into the state coffers, an article in The *Economist* stated, hundreds of millions of dollars being 'routed to a shell company in the British Virgin Islands.'

Deep-seated inefficiencies coupled with the plummeting price of aluminium have seen output nearly halve in the last five years, whilst transport costs have doubled. Following two judgements in foreign courts during the fall of 2013, the company is also saddled with a three hundred and fifty million dollar debt, owed in damages to Russian behemoth Rusal.

Having recorded losses of over forty million dollars in 2013 alone, in early 2014 Talco sacked over two thousand workers, cutting the wages of those that remained by thirty percent. With the situation looking dire, the enterprise has shed its social programmes and it's the town of Tursanzade, built for the plant's workers and their families, which has been hit the hardest. After-school sewing and dance classes, a sanatorium and a school for gifted children have all been handed over to the local authorities, whose promises to keep them running ring hollow. With the Tajik Finance Ministry claiming that the concern is on the verge of bankruptcy, some observers believe these assertions are down to nothing more than an internal power struggle. The Deputy Finance Minister, Djamoliddin Nuraliev is Rahmon's son-in-law, whilst Talco is run by his brother-in-law, Hasan Asadullozoda, whose position has generated resentment among the President's inner circle, particularly his children.

Despite not turning a profit since 2010, in what was termed a 'patriotic project' to promote national identity, the company still managed to sponsor the soaring new pennon in Dushanbe, temporarily sating the President's powerful case of flagpole envy. Rahmon and his family control most of the country's major business interests, including gemstone mining and the largest bank.

Their licence plates a mélange of Eurasian nations, trucks loaded with aluminium formed an unmoving kilometre-long queue at the border. Distracting the Tajik guards from a TV to hand over our documents, they were struck by an image of thatched cottages which decorated the inner cover of Stan's passport, a quaint government sponsored snapshot of a dying old England.

'Houses, Angliya,' Stan explained in answer to their pointing.
'Oooh,' they chorused, a little awestruck.

Eschewing their duties, their attention returned to the television screen, where Jennifer Lopez and a fleet of dancers were serenading Turkmen dictator Gurbanguly Berdimuhamedow with a rendition of 'Happy birthday, Mister President' for a fee in the region of ten million dollars.

'What country J. Lo? What language speaking?' a curious guard making a hash of correcting a clerical error with a desiccated bottle of Tipp-Ex asked us.
'Er, American?' I guessed; 'speaking English.'
'Oh,' he replied, his eyes drifting longingly back to her curvaceous form; 'J. Lo too much sexy.'

CHAPTER 16

Back to Oz'bekiston

Posters threatening jail time warned against trafficking, images show-ing children in manacles and human organs in jars. Emptying out our bags on the sterner Uzbek side of the border, we observed the pharmaceutical formalities, miming the purpose of every last pill and potion in our possession. With officials taking a shining to my tweezers, I simulated the action of plucking nose hairs to widespread bafflement. Indiscriminately examining the videos on my phone, a guard in camo was drawn to a clip of a toilet with a broken cistern.

'*Qayerda?* Where *khojat'hona?*' he grilled me, prodding at the screen.

I explained that it was my flat in London and I'd shot the footage to send to my landlord, but failing to comprehend, his interest waned.

Outside the exit, a few gold-toothed moneychangers buzzed around offering deals which made the official foreign exchange rate look good. Gold teeth weren't all about bling; dating back through centuries of nomadic tra-dition, they were also a convenient way of carrying one's wealth.

Queuing to leave Uzbekistan, a gaggle of women gawked at us as if we were a circus sideshow. Justifying their attention, as if on command the wheels fell off my Poundland suitcase. Coupled with the scraps of string holding my sandals together and an old woollen glove riddled with holes which was serving as my camera case, it was a pretty sorry state of affairs.

The usual ploy of walking away from the inflated initial overtures of taksi drivers proving successful - not that there were any other transport options - we were shepherded towards a row of baking Daewoo Nexias. Wading through deep sludge behind the vehicles, locals were gulping water from a rusty standpipe. Having run out of liquids some time ago, I was almost jealous of their iron stomachs.

Travelling at a hundred and forty kilometres an hour through flat fields cultivated with ripening awns of wheat, it was immediately apparent that rural Uzbeks enjoyed a higher standard of living than their Tajik country cousins. Their outfits smarter, farmers sat in tractor cabs stuffed with cosy floral cushions, agricultural machinery that most Tajik's could only fantasize about.

In the town of Denau - which boasted three storey buildings built from bricks and mortar - we stopped to pick up a boy and his mother, a large woman with short, spiky plum hair and a bleached cowlick at the front. Mopping herself down with wet wipes, big mama was instantly engaged in conversation with our driver, her tweenie son next to her already adept in manspreading, ball-cupping ways.

The paved road soon a distant memory, we laboured through arid scrub hills, ascending the off-white, boulder spattered canyons of the Boysuntau Mountains. Buttes lifted from the mesa in a landscape littered with caves which had been inhabited by Neanderthals some fifty thousand years ago. Removing his dark sunglasses to stare into the dust, with one hand on the gearstick and the other pressing his phone to his ear, our driver navigated through checkpoints, the abundance of which led me to the realization that shakedowns had only lessened on the major tourist routes.

With rude boys rubbernecking at the Derbent turnpike as our luggage was rifled through, the militsiya grudgingly replaced the back seat they'd wrenched out to search beneath. Choosing to take the middle of the rear for a spell, under the threat of my dusty trousers defiling his pristine drainpipe jeans, the son shelved his limb bifurcations

We'd been on the road for ten hours, passing through endless villages called Boston or Bustan - Persian for orchard - when our destination, Shakhrisabz (Verdant City) appeared on the horizon. Ejecting us at the edge of town, our driver explained that to go any further would create a 'politsiya problema.'

With no idea where we were, I'd just begun to drag my luggage along the ground when halted by a shrill cry.

'*Zhdat!*' the dark haired young boy from the taksi shouted as he raced down the street.

Catching up to us, he smiled disarmingly.

'Thank you, friend,' he said, one hand on his heart, as with the other he offered up the laptop I'd left behind on the parcel shelf.

The White Palace

At the Fayzullah Ravnakhi Museum B&B, we were welcomed with a thousand salutations by the dopy-hatted patriarch. Ushering us to a tapchan, as the sun began to set he brought out bowls of crystallized sugar, honey, raisins, dried chickpeas, walnuts and other unknown delicacies.

'E-yat, e-yat,' he encouraged us in faltering English.

A house of many generations, young women hung laundry whilst children skipped through the leafy courtyard. Shown to our room, the space was dominated by a large, gaudy painting of swans beneath an arched bridge, pink blossoms framing a reflective pool. A stack of photographs of Grandpa Ravnakhi through the decades spilled from a table. In the attached dining area, alcoves were filled with glazed ceramics and ornate choy sets. We couldn't work out how much our lodgings cost, but they were very nice indeed.

At dinner, dish after dish arrived, the wizened old man gesturing for us to chow down by moving a shaky hand towards his mouth. Ants, flies and other assorted bugs enjoyed the spread.

'Tut, tut,' he clicked upon his return, lowering his opaque eyes in disappointment and indicating the still heavily laden plates. 'Problema?'

All skin and bone, he wriggled an arm free from his sleeve, pointed at the food and pulled a strongman pose, absurd in his sagging greatcoat.

Hoping to become a little Samarkand, the provincial town of Shakhrisabz was in a state of renovation, readying itself for an influx of tourists that may never arrive. Writ large amongst the ruins of his hometown, between the remnants of the Ak-Saray Palace a gigantic statue of the crowned main man, Timur stood with a sword stashed at his side, no doubt ready to kill more Uzbeks. Following his capture of Konye-Urgench - now in Turkmenistan - in 1380, its artisans were dispatched to begin construction on Timur's 'White Palace,' the name symbolizing his noble descent, not the dominant colour. It took twenty-four years to complete this most ambitious of Timur's projects.

Now split asunder, two looming sections of the Summer Palace's *pishtaq* – the entrance portal - are all that remain. Colossal and evocative, the crumbling Ak-Saray had attracted coachloads of wedding day-trippers. A bride and groom passing through the vestiges of its axial blue majolica tilework, guests descended upon us, testing whatever English phrases they could muster.

'American? Oz'bekiston good? Shakhrisabz good? Like meat? Like fruit?'

Standing at a distance, a pack of youths laughed like hyenas, as one after another the wedding party took pictures with us. Careful to ensure they were never in the same shot, the two ladies who'd made the faux-pas of wearing identical dresses kept their distance from each other. Turquoise stripes were in vogue.

Attracted to the melee, others appeared, greeting us with bone-crushing handshakes.

'London? Oh, Manchester United!' a substantial fellow boomed authoritatively to murmurs of approval from his comrades.

Fleets of Daewoos rumbled past along Ipak Yoli, the 'Silk Road' to Samarkand. Tucked inside the mud and straw city walls which disintegrated to the touch, a fairground was visible between the two sections of the pishtaq. The lengthening shadows of antiquity never quite reaching them, a handful of gleeful toddlers rode a chintzy octopus merry-go-round ablaze with colour.

In an open-air teahouse of stone floors, wooden pillars and an elaborately carved roof, aksakals sat playing Matador dominoes over pots of choy. Behind his desk, the stout owner stared through a television show featuring children singing and dancing in front of the national flag. Bored, he flicked over to a Russian opera.

'Amerikanskiy?' a bearded young man in a long white thobe sidled over to ask us.

Putting aside human rights concerns for logistical support in the 'war on terror,' even in the minds of many not subject to decades of Soviet indoctrination, the reputation of the United States was now tarnished throughout Central Asia.

'Niet. English; Angliya,' I replied; but it was futile.

'Uh, Amerikanskiy,' the man whispered to his friends as he sat back down, a thinly veiled disgust upon his lips.

Great Ghosts

Encircled by panhandlers and their barefoot progeny, meat hooks reflected the truculent sun at the Chorsu (Crossroads) Bazaar. Sweating porters downing trolleys, old ladies shuffled cheap silver trinkets around displays fashioned from wolf pelts. In a shady alley off the main drag, the dusty mannequins fronting a row of bridal shops were draped in gowns once white, but no longer quite so pure.

Commissioned by the astrologer King Ulugbek to commemorate his father, the frescos of palm trees in the Kok Gumbaz (Blue Dome) Mosque were a composite of designs signature to the Indian and Iranian architects kidnapped by his grandfather, Timur. A light breeze whistling through the cool marble, there was a dream-like stillness in the grand, faded edifices of this burg waiting to wake from its long sleep.

Obscured behind Kok Gumbaz, a few traders dallied, burnt-out kettles and other hunks of scrap scattered across their table stalls. Angling away from their pitches, a path skirting a concrete football pitch led us to Dorus Siadat, the 'Seat of Might and Power,' final resting place of Timur's forebears. Tasked with piecing together the fragments of the tomb of Timur's favourite son, Jehangir, who was killed in a fall from his horse aged twenty-two, a pair of workmen looked lost amidst the slabs of this puzzle which would take them a lifetime to complete. Aside from them, we were the only visitors to this forgotten complex.

Sepulchres of descending size led to Ulugbek's reddish-brown House of Meditation, its unusual conical dome a magnet for birds. At the rear of the courtyard, a plain stone ossuary designed by Timur to be his final resting place lay undisturbed. Found when a child fell into it in 1943, cooing pigeons nested in a cracked lamp above its entrance. The interior damp and humid, there was nothing majestic about the crypt. Samarkand having requisitioned Timur's remains against his dying wishes, its casket lay empty.

The courtyard a fiery orange under the setting sun, back at the B&B the family were out in force. In addition to the eight daughters, with the English-speaking son having returned, we were even able to ascertain how much our stay had cost. Determined to fatten us up, with his starchy shirt done up to the top button, Grandpa Ravnakhi bumbled back and forth delivering mounds of food. It was good to see the elderly revered and central to proceedings, not discarded as is so often the case in the West.

Over shots of vodka after dinner, I got talking with a new guest, Mateus, a refugee analyst from Belgium.

'Do you get many asylum seekers from Central Asia?' I asked him.
'Oh, no, they're very rare,' he replied, stroking his wispy goatee. 'There was a Tajik mullah who said he was being persecuted, but it turned out he'd been embezzling from his mosque. Then we had a handful of Kyrgyz after the Osh riots, but they were all Bakiev's cronies who'd lost their positions of privilege. The only Central Asian we've accepted this decade, actually, is an Uzbek human rights campaigner whose family reported him to the police for being gay,' he concluded.

Illegal under Uzbek law, President Karimov decried homosexuality as 'disgusting' and democracies where it is accepted a threat to the 'moral purity' of his country. In practice, the law is only applied when the state feels there's a more pressing reason for punishment.

With the hour getting late, the ladies of the house were growing restive. Grandpa choosing to sleep on the tapchan, he needed his bed. Saying our goodnights, we retired to our room. Outside the wind began to sough, dogs howling in the streets of Shakhrisabz, a town of great ghosts and an uncertain future.

As part of the ongoing redevelopment, in the summer of 2015 the Fayzullah Ravnakhi Museum B&B was demolished along with all of the buildings lining the former main road, which is set to become a park and a shopping area.

Finger fares

Speaking in dollars with hand gestures, we negotiated a fare to Qarshi. Stan having bagsied the front seat, I shared the sticky back with two big-boned chaps, who despite being strangers were engaged in a jocose, semi-shouting exchange within seconds. Striking up a conversation was easy, pausing for breath unnecessary.

The gent next to me a real hand talker, unfortunately the conversation spread to his elbows, jabs to the ribs interspersed with the occasional blow to the face.

'I am Manchester United,' the gesticulator turned to arbitrarily inform me as we entered the town of Qarshi.

An indistinct transit hub of billboards and six-lane highways, newly built shops such as Gentlemen Burger® stood alongside an abundance of empty units, giving an air of expected expansion. Fenced off to the general public, a plethora of Astroturf tennis courts ensured that the President's elder daughter would always feel at home here.

In the thronging Qarshi Bazaar-cum-bus station, men dragging on cigarette butts were failing to sell burnt lepyoshka from the wicker baskets of prams. The last to board the marshrutka, with people literally perched on top of each other we sat facing backwards, all eyes boring into us for the duration of the journey onto Bukhara.

Blasts from the open window having buffeted my ears numb, the police pulled us over near the gas processing town of Muborak. Clambering about the vehicle, they flashed a picture of a fugitive whose face mirrored that of Arrested Development's Jeffrey Tambor; but which Bluth was it, George or Oscar?

Dropped at the North Bus Station outside of town, an aggressive taksi driver dragged our bags into his car.

'Five, five, ten dollar' he repeatedly barked, indicating the two of us with insistent fingers.

Ignoring his overtures, we reclaimed our luggage, biding our time whilst chatting to the first Tottenham fan we'd ever met in Central Asia, a sure sign of progress.

'Lloris, Walker, Bale…' young Muzaffar beamed as he rattled through the squad.

Football was a universal language.

Leaving impenetrable clouds in its wake, a banged-up white van shambled to a halt at the side of the road.

'Lyabi-Hauz?' I called to the driver.

'Da, da,' he replied, craning his neck and motioning for us to get in.

Wishing Muzaffar good luck, we hauled our belongings aboard, the scamming cabbie appearing crestfallen as we drew away. Passing our som forward, three minutes later we were in the old town, the journey having cost just twenty cents each.

CHAPTER 17

The Death of a Despot

The six-week tourist season not having begun yet, the streets of Bukhara were hushed, scant traders napping at their pitches. In search of a place to procure a cash advance on a credit card, we entered the lifeless foyer of the Hotel Asia, its reflective black glass doors held within a faux pishtaq. Photographs of actor Gerard Depardieu's stay at the state's expense oozed from the walls. In snapshots from his junket around the country - part of his disbursement for recording with Googoosha – the fulsome Frenchman, the President's daughter, the hotel director and various toadies posed around the sights of the historic centre.

On the internet, rumours were circulating that President Karimov had suffered a heart attack. As with all the other Central Asian dictators, no succession plans had been put in place. Gods don't foresee their own demise. With thirty generals and career politicians jockeying for position, at the time observers posited that the elite would likely split into three clan-based factions when the President died, civil war not out of the question as they fight tooth and nail for supremacy.

In a country where the idea of women's 'traditional role' has been promoted since the fall of the Soviet Union, Googoosha's chances of landing the top job were effectively ended when she took to Twitter to attack her mother for messing with her entourage and accuse her sister of sorcery. After tangling with the country's top security official, Rustam Inoyatov, and falling foul of one corruption scandal too many, by February 2014 Gulnara Karimova would be under house arrest, complaining in smuggled letters to a largely unsympathetic audience about the 'ugliness of what goes on here.'

On the night of the 1st of September 2016, the unthinkable happened, rumours circulating from sources on the ground that President Islam Karimov had died after suffering a cerebral haemorrhage. The next morning, the Uzbek government announced that the president was 'critically ill.' Within hours, western news outlets started to report the dictator›s passing.

With the city of Samarkand sealed off, preparations for a state funeral were well underway before the government's announcement. After puttering through the streets of Tashkent, Karimov's funeral procession arrived in his hometown to be greeted by delegations from around the country. A cast of thousands of men in dopys bowed their heads in mourning, wailing women throwing flowers as the coffin was carried past the Registan en route to Karimov's final resting place in the Shah-I-Zinda complex. Posting an article about the would-be successors and what might happen if they came to power, I fell afoul of a woman from the Ministry of Culture, who accused me of 'meddling in state politics' and besmirching the reputation of a 'great man.'

At the time of this book going to press, the leading candidate to replace Karimov is Shavkat Mirziyoyev, boss of the national cotton harvest and Prime Minister since 2003. An advocate of continuity and strengthening the 'security of the state,' in the words of Daniil Kislov, editor of the independent Fergana News Agency, 'he's the exact same kind of ruler as Islam Karimov, maybe even tougher, and I certainly think less intellectual.' Hailing from the same Samarkand Clan as Karimov, an advocate of better foreign relations –particularly with Moscow – Mirziyoyev headed the commission which oversaw the funeral, a position which signalled succession during Soviet times. Sensing a strategic opportunity, Russian President Vladimir Putin jetted into Uzbekistan on the 6th of September. His man was duly appointed interim leader two days later.

Other contenders for the election of December 4th 2016 include Rustam Azimov, First Deputy Prime Minister and Minister of Finance. A member of the Tashkent Clan, Azimov – who has served at the IMF and the Asian Development Bank – is seen as a business-friendly reformer who would boost global investment. Head of the feared National Security Service – successor to the KGB – Rustam Inoyatov was long seen as a natural replacement, but now 72 years of age, his advancing years may work against him. Karimov's younger daughter, Lola Karimova-Tillyaeva – the country's UNESCO representative – has also been mooted in some quarters, though she's always stressed her separation from the structures of state. Purportedly considered as heir by her father, she may be unlikely to want to leave her $58 million mansion in Beverly Hills to oversee a country that could easily slide into chaos.

Upon the death of Karimov, as part of a traditional remembrance feast called *khudoyi*, restaurants in Tashkent and Samarkand started serving up free plov. It wasn't long, however, before the authorities were pressuring locals to contribute to a fund to pay for the food. With custom dictating that the feast be repeated to mark the seventh, twentieth and fortieth day after his death, it seems that people may be out of pocket for some time.

There's Always Tomorrow

Alongside the Kalon Mosque, on what would become hawker alley during high season, we were greeted by a familiar cry from two traders hidden in the shadows.

'Hey meester, I remember you! When you look my shop?'

It was Nazokat, who Stan had purchased two unwanted shawls from ten months previously.

'Ah, tomorrow,' Stan lied.
'Tomorrow,' Nazokat echoed sadly, as if it was a refrain she'd heard far too often.
'Hey meester,' her colleague called out to the sunburnt Stan, 'why you look all red, like big tomato?'

With the city half asleep, the task of locating a reputable black market moneychanger proved problematic. Following a prolonged discussion, an old ice cream vendor in a long white thobe resignedly accepted our low denomination dollar bills.

'Tomorrow one hundred dollar,' he stated solemnly.
'Tomorrow one hundred dollars,' I agreed, mimicking the counting of endless small bills; 'one dollar, two dollars, three dollars...'
'Bwak, bwak, bwak,' he laughed like a chicken.

A neon strip light illuminating his concession stand and reflecting off his sequined skullcap, he loaded wads of som notes into his trusty counting machine, checking the amount five times. Exceedingly proud of this contraption, he clearly loved to count the money.

Between the triumvirate of the Kalon Mosque, Minaret and the Mir-I-Arab Madrasa, children bounced an underinflated beach ball off the hallowed walls. Others chased around the square on tricycles or in toy cars, doves above them circling the Madrasa's crescent moon.

Angle grinders breaking the calm, construction works were everywhere, new businesses including the Tyanet Shop hoping to be ready for the arrival of the summer coach parties. With edges rounded and surfaces smoothed, the old city was undergoing a facelift, the rift between change and continuity causing a pervading sense of unreality.

Back on the main drag, grandma was still perched behind her counter after dark, selling cigarettes, bananas and detergent. Since last year, *nebat -* crystallised sugar - had been added to her wares, though the 'Super Mini-Market' sign had gone.

'Banunchki bamunchki?' she asked as Stan bought a packet of cigarettes. 'Niet *banan?* Ah,' she reassured herself, 'to-mor-row.'

There's Always Tomorrow#2

Of mythic origins, the Ark of Bukhara dates back to at least the fifth century AD. When it was levelled in an aerial bombardment ordered by General

Frunze in 1920, the planes that reduced it to rubble were the first most Bukharans had ever seen. What survived the blitz was ordered destroyed by the fleeing Alim Khan. Shortly to be safe in Afghanistan with the city's teeming coffers, the last Emir bade that his harem should be blown up lest the Bolsheviks desecrate it. It is unclear whether the women of the harem were still inside at the time.

Planned reconstruction works on the vast, earthen-walled rectangle having been completed since our last visit, we walked up the ramp to its gateway and eighteenth-century towers. Our reticence to be extorted seeing the entrance fee reduced, we filed past display cases filled shards of pottery from antiquity and decaying taxidermied fowl, Karakul sheep and white desert rats.

Housed in the former living quarters of the Emir's Prime Minister, a mish-mash of artefacts constituted the Archaeology and Natural History Museum. Looking as if they'd been made as part of a kindergarten project, papier-mâché models of dinosaurs fighting gave way to more modern preoccupations. Above a plastic cotton bush, in a sepia photograph from 1997, President Karimov beamed as he cut the ceremonial cord at Bukhara's first oil refinery. Farther on, a sign suggested that an 'evil wind' had led to the decimation of the Aral Sea. A clumsily translated plaque quoting Goethe contradicted this supposition:

'One should not play tricks with nature. It is always fair, it is always strict, it is always serious; it is always right; it is a human being who is to blame for nature's errors.'

A path led through the former stables to the empty Coronation Court, a solitary stone lion keeping watch where Alim Khan had ascended the throne in 1910. Beyond this, in the overstaffed Protocol Court, attendants sat chin-wagging whilst knitting woollen socks. Glass cabinets contained colourful, overly large antique Bukharan paper money printed in Arabic script. Armour and iron helmets - heavy and hot for head frying - stood alongside the whips and weapons of historic manglers. A photograph of a vibrantly attired, pointy hatted dervish was accompanied by his club, like an outsized knobbly Nik Nak. In the portrait gallery, the only extant sketch of Charles Stoddart hung beside Arthur Connolly and their nemesis, Nasrullah Khan looking wild-eyed and positively insane.

In a final room, Mir Sayyid Alim Khan's gold and velvet throne stood upon a white dais surrounded by portraits. Decked in a blue silk robe, in a single colour photograph dated 1911, puffy eyelids obscured his dark and distant eyes. It seemed doubtful the last Emir's avoirdupois frame could have fit upon his ceremonial seat.

Across Bakhautdin Naqshband Ulitsa, in the shadow of the Arks imperious walls little appeared to have changed at the Pivo Centre. With the sun departing behind a disused Soviet water tower, men sprawled on kurpachas were engaged in games of chess, the proprietor buzzing around them offering skewers of shashlyk. The skull smashing extractor fan still jutting into the passageway leading to the toilet, judging from the puddles most people chose to relieve themselves on the stairwell.

"You know it's bad when you're mouth breathing and can still smell it," I observed as a horde of insects alit upon our tapchan.

Leaving the Pivo Centre, we saw a fight break out, five men pounding on a youth who was soon lying prostrate in a pool of blood. Cutting through the looming, moonlit backstreets, the 'burfph' of police sirens could be heard until we reached the main drag, where a throbbing beat took over.

An increase in the number of plastic camels was the measure of development in Lyabi-Hauz Square. The DJ had also been traded in for a younger model in a spangled silver jacket, the tunes on offer suffering as a result. There was still "Kim Ekan" to keep the big old girls dancing around the pond, though, much to the bemusement of the geese.

The stuffed swan in a sorrier state than ever, the now eye-patch clad Michael Jackson wannabe was still working at the chaikhana. Spending a full five minutes squinting into the mirror, he set the angle of his hat right before deeming his accoutrement fit to deal with the public. In an identical black ribboned fedora, there was even a mini-Michael now, a next generation clone all of twelve years old.

Irradiated fountains releasing a thin brume, men had candlelit dinners with their wives or mistresses, groups of old friends catching up over drinks.

Adorning the plastic tablecloths, Coca-Cola napkin holders featured simpering sweethearts, specks of dirt upon their teeth replicating decay. At the table next to us, a young couple sat in abject silence over a bottle of flat Libella, avoiding eye contact by playing with their phones.

'Worst date ever,' Stan remarked.

Stan's exam results having been released earlier that day, it was a night to celebrate, a night to remember, albeit only from pictures after the event. As the hours ticked by, we sampled our way through increasingly expensive vodkas. Eventually settling on Bukhara Gold - by far the best either of us had ever tasted - a few shots into the bottle things became fuzzy. Images attest that a jubilant Stan climbed upon a series of plastic camels before mounting the Holy Fool statue. Vague recollections of an hour long gesticulatory conversation with a shaven headed man carrying a small child were also later confirmed.

The worse for wear, in our room at the Hotel Rustam-Zukhra the next morning, we stared at Uzbek football on TV. Pakhtakor were gubbing Guliston, as they'd done the season before. The state sponsored 'Cotton Picker's' rarely lose.

For a while during the mid-noughties, Pakhtakor had seen their ascendancy challenged by FC Bunyodkor, 'creator' in Uzbek. Formed in 2005, the club bankrolled by the Gulnara affiliated business Zeromax splashed the cash, bringing in Brazilian World Cup-winning coach Luiz Felipe Scolari alongside ageing superstar Rivaldo on a salary of seven million dollars a year. Having trodden on the toes of too many officials, however, Zeromax hit the skids in 2010 and the money dried up. With the big names soon on their bikes, Rivaldo bemoaning 'broken promises,' Pakhtakor look set for another spell of domestic dominance.

'Say, weren't we supposed to leave today?' Stan asked blearily as another goal went in.
'Yes, but never mind,' I replied. 'There's always tomorrow.'

Goodbye Uzbekistan

Emerging from our room, I was accosted by a member of staff who we'd nicknamed "Fried Egg Monobrow" on account of her synophrys and the fact that, without fail, she always wore a sky blue dress with an ovoid pattern printed upon it.

'You Khiva, da?' she asked, beckoning for me to follow her to the kitchen, where the matriarch was waiting.

An anxious looking woman in bottle bottom glasses, on our first night I'd heard another guest refer to her as "Worrisome Goggles" and the name had stuck.

'Swedish girl go tomorrow,' she explained, stabbing the air with her finger. 'You go twenty-five, twenty-five; fifty dollar.'
'It's too expensive; we'll pay forty,' I countered.
'Hmm… I checking; maybe make special you. Don't tell Swedish price,' she susurrated, winking a swollen eye, but she still looked concerned.

At a quarter to seven the next morning, we were back on the A380 across the Kyzyl-Kum Desert, which had improved somewhat since the previous year.

'Germans make new road,' our driver explained, indicating idle machinery coated in sand.

Desert rats scuttled from our path, hurdling sections of the asphalt already melted into tyre track ridges. Oil-smeared men at work beneath their bonnets, we passed two broken down buses, passengers hunkered in the slither of shade the vehicles afforded them.

Waiting for the Swedes to navigate the free for all of the ticket office at the Urgench Vokzal, we crouched beneath a tree, making small talk with our driver.

'How much house Angliya?' he asked.
'For a one bedroom flat in Central London, perhaps half a million dollars,' Stan informed him.

Lurching back in as much surprise as the sapping heat would allow, he scanned our faces for signs of exaggeration.

'Oh,' he chortled, 'maybe I not live in Angliya.'

Making good on its moniker as the 'Museum City,' if things had altered in Bukhara, little had changed in Khiva, the only discernable development an extended network of security cameras. Obvious and incongruous, they peered from mud-brick towers. Sauntering beneath them along Rakhimova Street, boys used their phones to blast tinny music, a different theme tune for each person.

In 1997, both Bukhara and Khiva celebrated their 2,500 year anniversaries on a random date picked by a historian at the insistence of the government, though both cities are much older. President Karimov, foreign dignitaries and the director of UNESCO turned up in Khiva, but locals were ordered to stay inside for 'security reasons,' snipers lining the rooftops as the populace watched the festivities unfolding just outside their doors on television. The men employed to renovate monuments and erect scaffolds for lights and loudspeakers were never paid.

Setting out for the border with Turkmenistan at dawn, the road was a dust cloud of donkey carts. Home to a well-used concrete plant, the town of Shovot also boasted an entire bazaar dedicated to doors of different materials, shapes and sizes. Arriving at the Shovot-Dashoguz border, traders hawked melting ice cream and bottles of water.

'*Gaz, niz gaz?*' they called, competing for our last som, but with or without bubbles wasn't the problem.

Attracting curious glances from a breakfasting family, desperately in need of a toilet, I was ushered through their dirt-floored house.

'Shalom aleykum, *rakhmat*,' I thanked the head of the household, hand on my heart and much relieved, thinking he'd done me a huge favour; but without looking up, he just thrust out a calloused palm. 'Tyanet, five hundred som,' he demanded.

CHAPTER 18

Welcome to Turkmenistan

S melling of sweat and sewage, passport control at the Shovot-Dashoguz border post may have held jurisdiction over documents, but they didn't have a handle on odours. On the front of the building, a billboard featured a white dove taking flight as a waving President Gurbanguly Berdimuhamedow smiled down on visitors, welcoming them to Turkmenistan. Indoors, decked in khaki as he perlustrated their papers from a second portrait, he struck a more vigilant aspect.

With no entry forms in English available, we were happy to run into a mildly terrified, hoary British couple and their angsty teenage son.

'Where is your guide?' their ivory leisure-suited cicerone asked us.
'We don't have one,' I replied.
'No guide? May Allah help you,' he spluttered, eyebrows arched in astonishment as flapping a hand, he dismissed us as a lost cause.

A hooked index finger summoning us to the front desk, a clique of locals bayed in annoyance at our queue jumping, scarpering when a soldier turned to snarl at them.

'Fromly?' the starched bureaucrat barked at us.
'Angliya,' I replied.
'Murghh,' he sighed, revealing a grizzled overbite.

An intermittent power cut not helping matters, the official lumbered away to a back office, reluctantly reappearing almost an hour later when the whirring pedestal fans clicked back on.

'Which city go? Which hotel?' he probed.

I reeled off a ready-made list of unthreatening objectives.

'Hmm, if you go other place we deport you, understand?' he growled, fixing us with a bug-eyed glare. 'Now, welcome my country. You twelve dollar entry fee; each,' he exacted, signalling the next window, where a new pen pusher was waiting with a semblance of alacrity.

Progressing to the eighth stage of Passport Control, we emptied our bags and performed the now familiar medicine ritual. Ordered to switch on my laptop, I'd learnt from experience to hide contentious files, leaving little except photos of my kitten unconcealed.

'Ah,' a female guard cooed, cracking a smile at an image of its newborn, bat-like black head.

Choosing from a bevy of competing drivers, we inched into the rigid, Soviet built grid town of Dashoguz – translated as 'Stone Spring' - peeling blocks daubed in pink and peach providing a singular splash of colour. Overcast, uniform grey sky matching the industrial stagnation of the concrete and metal, people dressed in monotonal colours, the flat caps sported by men the only thing in town that wasn't square.

If the cab scrum at the border had lacked its usual vigour, it certainly didn't in Dashoguz. Prodding and poking, men with long Turkic faces and leathery skin attempted to wrest control of our luggage. Evading their clutches, much to their cheek puffing chagrin we boarded the bus and were soon rolling down the empty highway.

The other passengers paying us no mind, we pulled through parched sun-flower fields and scattered old Soviet era kolkhoz compounds. Renamed *dayhan berleshik* (peasant associations), the collective's directors still rely on brigade leaders to order workers (*kolkhozniks*) into action. Their plots leased from the state, the government then purchase the lucrative crops – mostly cotton - at a fixed rate which equates to indenture. Nowadays, with machinery long since broken down, almost all Turkmen cotton is laboriously harvested by hand.

Overcoming warring tribes, Russia conquered the land mass which now constitutes Turkmenistan in the 1880s. Despite sharing a common ancestry, the sedentary, semi-nomadic and nomadic people of the region spoke different dialects and had little by way of governance. Barely anything was done by the Tsars to alter this state of affairs.

Drawn up under Stalin's supervision in 1924, the borders of the Turkmen nation include a sizeable Uzbek minority. Working largely in agriculture, the Turkmen had few urban centres, so the heavily Uzbek cities of Dashoguz and Charjou - now Turkmenabat - were thrown in for good measure. Driven into these severe *gorods*, the Turkmen were Russified, their folklore, arts and crafts eradicated through propaganda, or failing that, by force.

I gazed from the window as a blur of agricultural land slipped past. Each new village announced by a triumphal arch which led to nothing in particular, the few extremely square houses may have been smarter than their Uzbek neighbour's dwellings across the border, but the jalopies remained unchanged. A flat, harsh land of unyielding geography, the Russian influence was immediately more apparent here, Turkmenistan favoured by its former masters for its oil and gas reserves and its security blanket of unremitting law and order. Keeping their own counsel, each passenger stared dead ahead, silence reigning on the bus for the entire journey. In Turkmenistan, ranked near the apex of most closed off and repressive countries in the world, regardless of appearances, anyone could be a government informer or a spy.

Old Urgench

On the outskirts of town, identic new pastel painted mansions were losing their sheen already. A smattering of militsiyamen patrolling the empty road, traffic light counters idled down for no one in particular. Signalling our arrival in the centre of Konye-Urgench, the flat-roofed mud-brick houses felt incongruous beneath a swathe of towering streetlights.

Ejected at the sleepy bazaar, our presence sparked debate. Any car was a hackney waiting to be hired, but nobody knew where the '*otel*' was. In homogenous flat caps, nylon slacks and striped short sleeve shirts, a host of men gathered round indicating different directions. Much to my surprise, they were joined by a hard as nails, cheroot-smoking lady; the first woman I'd ever seen behind the wheel in Central Asia. More than that, she too was a taksi driver too.

A confident young man eventually intimating to his colleagues' satisfaction that he knew where he was going, we were back on the road to Dashoguz, finding the Gürgenç Otel four kilometres out of town behind a row of stringy brown bushes we'd passed an hour earlier. Shocked to see us, the woman at the superior, probably only lodgings in Konye-Urgench ogled through our passports. In a padlocked shop attached to the foyer, the entire back shelves were devoted to bottles of vodka. Led to an oddly conjoined room set just off the main corridor, it didn't much matter that the key was steadfastly jammed in the sash lock or that the door didn't actually close; nobody else was likely to check in.

Hailing a car, I asked to be set down at the Nejameddin Kubra Mausoleum, but scanning a roughly sketched map as we drew through the wide streets, that clearly wasn't where we were headed. Repeating the name of our desired destination having no effect, I sat back and enjoyed the ride. Outside, the ashen sky was permeated with a sense of gloom. Eyes to the ground, women with heavy shopping bags shuffled beneath drooping telegraph lines. Where the fulvous roads gave way to fields, clumps of yellow-green myrtle crept from the desiccated earth.

'*Otkuda vy?* Fromly?' a fleshy man raced from a ticket booth to enquire as we stumbled from our cab fifteen minutes later wondering where we were.

Filling in boundless registration forms and stumping up eleven dollars each to see the ruins, it transpired that we'd been delivered to the southern monuments.

Once the centre of the Islamic world, the Aral Sea Basin remnants of Konye-Urgench are now largely forgotten. Besieged for six months by Jenghiz Khan's forces in 1221, defenders fought pitched battles in the burning streets after the Mongols broke through the city walls. Piqued by their resistance, Jenghiz Khan diverted the city's lifeblood, the Amu-Darya River to drown his enemies.

Reborn once more, Konye-Urgench became a vibrant trading hub, described by fourteenth-century traveller Ibn Battuta as the 'largest, grandest, most beautiful and most important city of the Turks.' Sensing a possible rival to his beloved Samarkand, however, Timur sacked Konye-Urgench. When the Amu-Darya changed its course in the sixteenth century, its residents admitted defeat, abandoning the settlement to the Kara-Kum Desert.

Today, scattered traces peek from the sands of this neglected town. Despite the structures usage being the subject of debate, it is generally agreed that the underside of the crumbling dome on the twelfth century Törebeg Khanym Complex functioned as a calendar. Representing the days of the year, the 365 sections of its glittering mosaic lead to twenty-four arches signifying the hours of the day, which now serve as a refuge for nesting pigeons.

Across the scrub, the tapering, pencil thin sixty-two metre Kutlug Timur Minaret – the tallest in Central Asia - leant ominously. Wrapped in wooden scaffolding, the self-commissioned Sultan Tekesh Mausoleum commemorated a ruler whose Khorezm Empire once reached into modern-day Iran and Afghanistan. On sacred Forty Mullahs Hill, scene of the last stand against the Mongol invaders - a mound of graves within a city of graves - young couples left offerings in acts of supplication for healthy offspring. Plastic dolls lay in miniature wooden cradles garlanded with knotted shawls, hairpins upon piled stone shrines. Completing the fertility ritual, woman sprinted downhill at breakneck speed, some losing their footing and becoming rumbling powdery balls as they rolled.

In lesser visited Konye-Urgench, from mild curiosity to outright gawking, with their sense of reserve cracking we became a diversion for interested locals. Fielding enquiries as to our nationality, photo opportunities were grasped by baseball cap clad boys. Their *koyneks* - ankle-length dresses with a brightly embroidered neckline - shapelier and more colourful in this hamlet than in industrialized Dashoguz, women shot shy smiles at us.

Hazarding a guess as to the most likely direction, having yet to procure any Turkmen manat, we walked back to town. Grit crunching between our teeth, an hour and a half later we were relieved to arrive back at the bazaar, where aksakals in long, olive drab coats and telpeks were picking through sacks of grain. Bare-headed women with round, Turkic faces haggled over bell peppers and tiny potatoes beneath the low sheet roof, the aroma of freshly baked *chorek* lifted from *tamdyrs*, revered bread ovens like giant clay kilns.

Given their notorious reluctance to give savers their money back, that my enquiries concerning the whereabouts of a bank were met with blank stares was no surprise. Directed down various side alleys, we circled in the heat, finding it difficult to see the town for the ballooning dust clouds. Taking pity on us, a toothless old man gave us a lift in his azure blue Lada, the seats thick with fur.

'No manat,' I tried to explain, expecting he'd want to be paid for his troubles, but he just shrugged and gave us a gummy smile.

When he passed us later that day, he craned from his car window waving frantically.

Night was falling by the time we reached our original destination. Tantalisingly close behind a construction site and a military barracks, it took us some time to get to the ancient Nejameddin Kubra and Sultan Ali Mausoleums. Facing across a courtyard, the eroded twin sandstone tombs bowed towards each other as if to finally touch.

A famous Khorezm poet and Muslim scholar, local legend tells how Nejameddin Kubra inadvertently sealed his own fate along with that of his people. Founder of the Sufic Kubra order, Nejameddin Kubra taught three hundred and sixty students, one for each geometric degree. He wanted to see things from all angles. When Shah Ala ad-Din Mohammed II had Kubra's star pupil executed following a false accusation, the holy man flew into a blind rage, damning the Shah. His invocation shortly came to pass.

In retaliation for the Shah having foolishly executed his envoys, Jenghiz Khan's army obliterated the Kingdom of Khorezm in one of the bloodiest massacres in recorded history. Kubra and his students fought in vain to protect the city, the mausoleum marking the spot where the holy man fell. With nowhere left to run, a few weeks later Shah Mohammed II died of pleurisy on an island in the Caspian Sea.

Nejameddin Kubra's remains lie in two tombs, one for his head and one for his body, separated by Jenghiz Khan. The graves of Kubra and the protégé who lies beside him are said to have healing properties, but that hadn't prevented one of the mausoleums domes collapsing on them some fifty years ago. Still unrestored, pilgrims intermittently come to pray at the debris.

Back in front of the military barracks, a gold-plated statue of former President Saparmurat Niyazov stood clutching his precious book, the *Ruhnama*. Suited and booted, an illuminated portrait of current President Bcrdimuhamedow stared down at him. Meet the new boss. Wherever statues of Niyazov remain, in a bizarre game of one-upmanship, Berdimuhamedow had ensured that his image was hoisted higher still. Soliciting suspicious glances from the militsiya as I scribbled observations, I soon put my notebook away. Turkmenistan, it appeared, would have to be drawn from memory.

The Golden Age

In 1948, an earthquake measuring 7.3 on the Richter scale struck near Ashgabat. Lasting only a few seconds, its effects were nonetheless devastating, rumours spreading that an atomic bomb had levelled the city. Barely reported in the Soviet media, in a statement eventually released by Moscow, ten thousand were declared to have died. Orphaned in the earthquake, post-independence dictator Niyazov would write in his book, the *Ruhnama*, that 'in one night, out of a population of 198,000 people in our capital city, 176,000 were martyred,' figures perhaps closer to the truth.

Raised in an orphanage, the young Niyazov took a job at a power plant and resolved to join the Communist Party, the decision that would shape his life. With foundlings often favoured by the Soviets as they had no problematic clan or kinship ties, the portly apparatchik with a penchant for fine cognac quickly ascended through the ranks. Charming, integrating and servile with a flair for sidelining opponents, by the age of forty-five, Niyazov was First Minister of Soviet Turkmenistan.

Alarmed by perestroika and desirous of a return to simpler, more authoritarian times, Niyazov supported the attempted coup against Mikhail Gorbachev by hardliners in 1991. Neither the Turkmen elite nor its people welcomed the dissolution of the USSR, ninety-seven percent voting against independence in a referendum held in March of that year. With the union crumbling, however, Niyazov declared independence on the 27th of October 1991, ninety-four percent of Turkmens now purportedly supporting his volte-face in a second plebiscite.

Winning the Presidential election of 1992 unopposed, Niyazov declared himself 'Turkmenbashi,' meaning Father of the Turkmen. Eager to foster a cult of personality despite his reclusive nature, statues of the benevolent ruler began to sprout across the country. Atop a rocket-shaped monument called the Arch of Neutrality, his twelve-metre-tall golden likeness rotated to face the sun, or as a Turkmen saying had it, the sun revolved to face him.

'My countrymen worshipped Lenin, then Stalin,' Niyazov ruminated. 'Now it'll either be Allah or myself. It had better be me.'

Billboards of the President powerwalking in gaudy flannel tracksuits reared from the desert. Guards stood sentry over marble fountains and effigies of the beloved leader, his arms outstretched to embrace streets devoid of people. Even in toilets, with a pinhead of angels at his shoulder, Turkmenbashi was there to watch you piss.

'If I was a worker and my President gave me all the things they have here in Turkmenistan, I would not only paint his picture, I would have his picture on my shoulder, or on my clothing,' Niyazov avowed during a rare interview with *60 Minutes* on CBS News. 'I'm personally against seeing my pictures and statues in the streets, but it's what the people want.'

A 1994 referendum to extend his mandate approved by 99.9 percent of voters in a farcically rigged poll, by now the emboldened Niyazov was free to do as he pleased. His solutions were manifold; amongst a cavalcade of decrees were bans on lip-synching, car radios, cinema, clowns and the playing of recorded music at weddings. Long hair on men and beards were outlawed, citizens with gold teeth ordered to have them extracted.

'I watched young dogs when I was young,' Niyazov philosophised. 'They were given bones to gnaw to strengthen their teeth. Those of you whose teeth have fallen out did not chew on bones. This is my advice.'

Compulsory education was cut by a year so students could no longer qualify to study abroad. The opera house and ballet boarded up, in place of culture came such fanciful projects as the fifty million dollar Turkmenbashi's World of Fairytales theme park and the world's largest shoe. Six metres long and one and a half metres tall, it was manufactured to symbolise the 'great strides' Turkmenistan had made under Niyazov's leadership.

Having pronounced his nation too immature for democracy, in 1999 Niyazov's rubberstamp legislature fashioned the man they'd declared to be their 'teacher, magic crystal,' President for life. 'With long and excited applause, delegates to the supreme governmental body literally forced Niyazov to accept the title,' state-run media reported.

Liberated from all constraints, Niyazov steered his nation towards a new era of international isolation. Purges and choreographed show trials Stalin would've been proud of played live on government TV channels. Shaking with fear as they read from prepared scripts, figures such as former Foreign Minister Boris Shikhmuradov - who'd had drugs planted on him - admitted to being an 'addict' and a 'thug.' Referring to the President as a 'gift from the heavens' didn't spare him or his relatives from incarceration, though. Despite Turkmenistan being a signatory to the International Covenant on Civil and Political Rights, as of March 2015 no information is available as to what became of dozens of political prisoners who "disappeared."

By now untouchable, Turkmenbashi pursued ever greater follies, as epitomised by his self-aggrandizing *Ruhnama*, his very own version of Mao's Little Red Book.

'I, by means of the "Ruhnama" string the past, present and future on a single rope,' the barely literate President's ghostwriter penned.

He'd certainly strung his people up.

A heady cocktail of pseudo-spiritual cogitations and revisionist history, the 'Book of the Soul' claimed the Turkmen people to be the inventors of the wheel and heirs to Earth's oldest civilisation. Within a year, most bookstores carried nothing but the *Ruhnama*, previous greats of the Turkmen literary cannon removed from libraries and ceremonially burnt. Novelists were arrested as the literary bug caught hold of Niyazov, who published volume after volume of his poesy, which critics fell over themselves to laud. By 2005, all libraries outside of the National in Ashgabat were ordered closed, as people should already own all the reading material they would ever need.

Officially declared the 'Thirteenth Prophet' by parliament, Niyazov pronounced himself 'the direct descendant of Mohammed and Jenghiz Khan... All who read the Ruhnama three times, Turkmenistan's literary masterpiece,' he promised, 'are assured of going to Paradise.'

Displayed at all places of worship, where it was to be kissed by visitors, the 'Holy Ruhnama,' the books official website claimed, was 'on par with the Bible and the Koran.' With the last Imam of Turkmenistan imprisoned for twenty-five years for refusing to preach its lessons, Niyazov even paid the Russian Space Agency to put a copy into orbit. 'The book that conquered the hearts of millions on Earth is now conquering space,' the country's only newspaper, the four-page government mouthpiece *Neutral Turkmenistan* gushed.

Crafting arguably the most fully developed cult of personality ever, Niyazov's face adorned everything from watches and perfumes to bottles of vodka. Even in alcohol, there was to be no forgetfulness. The month of January renamed after him, September was rebranded Ruhnama, the Turkmen words for April and bread replaced with the name of his late mother. Planted around Ashgabat, a Dahlia christened after him led to a decree that residents could only own a single cat, dog or bird, as the animals scent might overpower its ambrosial fragrance.

Ramping up his drive to create a brainwashed, nationalistic generation, on top of the three months a year lost to compulsory cotton picking, Niyazov decreed that two-thirds of every school week should be devoted to studying the *Ruhnama*. Teachers were made to sit exams on the book and write articles praising his leadership. With almost all jobs being in the public sector, failure to comply was unthinkable.

Sacking fifteen thousand doctors and nurses and replacing them with conscripted soldiers - for whom it made a change from picking cotton - the President next turned his attention to healthcare. Forced to swear a Hippocratic Oath to his 'great genius' and banned from discussing infectious diseases, doctors were only allowed to study the writings of their President and that of an ancient Persian hero. With illness and mortality rates soaring to rank among the worst on the planet, a resultant outbreak of plague in 2004 saw the word 'plague' declared illegal.

Still not content with his handiwork, in 2005 Niyazov ordered all hospitals outside of Ashgabat shut, instead spending the nation's health budget on a gleaming new leisure centre for horses. Equipped with medical facilities and a swimming pool, the twenty million dollar complex also featured air-conditioning, keeping the stables cool. Niyazov, meanwhile, was treated by German doctors at his own specially built facility.

Upon independence, Niyazov had pledged to turn his desert nation with one of the world's largest reserves of natural gas into the 'Kuwait of Central Asia.' Each family, he promised, would receive 'free bread and a new Mercedes.' In actuality, every year all top officials were given a new Mercedes, the theory being that these would eventually trickle down.

Niyazov may have declared his time a 'Golden Age,' but in reality, their savings decimated by spiralling inflation, his people sank into destitution. An endemic response to crippling poverty, crime skyrocketed, the old days of the USSR remembered fondly. With Niyazov accumulating an estimated two billion dollars in his offshore accounts, in 2006 Global Witness reported that 'no money from the sale of Turkmen gas [ever made] it into the national budget.'

Despite all this and the country's worsening human rights, in its hunger for investment opportunities, the European Union quoted the *Ruhnama* in its correspondence with the regime, nearly doubling aid to Turkmenistan from 2004. Stooping for profit, foreign companies even paid to have the *Ruhnama* translated. Natural resources had become an obstacle to change.

As he grew older, Niyazov turned his guns on ageing. Adolescence now officially lasted until twenty-five, youth until thirty-seven and old age didn't begin until eighty-five, far beyond the average life expectancy. His war on nature couldn't save him, though. On the 21ˢᵗ of December 2006, Turkmenbashi died at the age of sixty-six, the 'age of inspiration.' The official cause of death reported as heart failure, rumours persist that he was poisoned.

Mourners wailing and fainting as they passed his open coffin, Niyazov's body lay in state before being buried next to his mother in an enormous, ready prepared marble tomb in his home village of Gypjak. Inlaid with scripts from the *Ruhnama*, it had cost a hundred million dollars to construct. Despite fifty-eight percent of his people living below the poverty line, by the time of Niyazov's death there were ten thousand new statues in Turkmenistan, largely of him and his family.

Night at the Otel Gürgenç

The taksi driver having no idea where the Otel Gürgenç was located, we circled aimlessly for some time. It didn't really matter, petrol was state subsidized. With gasoline costing less than a bottle of water, smuggling fuel into

Uzbekistan was a vocational mainstay in Turkmenistan. With unemployment running at fifty percent, however, as of 2017 the powers that be have decided to end subsidies on gas, water and electricity. Having changed the constitution meanwhile, Arkadag is set for another seven years in office.

Its' musty walls redolent of despair, the Gürgenç was one of those decrepit old Soviet joints that simply demands vodka. Spotting us peering through the darkened shop window, the hotelier, Ogulgerek's lifeless eyes suddenly lit up.

'Good, good,' she cried enthusiastically, unlocking the door and hoicking dusty bottles from the shelves.

One of numerous Turkmen naming protocols, with Ogulgerek literally translating as 'we need a son,' I presumed our hostess must have many sisters.

We settled on unbranded vodka and a warm beer called Ak Ayy, its label featuring an irate, cartoonish Polar Bear. Tasting it, one understood why the bear was angry. Smelling like ditch water, it was aptly named for the sound one made whilst drinking it. Good, it wasn't.

On the horizon, a storm was threatening to arrive. Sitting with the now melancholy proprietor and her mother on the concrete steps out front of the deserted hotel as dusk fell, we watched the traffic going by, presumably to somewhere better.

Later that evening, Ogulgerek had a gentleman caller. The wind sighing through a gap in the front door, illuminated by distant lightning as she twitched at the net curtains, Mother eavesdropped from the foyer. Past midnight we heard an eerie banging emanating from the room adjoining ours. Escaping the prying eyes of her mother, it was Ogulgerek and her boyfriend.

CHAPTER 19

The Journey to Hell

There was no difficulty in getting a car to Darvaza.

'Gaz? Gaz? Gaz?' the cries rang out, as scuttling from onrushing traffic, I dragged my wheel-less suitcase across the sandy highway.

A charge of prospective drivers surrounding us to extol the virtues of their respective vehicles, my luggage was hurled in the trunk of a surly fellow's Lada before I could argue. By virtue of his decent English and less pushy nature, Stan and I chose a pimped out ride belonging to an ebullient, swarthy fellow called Shikrullah, the driver whose boot I'd yanked my belongings from tapping at the window disconsolately.

'Goodbye Shazam, fuck you,' Shikrullah laughed, waving at the man whose fare he'd usurped as we pulled away.

On a small monitor suspended from the windscreen mirror, a video of dancing at random weddings shot on shaky hand-cams played. A Turkish flavour pervading the pop music, proper nice boys in shirts and ties crooned, old ladies clapping along as they swayed from side to side. Twirling on the dance floor, the bride's gowns were eye-gouging technicolour dream coats; their po-faced groom's suits a more staid affair.

The practice of bride kidnapping takes an interesting twist in Turkmen culture. Meticulously planned, weddings involve a long-winded back and forth between families, each part of the process having an attached ritual. Even after the parents reach an accord, aunts and sisters-in-law must still visit the prospective groom's family to establish good relations. When the nuptial day is finally set, the girl's family traditionally sing one of many ceremonial songs.

We've seen our future son-in-law. He doesn't look worse than our girl, ya-ya. We've tasted their dish, ya-ya. It's better than grapes, ya-ya.

Despite all this rigmarole, the suitor must still pursue and capture the bride. Originally undertaken on horseback, then by donkey cart, nowadays this rite mostly takes the form of a high-speed car chase.

Infrequently broken by sickly wheat fields, the ravenous desert swiftly engulfed us. Weaving through a series of adjoined potholes and scrub side tracks, severe jolts were greeted by Shikrullah, a moonlighting history teacher, with gleeful hollers.

'Whoop it Gangham style!' he cried.

In the back with me, his 'great friend' Kemran - a Turkmen language teacher aged forty who could easily have passed for seventy - offered me a soggy somsa. My rebuff causing bafflement and some offence, he waved the meaty goodie at me repeatedly in case I'd misunderstood. Flakes of greasy pastry falling on the girl wedged between us, she tolerated her compatriot's school-boy antics in stoic silence.

An incessant talker, the beaming Shikrullah was soon grilling us on the finer points of history.

'Who discover Australia? Who discover America?' he asked.

If he were indeed a history teacher, one would hope he already knew this, though perhaps in Turkmen textbooks, Turkmenbashi was that great explorer.

Pools of sweat building under his armpits, the jet-black haired Shikrullah enquired as to whether we had any children, voicing his heartfelt condolences to our negative replies.

'Wife?' he continued to probe.

'No wife,' replied Stan.

'No wife? Take please Turkmen girl,' he suggested. 'We can find for you, yes?'

It wouldn't be easy, though. By decree courtesy of Niyazov, until a few years ago any foreigner wanting to marry a Turkmen woman had to pay the state fifty thousand US dollars for the privilege. Now, outsiders have to live in Turkmenistan for at least a year before the wedding, and there's a mandatory three-month engagement period following the proposal.

'Sex man two wives,' Shikrullah laughed, indicating Kemran, who having fallen asleep was humming like a generator as he drooled on silent girl.

'Turkmen cigar good, make sexy,' Shikrullah asserted, rolling himself some *nas*, the popular green powder made of mysterious ingredients said to include opium and chicken faeces.

Slowing to a crawl as Stan declined his offer of a smoke, we hit the back of a jam, a train of amber brown dromedary camels blocking the highway.

'*Anglische* camel?' Shikrullah queried, shocked when we informed him that no, we didn't have herds of camels roaming the English countryside.

We talked jobs and earnings, gasps solicited at the price of petrol in the West. Joggled awake, Kemran looked very pleased with himself, the cab falling into a deferential hush of expectation as he lifted his finger as if to make some profound and salient point.

'Melody,' he chipped in, pointing to the stereo, from whence Madonna was squawking her way through her eighties repertoire.

It was the only word he spoke in English for the entire duration of the journey.

Suspicion suddenly rearing its head in a land where spies were everywhere, the loud grumbling and gesticulating of Kemran resulted in Shikrullah asking Stan why I kept tapping at my phone when there hadn't been any reception for hours. Desisting from taking notes, I put the device away as we drew to a halt to inspect a far-flung bronze statue dedicated to a fourteenth-century musician. Corroded by rust, a giant *dutar* - the two-stringed guitar like Turkmen instrument - towered over the undulating desert.

'Father of music, hero of love,' Shikrullah commented reverentially, he and Kemran pressing their hard earned manat into a collection box some local official would undoubtedly empty into his pocket.

A haze settled over the pale ridges of the Kara-Kum Desert. Low windbreakers made of twigs having little effect, gusts whipped sand clouds across the featureless horizon. Away to the west lay Golden Age Lake, another ambitious, yet ultimately harebrained scheme of Niyazov's, its aim to reclaim the barren wasteland for agricultural purposes.

Constructed at an initial cost of eight billion dollars, Niyazov's idea was to build a two thousand square kilometre lake in the Karashor Salt Depression in the middle of the desert. Renamed the Grand Turkmen Lake under Berdimuhamedow, planners hope this artificial sea will enable 450,000 tonnes of cotton and 300,000 tonnes of grain to be grown, turning the area into a blossoming oasis replete with a 'recreational zone' hundreds of kilometres from the nearest population centre.

In 2009, a thousand strong crowd of telpek-clad men gathered in the heat to watch Berdimuhamedow release the first trickle from a tributary canal, draining the country's only source of water, the Amu-Darya River which it shares with Uzbekistan. At a cost of a further four and a half billion dollars, the lake will take fifteen years to fill.

'I am convinced that our great deeds will be recalled by glory,' Berdimuhamedow bellowed at the assembled throng, before riding into the sunset on his jewel-bedecked stallion and boarding his private helicopter back to Ashgabat.

Temperatures in the Kara-Kum Desert regularly reaching fifty-eight degrees Celsius for months at a time, the lake will, of course, evaporate, what remains becoming contaminated with salt, fertilisers and toxic pesticides.

Back on the road, irrigated cotton fields signalled the outskirts of Ruhubelent, an isolated, decree built bizniz centre of uniform two storey white buildings. Hiding behind a spindly bush, two militsiyamen stood pointing speed guns at the road. Slowing until safely past them, Shikrullah turned to flash his middle finger back towards the impromptu checkpoint.

'Fucking idiots,' he laughed drily.

The Gate to Hell

Dropped at a truck stop, we surveyed our surroundings. Darvaza town consisted of eight buildings, two of those crumbling to the ground with caved in roofs. Tamdyrs, considered too holy to be destroyed, peeked from the sands where consumptive camels circled. Altocumulus clouds floated across the hazy blue sky, the most remarkable feature of this flat expanse.

Darvaza, meaning 'gate' in Turkmen, is the closest settlement to a Russian gas rig which collapsed in 1971, the entire drilling station disappearing into the cavernous pit beneath it. Given the Soviets proclivity for cover-ups, little else is known about the disaster. As to the fire that has been burning in the desert crater ever since, some say the Russians started it to burn off the gas, others that a shepherd, fed up with the fumes poisoning his sheep, set a tyre alight and rolled it into the hole.

Flying over the settlement of Darvaza in 2004, President Niyazov was struck by its privation.

'I do not want to see this next time I fly over,' he said. The bulldozers soon moved in, three thousand villagers given an hour to pack before being forcibly displaced by soldiers. Expelled in silence from their family homes, they knew better than to argue.

Undeterred and uncompensated, a handful of Darvaza's residents built an even more deprived encampment away from the President's flight path, their tents sprouting walls built with whatever came to hand as the years passed. Now, President Berdimuhamedow has ordered the flames, one of their only sources of income, be extinguished.

In the truck stop parking area, those with newer cars took one look at their environs and sped away. Angry men shouting at me for aiming my camera at their partly crushed lorry, we were ushered inside by the boss, Timur, a tall, round-faced, muscular fellow in a mismatched tracksuit and an FBI cap.

Our eyes growing accustomed to the dim light thrown from a generator-powered television, we were greeted by a mixture of full on stares and furtive, suspicious glances from a burly, sweaty bunch of men. Considering the ban, sets of gold chompers were plentiful here. The ramshackle buildings once whitewashed walls spattered with grimy handprints, mismatched scraps of threadbare rugs and plastic covered tables took up the floor space. There was no running water.

'Where does water come from in the middle of the Kara-Kum Desert?' I murmured, but with Stan preoccupied with a bunko artist, my question fell on deaf ears.

Having negotiated and paid Timur for a jeep to the crater, he was happy for this second character to attempt to fleece us. Selling cheap food and drink or camel herding being the only career paths left for the few that remain in Darvaza, I couldn't blame him for trying. If the authorities thought to market it as an attraction, the crater could probably become reasonably lucrative, but Turkmenistan being arguably the second most insular state in the world after North Korea, they're not really in the market for tourists.

Settling for a measly eight manat, the hustler eventually drifted away, leaving us to the excitable Vladi. Female members of staff confusingly calling him by his patronym, Sergei - Russian lineage loves to bestow many names - Vladi was a sun-baked man-child with bright blue eyes and a shock of blonde hair. A simple whipping boy, the ladies of the establishment chased him away with kicks to the arse, but whatever else Vladi lacked, he was persistent. Following us outside, through a combination of sign language and etching on the ground, he told us his story.

When the Soviet Union dissolved in 1991, Vladi and his father had been in Ashgabat. Non-ethnic Turkmen not feeling particularly welcome post-independence, most Russians went home, but during their passage back to the city of Kazan in Tatarstan, Russia, Vladi and his father had become separated. With no passport, Vladi was landless, an illegal alien who couldn't return home. Thirty-one years old, though the lines on his face made him look well over forty, he'd been in Darvaza for eleven years. Nationality in Central Asia being about blood, bonds and history, he'd never be fully accepted here.

Statelessness is an issue throughout the region, the number of those with expired or invalid papers difficult to gauge with any degree of certainty. Particularly badly affected are the so-called 'border brides,' those who've married across national frontiers and found themselves legal in neither country. In a surprise move, Turkmenistan has become the first country in the region to begin granting citizenship to stateless people, though the three thousand registered so far are a drop in the ocean, a world away from Vladi and his predicament.

Niet Machina

Summoned back inside by grisly, shouty Abdullah, Timur's number two, we were soon everybody's new best friends. Passing round our cameras, we regaled the staff with pictures from our trip, the increasingly hammered Abdullah pulling moody poses for photos he demanded I take. Shy in our presence despite their normal bullishness, draped in long, florid robes, the dark-eyed ladies of the flophouse were particularly keen to have their pictures taken with Stan.

The next nine hours passed slowly, our repeated refrain of 'Niet Russki' growing increasingly tiresome; but still there was no jeep. My designs on seeing the gas crater at sunset a distant memory, pacing up and down kicking at the earth in mounting agitation I was starting to annoy the scowling Timur. It was gone ten PM by the time he summoned me.

'Problema. Niet *machina*,' he flatly declared.

Following some commotion, we were transported a few hundred metres down the road by one of Timur's minions, disembarking at a wooden shack where a litter of kittens, a mangy dog and a listless camel were milling about. Huddled around a campfire, a couple kept a watchful eye on two toddlers who were crawling in the sand. Another hour passed before it became apparent that our jeep had morphed into motorbikes, which then became a single motorbike. Despite the best efforts of those assembled, however, it was patently obvious that we weren't going to be able to traverse over ten kilometres of dunes with three on a bike.

At this juncture a second motorbike arrived, Stan's ride tearing off into the desert. As I eagerly mounted my metal steed, with a sharp clank the front light fell off. Much pointing and gesticulating ensuing as the headlight was secured with Sellotape, I got the sense that my driver had never been to the crater before, a feeling shortly compounded by his frantic circling in the pitch dark sand drifts. My ankles cut to shreds as we slid through low scrub, I clung to his paunchy belly for dear life no longer caring if we found the crater or not, just not wanting to die in the black desert night. When he finally saw a faint glow on the horizon, my driver couldn't contain his excitement.

'Gaz! Gaz!' he screaked.

Arriving at the gaping wound which is the crater, it felt as if I'd reached the back of beyond. Locating Stan - who'd feared the worst given my protracted delay - we navigated our way around its two hundred metre circumference.

A smouldering heat haze rising from the fiery pit to blur the sky, the stench of gas was overpowering. From a depth of thirty metres, methane seeped out of the rocky ground, fireballs erupting from white hot embers. Its hardened sand walls ablaze with yellow flames, a lone rusted tamdyr and a twisted metal strut were the only indications that the rig had ever existed.

A thin slither of moon above us, we sat on a high escarpment with the otherworldly gate to hell burning spectrally below. Adamant in their desire to leave, we stalled our drivers for as long as possible, before eventually being forced to admit defeat. Determined to keep pace with his mate this time, my driver jumped and skid from dune to dune, depositing me back at the flophouse a hair-raising twenty-five minutes later.

The generator cranked up, the male staff surrounded us, determined to show off the virtues of Turkmen porn. Following me, a twelve-year-old boy flashed videos of penetration at me on his mobile, mimicking the action of fucking with urgent hand gestures. My initial impression of Turkmens being the quiet Central Asians well wide of the mark, they were anything but when the police weren't around.

Much to their confusion and dismay, we escaped the buzzing smut show, sitting outside on the tapchan, where new friends were inevitably made. Piling from their Opel Vectra, a patriarch with wispy grey hair was followed by five of his broad-shouldered sons. Introducing himself as Achir Berdiyevich, he plied us with bottles of warm Berk pivo and shots of vodka, indicating his children with an outstretched talon as they gathered round.

'Ìàêñèì, Misha, Albert, Alty, Yedy,' he introduced them.

Gauging from his dactylology that he had seven sons in total, he must have grown tired of dreaming up names for them by the time the last two were born, their monikers literally translating as 'six' and 'seven.'

By now adept at gesticulatory conversations, it wasn't long before Achir discovered that we had nowhere booked to stay in Ashgabat. Taking my notebook, he scratched out the contact details of his family in the capital, who he assured us would be most accommodating. A model of hospitality, his only regret was that headed in the opposite direction, he was unable to offer us a lift.

Raised voices indicating some kerfuffle amongst the staff, Achir and his sons said their farewells as the underlings of the establishment yanked us back inside. Either there was a problema, or Timur wanted to pass out on the tapchan.

The Road to Ashgabat

Shaken from my fitful dreams on the cold stone floor at an ungodly hour, the twelve-year-old pointed insistently towards the exit. Angry Abdullah already at the vodka, barking instructions as he drained deep measures from a chipped chay bowl, it seemed we'd outstayed our welcome. Fragile and distinctly the worse for wear, I scraped my belongings together and headed out into the blinding sun.

'Angliyskiy? Angliyskiy?' early morning punters chorused at us, a man in high rubber boots taking pity on our dishevelled state and making a gift of a lump of stale chorek.

As we attempted to thumb a ride in the surging heat, lorries blew dust into our faces as they veered, shade finally afforded only when a vehicle broke down. Out of water, we hunkered in its welcoming, if slim shadow. We remained no closer to our objective of hitching a lift, however, until arriving like a mirage along the shimmering highway, there was Shikrullah on his return journey to Konye-Urgench.

'Ha ha!' he greeted us with a hearty belly laugh, 'transport problema?'
Striding imperiously into the middle of the road, he flagged down the first truck which approached, achieving in an instant what we'd been trying to for the last ninety minutes. Climbing into the extended orange cab-over with hand painted go faster stripes, I discovered that

the area behind the front seats contained an immensely alluring blood-stained mattress. Offering our sincerest gratitude to Shikrullah, we raised our hands in valediction as we left Darvaza behind.

Swathed in bandages against the wind and sand, figures that looked like the invisible man zipped past on motorbikes, signs warning of camels crossing dotted along the roadside. Austere music spilt from the stereo, a lot of wailing and gnashing of teeth about what sounded like 'Chicken-eyed Jamal.'

A brief stop at the town of Jelandy's premier shashlyk stand rousing me, I gazed out past the scattered mud-brick shacks into the void. Travelling through Turkmenistan in 1888, British MP George Curzon had written that the sands were like a 'sea of troubled waves, billow succeeding billow in melancholy succession.' Finding the land to be 'the sorriest waste that ever met the human eye,' Curzon noted that 'the Turckmans themselves are unaware that such a gloomy impression can at any time be conveyed by their country. They have a proverb which says that Adam, when driven from Eden, never found a finer place for settlement.'

Four hours later, we entered the outskirts of Ashgabat, the tectonic plate of the Kopet Dag Mountains demarcating the border with Iran glimmering in the distance. Our friendly drivers flagging us down a ride from the truck depot turn off, we continued along the six-lane superhighway through conurbations lined with parched earth coloured tanks. Consumed by the megalopolis, our taksi sped through Niyazov's hometown of Gypjak. Its minarets reaching to the sky, his sixty-metre wide tomb, the gold-domed Gypjak Mosque dominated the landscape.

'Ashgabat beautiful,' Shikrullah had declared.

As we approached the centre, a giant billboard of President Berdimuhamedow offered his welcome to the capital, endless white marble towers spreading out before us like a virus.

CHAPTER 20

The City of Love

In the foyer of the Dayhan Hotel, the cheerless receptionist took her time evaluating this new bunch of filthy ne'er-do-wells. Tapping a long fingernail upon a desk indented through years of practice, she fixed us in the crosshairs of her withering gaze. A lone fly buzzing, the hands of a clock ticked to the pedestrian pace of her drumming. Finally ending the stand-off with a derisive snort, she decided to do us a favour, allowing to be gouged by their bedsprings.

'Fifteen dollar,' her slightly friendlier assistant snapped, nose pressed against the smudged glass of the reception booth.

This would've been remarkably cheap.

The waters grew muddier, however, when she pointed to a second time-piece, its static hands fixed at noon.

'Check out twenty o'clock,' she bellowed, like an imbecile talking ever louder to the deaf.

Scrutinised by security cameras, we dragged our bags up two flights of stairs where faux crystal chandeliers grasped at glamour. Flickering lights in the slender hallways causing disequilibrium, portraits of a smug looking Berdimuhamedow lined the walls. It being unclear if our room was bugged, as many hotels, cafés and public places in Ashgabat are, I decided to keep my own counsel as to my first impressions.

Air-con units spewing more sapping heat into the mix, outside the hotel on 2022 Street, three vodka emporiums in a line were followed by the City

Bar and the Bar Bar. Beyond this, a protracted procession of white marble towers like Styrofoam monoliths, meticulous, indistinguishable and straight as bed bug bites took over. Triumphal arches leading nowhere, ubiquitous statues and fountains abounded, the surreal city silent save for the splashing of wasted water. Redundant soldiers sweltering on every corner, gardeners kept the deserted parks pristine. We had reached cult central, the apex of autocratic megalomania.

'I want Ashgabat to become the city of my dreams,' Niyazov had declared upon independence.

It became the city of other's nightmares, the city that never woke up.

A moderately young metropolis, its appellation meaning 'City of Love' in Persian, Ashgabat developed around a Russian garrison during the 1880s. Levelled in the earthquake of 1948, prefab Soviet blocks soon sprung from the debris. Shaping his vision, Niyazov had these *kommunalkas* torn down and replaced by boxy, flat-topped marble towers with dazzling, reflective windows, the occasional one wearing a tiny dome like a skullcap. Largely of a uniform eleven storeys, their showy ostentation lacked any semblance of functionality, endless ministry buildings standing unoccupied, overpriced residential blocks home to an affluent few.

Their neighbourhoods destroyed with no compensation or allocation for rehousing, people had no connection to this alien new world, and so its manicured lawns just sat there baking in the sun. A fever dream of a city, its ostentatious puppet theatre unloved and its World of Fairytales theme park rarely open, Ashgabat had been transformed into a temple of kitsch. Beneath endless graven likenesses Niyazov had dedicated to himself, the police guarded this retro-futuristic fantasy against no one.

Strolling through the streets of his vision incarnate, Niyazov's eight-year-old granddaughter, Julia had been struck by the city's panorama.

'Grandpa, why are your portraits and statues everywhere?' she naively asked.

Unwilling to accept this innocent challenge to his God-like station, the Great Turkmenbashi never spoke to her again.

Foto Problema

Offering respite from the scorching sun, but unnecessary in terms of traffic, underpasses adorned with stars led to the Earthquake Monument. Niyazov's father having died during World War II - gossip contends that he went AWOL and was sentenced to death by a military court - the cataclysm of 1948 killed his mother and two brothers. According to the *Ruhnama*, young Saparmurat sat alone in their ruined home for six days before being pulled from the rubble.

A globe gored upon its horns, the Earthquake Monument featured a black bull seemingly borrowed from the Bank of America Merrill Lynch logo. Emerging from a crack in its surface, Mary-like in her shroud, there was Niyazov's mother, Gurbansoltan lifting her golden child from the misshapen orb. Glared at by bored militsiya, I tugged at the doors of the Earthquake Museum, but as a hobbyhorse of the former dictator, its entrance was locked steadfastly shut, perhaps permanently.

Across a sizeable parade ground lay lavish and gaudy Independence Square, its structures erected by the French corporation Bouygues, court builder to Niyazov. A tangle of right angles and star polygons, ornate lampposts encircled aureolin yellow flowerbeds. The Kopet Dag Mountains its backdrop, a bronze statue of Niyazov's mother stood in front of the Ministry of Fairness toying with scales of justice which would never deliver. A single bird circumnavigating turquoise domes redolent of upturned chay piyolas, the Tuscan columns of the seldom used Ruhyyet Palace stretched for city blocks.

Facing the vacant square, the Presidential Palace had cost more to construct than the nation's annual health budget. Aptly obscured behind this, the rubberstamp parliament was one of a row of flag topped, gold-domed marble buildings trailing off in a relentless succession.

There'd be photo skulking to be done here.

'How many pictures do you think I can take before the police stop me?' I asked the nervous looking Stan.

The answer was eight.

Blasting on his whistle and summoning me over, a red-cheeked militsiyaman shook my hand before taking my camera. It being unclear whether one was technically allowed to visit Darvaza, I was a bit concerned about the first photos he sifted through; that is until I realised he didn't know where Darvaza was.

'Not Turkmenistan,' he stated, eyeing the fiery pit.
'Da, Darvaza, Turkmenistan,' I couldn't resist correcting him.
'Niet, not Turkmenistan!' he shouted authoritatively, lingering to scroll through snapshots of the truck stop ladies.

A muster of peak capped soldiers descending upon us, he inevitably came across the offending images of the Presidential Palace and attendant ministerial buildings.

'Foto problema. *Udalyat!* Delete!' he demanded tetchily, disposition deteriorating as he fondled the handcuffs dangling from his belt.

Feigning ignorance of my transgression, I meekly followed his instructions.

Deciding it would be prudent to lie low for a while, we slunk into an air-conditioned mall to take in the delights of a local eatery. Among the dishes on offer were *Shurpa* - mutton broth with potatoes, to be mopped up with *Yagly* nan - mutton fat bread. This could then be washed down with *Chal* - fermented camel's milk mixed with soda water. Feeling unadventurous, I played it safe and ordered a spinach omelette, except it transpired that spinach was a type of ham. Picking out the pieces and piling them on the side of my plate, when the bill arrived there was a mysterious fifteen percent discount. Perhaps the meat could be recycled.

Emerging back onto the streets, the expansive highways were all still empty, marble bus stops uninhabited. Surveillance cameras everywhere, mirrored glass buildings magnified the heat. There were no trees to offer shade, nowhere to hide. Uninterrupted strips of fountains diffusing a tantalising mist, the ever vigilant police peered from every nook and cranny.

At the far end of Ten Years of Independence Park, Turkmenbashi's World of Fairytales was situated behind by a wall painted with sights from around the globe: the Parthenon, the Pyramids, the Statue of Liberty and Niyazov's Arch of Neutrality among them. Occupying twenty spaces in the car park, a hulking carnival float like a tugboat on wheels lay marooned and forgotten. A toy train circling the grounds, a rusted stairwell led to a stationary rollercoaster, the obligatory Ferris wheel less than half the height of the towers which overshadowed the site.

Back in the park, gardeners in orange and blue uniforms were engaged in sculpting the grass with pairs of scissors. In addition to featuring in the centre of the National Seal and having a beauty contest and a national holiday dedicated to them, the traditional Turkmen horse, the Akhal Teke had also scored their own monument. Rearing from a plinth they were ensnared by fountains, beached behind a golden Niyazov in a suit and flowing superhero cape. His name repeated like a mantra, multilingual signage let it be known that these simulacrums had been sculpted upon resolutions passed and inaugurated by the 'First President of Turkmenistan, Great Saparmurat Turkmenbashi.' Perched higher still, where there was Niyazov, there without fail was Berdimuhamedow. On a billboard standing twenty metres tall, he grinned and waved from an arch.

Passing the Presidential Palace once more, the urge to retake the photos I'd been forced to delete proved too great to resist. Materialising from an alcove, a militsiyaman whistled furiously, shaking his fist and chasing after us. With the Benny Hill theme music playing in my head, we fled in panic, scurrying away between towers. Losing our pursuer, I was glad to reach the relative safety of the Dayhan.

'I just don't get it,' I wheezed at Stan as I bolted the door. 'I mean, what's the point in banning pictures of the Presidential Palace when it's featured on the banknotes?'

The Berdy Man Can

Far from being next in line, Gurbanguly Berdimuhamedow came to power in an effective coup. Wooing him in order to gain access to natural resources, the international community turned a blind eye as the Turkmen constitution was amended, and one by one his former allies and enemies alike were arrested. It wasn't as if he could be any worse than his predecessor, after all.

With all seven 'opposition' candidates declaring their loyalty to him, Berdimuhamedow won eighty-nine percent of the vote in window dressing elections of 2006. State company bosses openly calling on workers to vote for him, one even referred to him as 'our King.' Describing him as a 'vain, fastidious, vindictive... micro-manager,' a leaked US diplomatic cable reached the conclusion that Berdimuhamedow 'does not like people who are smarter than he is. Since he's not a very bright guy... he is suspicious of a lot of people.'

Initially foregoing statues, perhaps in an effort to set himself apart from the man he'd replaced, photographs of Berdimuhamedow were sprinkled throughout the land instead, even newlyweds posing for keepsakes next to his portraits. Rumoured to be the illegitimate son of Niyazov, who he served as a dentist, in reality any differences between the two dictators are chiefly cosmetic. Where Niyazov fashioned himself Turkmenbashi, Berdimuhamedow prefers to be called 'Arkadag' (Protector). In Niyazov's time, people were living in the 'Golden Age' - at least in terms of his statues - now they live in the so-called 'Era of Supreme Happiness of the Stable State.'

Promising a review of pensions, a return to ten-year basic education and internet access for all, the change Berdimuhamedow spoke of upon his inauguration has been largely unforthcoming. Steadily dismantling the trappings of his predecessor, the reach of the *Ruhnama* has lessened only to be substituted with his own books, forty of them to date. Eventually allowed into the country, the internet remains rigidly controlled, visitors to internet cafés having to show their passports and register in a logbook. Social media and streaming websites remain banned, private internet connections costing up to seven thousand US dollars a month.

'There is still no political life... no civil society,' Tajigul Bermetova of the human rights group, the Turkmenistan Helsinki Foundation observed. 'Berdimuhamedov grew up and made his political career under President Niyazov. At that time, ministers were not allowed to travel, so Berdimuhamedov is not familiar with any other form of governance.'

In other words, he's doomed to repeat the follies of his antecedent.

His self-satisfied smirk, pudgy cheeks and immovable shiny black hair having replaced Niyazov's as a permanent fixture on state television, government minister's bow as they diligently scribe his words of wisdom. Echoing Turkmenbashi, Berdimuhamedow is also fixated on immortalising the man who raised him, effigies of his father, a former prison guard popping up all over the country.

In addition to writing books – which include a novel about his father – being a pilot and crooning ballads on state TV, Berdimuhamedow is presented as a sportsman of immense ability. Having won the inaugural Tour de Ashgabat on his custom green mountain bike, in 2013 the Berdy Man ordered all able-bodied citizens to purchase bicycles ahead of a national race, the threat of redundancy hanging over anyone foolhardy enough not to comply. With summer temperatures hovering around thirty-eight degrees Celsius, the inherent risk of heatstroke was summarily dismissed.

'In the Era of Might and Happiness... shaping a generation that is physically healthy and spiritually perfect' is a priority, the government news agency recounted, conveying the announcement of enforced calisthenics as part of a 'Week of Health and Happiness.' Citizens of this desert nation were also strongly encouraged to take up ice hockey.

With his competitor's tugging at their reins for dear life in fear of beating him, in April 2013 upon a steed called 'Mighty,' the fifty-six-year-old

President was victorious in one of Turkmenistan's most prestigious horse races. An omnicompetent dynamo, if anyone can, the Berdy Man can.

With the President taking a comedy spill immortalised on *YouTube* just seconds after crossing the finish line, a dumbfounded silence descended over the crowd. Fifty dark-suited secret service agents wearing worried expressions scampered onto the track. The sheepskin telpek and kaftan-clad Berdy Man was soon back on his feet though, waving to his vassals as he claimed the eleven million dollar first prize.

Unsurprisingly, Berdimuhamedow won the event again in 2014, his victory, reported the State News Agency of Turkmenistan, greeted with the 'wild, lasting ovation' befitting the 'great mastery of an experienced and brave rider.'

Ashgabat at Night

Back in Independence Square, a military parade was taking place. Salamander green trousers tucked into their thigh-high gumboots, goose-stepping like characters from Monty Python's "Ministry of Silly Walks," soldiers caressed their rifles through thin white gloves. The pounding of their feet echoing through the still, late afternoon, we were the sole spectators.

At the Russian Bazaar, there was at least some civilian activity, punters emerging into the car park from O Limp Sport with rustling shopping bags to hand. Still required to pass a sixteen-hour course on the *Ruhnama* in order to procure a driving licence, a plethora of signs ensured that long-suffering citizens were aware that use of the horn had been outlawed by decree. All eyes and ears, from their station beneath the disembodied head of the Berdy Man floating on a behemoth of a screen, the militsiya emerged to examine driver's documents, ensuring that the law was rigorously adhered to.

Farther along 2011 Street, a twitchy sentry whistled testily, shooing us onto the pavement opposite. There appeared to be a ban on walking too close to this particular faceless edifice, presumably yet another military installation. Cutting through a park behind the heavily guarded compound, the soldier watched as we passed an incongruous looking statue of a diminutive Lenin, cut down to size on a vaunted, crimson tiled plinth.

In the dying twilight, some signs of normality finally surfaced on a slim green traffic island on 2022 Street. Overlooked by a rash of casinos, children on illuminated neon rollerblades darted about. Carefully minding their own business, chic women in kitten heels and singlets sat on benches staring dead ahead, their well-groomed partners occasionally offering reserved, grunted greetings to their comrades.

Adjoining 2022 Street, the domed palaces of the city within a city covered an area so vast one could easily get lost. Picked out by dazzling spotlights, the imposing Ministry of Defence building cast a voluminous shadow, when the only thing anyone needed protection from was the regime itself. At the far end of surreal, rectangular Independence Square, the Crying Mother Monument stood eerie and alone in the gathering gloom.

As we stumbled in the dark, retracing our steps towards the thin shoots of life we'd witnessed, a young woman in a mini-skirt with a pimple-scarred face clocked our approach.

'Vy govorit'e pa-Russki, da? Niet? Ah, Angliyskiy!' she surmised, tottering towards us on open toed blood red stilettos. 'Hello welcome, I am from Ukraine. This my number. Call me,' she smiled, handing me a business card. 'For sex. Hundred dollar, da. I have friend also, very, very beautiful. Militsia, niet problema. What hotel you stay?'

'Er, the Dayhan,' I replied, unable to come up with another name off the top of my head.

'Ah, no good place, no good there,' she said, shaking her head, a mane of greasy, waist length blonde hair whipping at us. 'This very good hotel,' she continued, indicating the lavish Grand Turkmen, which was lit up like a Christmas tree. 'Pay security only thirty dollar, they don't looking.'

Making our excuses, we scuttled into the Bar Bar, a place where trendy young things liked to go for cheap drinks. Ignored by the staff, it quickly became clear that table service wasn't for the likes of us. Ordering two pivos in a timber building that resembled a youth club, we settled in the garden beneath a Coca-Cola umbrella which had trapped the heat of the day. On a makeshift stage, a DJ was singing along karaoke style to records already containing vocals, fizzing speakers carrying the thumping beat through the concrete floor.

At precisely ten thirty PM, with a sharp scratch, the music stopped mid-song, replaced by a deafening hush as both staff and patrons melted away. Rising to leave, I noticed a throng of agitated, well-oiled men pressed against the bars exit. Apparently the victims of an involuntary lock-in, they pushed at the doors to no avail, their expressions somewhere between fury and wide-eyed panic.

In Marble

Up at the crack of dawn, we hailed a taksi to the State Bank for Foreign Economic Affairs. It was our last full day in Ashgabat and we had a grand total of three dollars left between us. ATMs which didn't accept international cards mocking us from street corners, the State Bank was one of only two places in the country where foreigners could obtain cash, one solely for Visa transactions, the other for MasterCard.

Lingering at the teller's window – one-way glass ensuring you couldn't see if a member of staff was there or not - I patted down my pockets, realising that my phone had fallen out in the back of the cab. Its singular use being as an alarm clock, it didn't matter greatly. Barred from connecting to a network, I hadn't had reception since we'd crossed the border into Turkmenistan.

En route to the bank, I'd spotted the Arch of Neutrality on the distant horizon; which was a boon. Recently moved from the city centre to the suburbs, our efforts to reach it had been thwarted by drivers not having a clue what we were yammering on about. Shooting quizzical glances, they'd shrug before pulling away.

Heading determinedly in the vague direction of our no longer visible goal, I marched Stan along shadeless streets where spindly saplings had been planted, perhaps to offer respite from the sun to future generations. Every few hundred metres there were air-conditioned bus stops, but no buses, the space age *telefon* boxes like teleportation booths containing no telephones.

The City of Love holding the record for the highest concentration of white marble buildings in the world – 4.5 million square metres of them – many bore an embossed bust of Niyazov, attached to the top corner like a postage stamp. Their architectural style alternately described as 'Walmart-meets-desert-emirate' or 'somewhere between Las Vegas and Pyongyang,' the towers bore the logos of Western and Korean companies: Coca-Cola, LG, Samsung. Sponsored, yet barely occupied, their expansive car parks stood empty. A marmoreal chimaera not constructed from solid marble, the tiles had fallen from some high-rises, others slanted through subsidence.

The consummately straight roads peopled only by conscripts and the occasional horticulturist sweating as they toiled, a two-hour walk led us to the Arch that wasn't an arch. Looking like something from the set of 'Lost in Space' that could never hope to leave the Earth, Niyazov had spent twelve million dollars on his seventy-five-metre tall rocket. At its apex, a twelve-metre gold statue of him was planted, arms aloft as if receiving plaudits. No longer turning to face the sun, the father of the nation had been downgraded.

Dumped in the outskirts, its aureate core and wooden rings were adorned with *guls*, emblems of the five tribes of Turkmenistan. The lift upon its marble frame long since out of commission, two soldiers stood like mannequins in glass boxes at its feet. The ticket booth closed, nobody was going to come. The sun had set on Niyazov's golden age.

It was ten thirty AM and forty-three degrees in the non-existent shade already. Swinging batons, sweltering militsiya in blues, greens and khakis loitered at the side of the roads. Unstaffed ministry buildings stretching to eternity, the Ministry of Deserts was shortly followed by the State Joint-Stock Corporation for Carpets and the State Konserni for Turkmen Horses. Given the pace at which more were being built, it didn't seem to concern the regime that there was such a glut of vacant towers.

Cranes busy extending the madness, we headed towards the Alem (Universe) Cultural and Entertainment Centre. Puttering along at fifteen kilometres an hour, our gummy driver was befuddled by the construction. Circling dizzily at roundabouts, neither he nor the other passengers wedged in the back were able to fathom out how to get there. They weren't alone; you couldn't. A recently completed multi-million dollar complex boasting the world's tallest enclosed Ferris wheel, it had been cut adrift, new worksites offering no way through.

Disembarking no closer to our target, we endeavoured to cross a barren patch of land awaiting a new tower, only to be barked at by a policeman who waved his arms as if attempting to take flight. Another detour ultimately leading to the Alem Centre's enormous deserted parking lot, the green and red flag of Turkmenistan with a crescent moon, stars and guls fluttered in abundance from soaring masts. Predictably wrought in white and gold and embellished with the ever popular star motif, the giant Ferris wheel mostly resembled a gargantuan clock face.

Given the tumbleweeds, it looked as if the attraction was closed, but a tug on the handle of its mirrored door brought forth a guard.

'Niet *inostranets*!' he growled authoritatively, raising a palm in Stan's face.

Would the entertainment blow our minds? Would we stumble across state secrets? Either way, as foreigners we weren't going to be admitted.

Having run out of water over an hour ago, doing my best charade of dehydration, I pleaded with the sentinel. Reluctantly deciding to admit one of us, he called over a maintenance man in a boilersuit and baseball cap. His mop leaving puddles as he dragged it behind him, he led me to a rusty, dripping tap, but having come this far without being poisoned, I wasn't going to risk it now. Brandishing my water bottle at him and smiling inanely, he begrudgingly trudged past a succession of shut down kafes with decorative plastic birds hanging from the ceiling. Beyond a gaudy carousel which didn't look particularly entertaining, on the third-floor success was had at an unfrequented shashlyk stand, the woman behind the counter wiping a layer of dust from two small bottles.

Through a window, I noted that although its pods hadn't moved, there was the odd person sitting on the Ferris wheel, waiting patiently to be afforded a view of towers, saplings and cranes. Like the new mass weddings compound, the Palace of Happiness - the world's largest star shaped architectural feature, stuck on a scorched hill at the edge of town - it all struck a rather glum aspect.

Back in the ceaseless sun and hair drier wind, our water rapidly boiled and evaporated. Followed by two militsiyamen, we finally thumbed a ride in a random car circling the city. With everyone observing the speed limit during daylight hours, tyres screeched softly on the melting tarmac. Upon a giant LCD TV screen, an advert for the Alem Centre was playing, the lights, bling and excitement a far cry from the lustreless reality.

Berzengi

Except for nine highways which bore the moniker of Niyazov, his family and personal heroes, the wide thoroughfares of Ashgabat had all been renamed by number. This being the fourth name change since the nineties, it came as no surprise that our taksi driver didn't know where he was going. Nobody knew where anything was.

Its arcs like a titanic clam shell, we drove past the optimistically named Olympic Stadium. On Independence Day, North Korean style celebrations would take place here, children who'd been excused from school for weeks to learn dance routines parading beneath the President' s skybox. With soldiers handing out flags and orchestrating cheers, leaving early was not an option for those forced to attend.

Losing faith in our leadfoot, we decided to hike across an anomalously overgrown section of Independence Park to the Altyn Asyr (Golden Age) Shopping Centre in Ashgabat's Berzengi District. Resembling a colossal, seven-tiered wedding cake, until recently it had claimed the world's largest fountain, but having been outdone by South Korea, the water features were summarily switched off. The antenna-topped forty million dollar marble pyramid reflected in its now still pools, figures of pert breasted women with long braided hair held aloft dry ewers. Ashgabat has the most fountains of any city in the world, this contrasting sharply with the life of most residents, who don't have unbroken access to running water.

The bulk of its metal shutters firmly drawn, inside most of the units were vacant, the remaining staff pacing somnolently. A gold-plated elevator replete with a piped muzak version of 'Somewhere over the rainbow' took us to the fifth floor Minara Restaurant, purportedly one of the capital's finest dining establishments. We were the only patrons. Through the restaurant's filthy windows, a panoramic view of Ashgabat revealed residential areas. Concrete jungles reminiscent of a prison, satellite dishes - a lone connection to the outside world - vied for space on the rooftops. In the distance, clouds were billowing from a slew of construction sites, more towers set to rise.

Back in Independence Park, giant monitors showing men in white telpeks dancing for their President played to no one. Everything was flawless beneath the cloudless sky, not a stone out of place in the litter-free synthetic city. Fountains gushed wastefully along perfectly linear paths that led to nowhere in particular. Turkmenistan is two and a half times more profligate in its use of water than the next worst culprit in the world.

Sudden and urgent diarrhoea overcoming Stan, there was no making it back to the Altyn Asyr. With limited tree cover, he hunkered down on the grass and delivered his payload. The lack of privacy wasn't too big of an issue; there wasn't a soul to be seen. When a gardener did appear some time later, Stan looked sheepish about the dirty gift that awaited this hapless soul.

'I had no choice in the matter,' he assured me.

The immaculate junkyard of futuristic kitsch, Roman Doric columns, domes and pinnacles stretching on for klicks, every fifty metres public address speakers sprung from the soil on tall metal struts, ensuring the good word of the President would be heard by all. At the far end of the park lurked the unfrequented Ashgabat Independence Monument. An architectural monstrosity illuminated in hot pink at night, its round base and single lofty column had resulted in its apt nickname of "the plunger."

We circled back to the pink and green Ruhnama Monument, an outsized testament to the once holy book. Ringed with gold, at its centre sat a bust of Turkmenbashi, looking far more dapper than he'd ever done in real life. At the foot of the sculpture a multi-headed eagle, similar to that used by the Hittites, Romans and the Russian Emperor had an added Medusa effect. More was better.

In the dying evening light, we lingered for some time wondering if the fabled book would open as promised in documentaries to display episodes from Turkmen history on its movie screen pages, or if its motor was currently burnt out. With nobody to ask, though, and it being unlikely they'd know even if there was, we left the book to its solitary spot, consigned to a past most would rather forget.

With the Kopet Dag Mountains to the south and new marble monoliths on its flanks, the north of Independence Park was fronted by the Mir 2 residential district. In the parking lots of smarter estates bordering the park, freshly waxed Lexus and Hyundai gleamed. Behind these blocks, older digs were concealed. Faceless and monotonous, Constructivist strips with porthole windows were demarcated into areas by their faded paintwork, the peach zone giving way to the yellow zone, the green to the pink. Grime clogged air-con units projecting from the walls, lines of laundry were strung storeys high across adjacent blocks roofed with asbestos sheets. Herded into these cramped living quarters when Ashgabat's traditional locales were bulldozed, there was simply no other space left for people after the ministries and monuments had been erected.

Turkmenistan Good

Sweating over a last few jars of frosty Zip pivo in the Bar Bar, we wondered whether we'd be able to hail a ride to the airport in the middle of the night and, if so, whether we could afford to pay for it. Checking out at four thirty

AM, though, our concerns proved to have been unfounded, the only two cars on the street affecting screeching U-turns to compete for our business.

'Turkmenistan beautiful,' I said, giving the thumbs-up in an attempt to befriend our driver and procure a fare we could manage.
'Beautiful? No,' he answered, dolefully shaking his head. 'No.'

At Saparmurat Turkmenbashi International Airport, with the control tower having been built on the wrong side of the runway, the angular terminal building blocked the view of air traffic controller's attempting to guide pilots. Warned of this flaw, the authorities had simply responded, 'it looks better this way.'

Four bag scans and seven passport checks followed. The last three checkpoints situated within forty metres of each other, officials watched comrades perform their duties before diligently repeating the process. Flicking interminably through my passport, the final bureaucrat gazed at the array of stamps and stickers before wearily mumbling,

' *Tranzitnaya viza* problema.'

His cautionary words ringing in our ears, he disappeared with our documents.

'What are they going to do,' I whispered to Stan as the minutes ticked by, 'not let us leave? Extort us for our last three manat?'

Returning from a mirrored office, the sombre official eased his cheeks back into a squeaky plastic highchair.

'Turkmenistan good?' he asked, as his exit stamp finally fell.

PART **III**

CHAPTER 21

Transit Blues

On the flight out of Istanbul, a scuffle broke out over whose bag had most right to occupy the chock-full overhead luggage compartment.

'Calm down!' a distinctly agitated man shouted.

'You! You calm down!' the other hollered, bristling moustache up close and personal in the first fellow's face.

'You make my daughters cry! My daughter's crying because of you,' a woman lamented, wringing her hands.

'I call the police,' another man interjected, as escalating into handbags, the storage wars continued.

Escorted away by a steward with his offending knapsack in tow, the loser's porpoise grey eyes shot daggers, sweat streaming from behind his ears and glistening as it trickled down the nape of his neck.

Five and a half hours later, we landed in the Kazakh second city of Almaty, skimming like a stone along the runway to spontaneous applause.

Buffeted by the throng, we arrived at Passport Control, where citizens of partner nations forming the new Eurasian Customs Union – all Russians – were fast-tracked through. Resignedly forming a rigidly straight queue in order to be permitted back into their homeland, the Kazakhs inched towards the double lateral booth.

Following extensive scrutiny, we emerged from the terminal building to be greeted by a stock of eager biznizmen.

'Vy govorit'e pa Russki?' a tout blurted. 'Taksi, da? Taksi *myetr,*' he continued, unfazed by our limited comprehension.

Patting me on the back, he broke into a doom-laden laugher.

'*Traffik problemy,*' he pressed, tapping at his watch to indicate that although it was only five AM, rush hour would soon begin.

Angling away from the airport, the wide roads featured the standard array of pre-fab blocks. On islands in the highway, French marigolds bloomed at the white painted feet of perfectly round topiary trees. As we headed towards the distant, snow-capped Tien Shan Mountains, the sun rose over the outskirts of Almaty. English language pop songs cutting in and out on the radio, Beemas, Land Cruisers and rusting relics mingled on the freshly laid asphalt. Speed guns to hand as they stood beside their standard issue Lada Nivas, the politsiya had gotten a bum deal in the vehicle stakes.

Sprawling suburban blocks replaced by a twilight zone, the streets became flooded with casinos and car showrooms. Multiple Aqualand outlets appeared, giant plastic pools propped against storefronts. A statue of a warrior on horseback and the golden dome of the Central Mosque on Pushkin Street marking our arrival in the city centre, we drew to a halt at the Hotel Turkistan, the cheapest digs in town.

Snatching a pen from his dashboard, the oblong-faced driver scratched a figure on a piece of paper, drumming upon it insistently. Craning from the backseat, I noted with consternation that he'd scribbled '13,000' - over seventy US dollars - for a twenty-minute ride. Anticipating our protests, he reached for the glove box, producing a well-worn document in Cyrillic which probably stated that it was one thousand tenge per kilometre. Unable to read it, but too exhausted to do anything but steam and slam the doors, we acquiesced. It was robbery by laminate.

Trade and Transgression

Permitted to check into the neglected hotel six hours early, with neither of the elevators working, we hauled our bags up the deliciously pink stairwell.

Obscured behind a pile of dirty dishes, our room was located on the fifth floor in a long, tenebrous corridor. Tossing my bag upon the bed, I took in our surroundings. A single plug socket dangled from the watermarked wall above a boxy television which picked up no channels. Given a whack, the air-con unit whirred into life, spurting creamy goo over the balcony doors.

'All told, it's not so bad,' I said.
'We've stayed in far worse,' Stan concurred.

Beyond a slim, perilously low balustrade, our accommodations looked out over the corrugated roofs of the turquoise painted Zelyony Bazaar, almost pretty beneath serried, thistle-grey clouds. It was a quarter to six in the morning and stallholders were beginning to arrive, pausing at a canteen for a quick breakfast of horsemeat sausage and a bowl of sour cream, cardamom and fennel chay. Propelling himself upon stubby sticks, an amputee beggar left a trail of polyurethane, padding spilling from his polymer wrapped stumps. Settling on a position he hoped would prove advantageous, he placed a tin mug upon the ground.

With its oblique pyramids of dried fruit and hall of butchers in blood-smeared white coats, Zelyony was fast becoming Almaty's largest bazaar, largely because its chief rival, Barakholka kept going up in flames. Hugely profitable and completely unregulated, at its peak 180,000 people worked in the Barakholka complex, but a power struggle in the grey area between government and organised crime has seen traders fall on hard times.

Seven fires having struck in the space of fourteen months, witnesses told STV's *Territory Accidents* that when a blaze broke out in November 2013, security guards sat on their hands for over an hour before calling the emergency services. Costing billions of tenge in damage, eight weeks earlier another incident had caused pillars of smoke visible throughout Almaty, helicopters assisting 1,518 firefighters to extinguish the conflagration. Blamed on a range of causes from 'incautious welding' to an 'unattended candle,' the single episode officially adjudged arson was ruled to have been an inside job. Despite the fact this is highly unlikely, the Tengri News network dutifully reported that 'during the fire outsiders was not there.'

We took a bus to Barakholka, rumbling down the ten lane highway. Abaft of the rubble-strewn periphery, rows of blackened sheds and shipping containers led to a warren of metal pitches. Porters shoved overstuffed carts, bawling at us if we got in their way. From pageant dresses and knitted woollen bobble slippers to gleaming meat cleavers and two-dimensional paintings of horses, if you wanted it, chances are it was there.

At the entrance to a building resembling an aircraft hangar, two competing DJ's pumping their tunes sat with CD mixers balanced upon pairs of speakers. Inside, a woman with sagging jowls sat sandwiched between the display racks of her stall. The only merchant we encountered that could speak English, between half-heartedly trying to interest us in knock-off Chinese sunglasses, she bellyached above the din about her plight.

'Nobody here,' she grumbled, throwing her hands. 'Nobody know Barakholka open. Everybody think we all burned.'

The government long having planned to demolish the bazaar and replace it with a gentrified mall somewhere between a spaceport and a humongous white snail in appearance, those whose livelihoods depend upon Barakholka smell a conspiracy. Vendors would be welcome to return once the new structure is completed, the authorities have assured them, but only at vastly inflated rents.

As Barakholka struggles, a massive free trade zone has opened in the barrens of Khorgos on the Chinese border. A bone-crunching five hours from Almaty - the nearest Kazakh city of note - it was designed as a visa and tax-free arena where citizens of the two countries could shop and enjoy local entertainments. On the Chinese side, one can buy the latest tech and stay in a choice of upmarket hotels. With plans for a Disneyland-style theme park having stalled, on the Kazakh side a limited selection of candy is offered from a sprinkling of shipping containers.

The Kazakh government having put more effort into barricades than facilitating commerce, a line of barbed wire fences lay underground beneath a rubber seal, ready to spring into action. Corruption hasn't helped matters;

the Head of Customs at Khorgos was arrested in 2011 as part of a massive smuggling ring. A few days later, the sacking of the country's Customs Chief for his alleged complicity was announced via Twitter. Unsurprisingly, neither man has been heard from since being taken into custody.

Panfilov Park

A block behind the Zelyony Bazaar, at the entrance to Panfilov Park stood a statue of Bauyrzhan Momyshuly, Kazakh-born soldier, author and Hero of the Soviet Union. Momyshuly served under Major General Ivan Panfilov, whose name now graces parks throughout the region. Volunteering for the campaign to put down the Basmachi revolt, a series of promotions saw Panfilov named Chief of Staff of the Central Asian Military District in 1937. Redeployed to the Battle of Moscow in 1941, under threat of execution should they retreat, Panfilov's 316th Rifle Division suffered heavy losses. An overblown but popular story tells how twenty-eight of Panfilov's men destroyed eighteen German tanks, grinding the Nazi advance to a standstill. With the People's Commissar of Defence passing a decree that his unit's status be upgraded in recognition of their service, Panfilov called a press conference, during which he was killed in a mortar attack.

On a plinth next to the Jinnah-capped Momyshuly, youngsters scaled the chamber of a divisional "Stalin gun." Women in jogging bottoms and big, dark sunglasses wheeled pushchairs down paths shaded by tall evergreens which stretched onto Almaty's premier sight, the Ascension Cathedral. Also known as the Zenkov after its designer, beneath its candy chequered domes and golden turrets, the cathedral glowed in shades of yellow, the lower levels that could be reached without a ladder having seen a lick of paint more recently.

Completed in 1907, the church is one of the few Tsarist era buildings to have survived a massive earthquake which struck Almaty in 1911, this despite being made entirely of wood, right down to the nails. At the time of the quake, bishops swore it must have been saved by God, but this didn't stop the authorities using it as a concert hall and then to house radio transmitters before boarding it up completely. The structure was finally returned to the Russian Orthodox Church in 1995.

Hovering in the narthex of the church, a couple of men with cattail whips were enjoying a spot of self-flagellation. In the nave, women in headscarves that appeared to be Muslims crossed themselves beneath a burnished iconostasis. Perhaps it was a shared superstition, but there was no harm in hedging one's bets. Either way, in their long, black vestments, despite their acerbic countenances, the priests looked immensely satisfied.

Outside the cathedral, traders hawked caged doves to be released by the faithful for a price. Other entrepreneurs had hauled out life-sized models of Shrek and Donkey for toddlers to have their pictures taken with. Speeding in and out of photographer's shots, children on rollerblades watched as their older brothers pulled stunts on neon framed BMX bikes, feats they hoped to one day emulate.

Circumnavigating the park, a gilded carriage was propelled by two graceful white mares.

'I bet they'll end up in a tin,' remarked Stan.

We followed the droshky west to a formidable war memorial featuring soldiers from each of the fifteen Soviet Socialist Republics. Bursting forth from a map of the dead empire, their muscular forms surveyed a pink tuff square centred on an eternal flame so small it could've been a genie in a matchbox. Drawn like moths to a candle, successions of wedding guests were having their portraits taken. In puffy white dresses, the brides seemed reasonably eager. Lingering on the tree lined periphery in tight cream suits and lime green ties, their chain-smoking, balding blonde Russian grooms looked less enthusiastic.

Father of Apples

I'd heard that Almaty was Central Asia's most cosmopolitan city, vibrant, oil-rich and shimmering with glassy new skyscrapers, but any thoughts of a space age

Dubai were quickly dispelled. On the concrete thoroughfares, the few pedestrians appeared drowsy from the humid midsummer heat. Portraits of local dignitaries kept watch over neglected gardens, where malformed plastic models of foals were planted in front of derelict buildings. Sprouting from an empty car park, a scale replica of the Eiffel Tower dwarfed a five storey mall once dedicated solely to French perfumes. The capital having been moved to the hinterlands of Astana on a whim of the President, most officials and their families had left Almaty, the former capital exuding a feeling that life was now elsewhere.

The site of a Silk Road oasis laid waste by the Mongols, the modern history of Alma-Ata - literally 'Father of Apples' - began with the construction of a Russian piedmont fort in 1854, around which a minor provincial centre grew. Upon hearing that Trotsky had been exiled to Alma-Ata in 1928, one of his enemies quipped that 'even if he dies there, we won't hear of it soon.' Married to the outside world by the arrival of the Turkestan-Siberia Railway in 1930, the advent of World War II saw Nazi-threatened factories and their workforces relocated from the Eastern Bloc. At the same time, an influx of forcibly resettled Koreans arrived from Russia's Far-East, the population of the city increasing tenfold within thirty years.

Against a backdrop of show trials and purges, between August and October of 1937, 171,781 ethnic Korean-Soviet citizens were deported to Kazakhstan and Uzbekistan. Distrustful of where their loyalties lay, the official rationale behind the first mass transfer of an entire nationality within the USSR was to stem the 'penetration of Japanese espionage into the Far Eastern Krai.' Deposited throughout the steppe, often without food and shelter, thousands perished before the first wave of refugees began to find their way to Alma-Ata. Approximately half a million ethnic Koreans still reside in the former Soviet Union, primarily in Central Asia.

Passing one of Almaty's numerous Korean restaurants, we chanced upon the building which had served as Trotsky's first residence in the city. Then the Hotel Dzheysya, today it is a nondescript district sanitary surveillance office.

'The town had no central waterworks, no lights, and no paved roads,' Trotsky wrote of his time in Alma-Ata. 'In the bazaar in the centre of town, the Kirghizes sat in the mud at the doorsteps of their shops, warming themselves in the sun and searching their bodies for vermin. Malaria was rampant. There was also pestilence, and during the summer months an extraordinary number of mad dogs. The newspapers reported many cases of leprosy in this region.'

In the south of the city, where Almaty rises towards the Tien Shan Mountains, Respublika Alangy is the Soviet era ceremonial centre of the old capital. In this wide open space, a clutch of new monuments celebrate the nationhood Kazakhs once so vehemently opposed, ninety-five percent of respondents voting to preserve the USSR in a referendum of March 1991.

At the foot of the Monument to Independence, a semi-circular bronze relief depicts ten scenes from Kazakh history. Never one to underplay his importance, on the final panel President Nazarbayev stands at a lectern, his people in receding rows behind him. Atop a lofty column, a replica of the popular national symbol, the Golden Man soars upon a winged snow leopard. Discovered in 1969, bedecked in an ornate ceremonial suit, this figure dating from 500BC was largely ignored at the time as it didn't fit with Soviet historiography. Warrior chieftains being proletarian, it would've been politically incorrect for one to be found in a bourgeois Scythian burial kurgan.

Using permafrost to preserve the deceased, the kurgan was a tumulus - a mound of stones heaped over a deep wooden chamber - into which the dead were laid to rest surrounded by their horses, the number of steeds a reflection of their status. Believers in the afterlife, horses acted as psychopomps to the Scythians, leading souls to the next realm.

Rivalling the relics of Ancient Egypt, the workmanship of the Golden Man artefacts reveals a philosophical people with a strong mythology and an understanding of the cosmos. Recently, some archaeologists have begun to posit that the Golden Man may, in fact, be a woman. Queens, leaders and formidable combatants, the Greek legend of the Amazons was likely based upon the Scythians. Whatever the truth may be, in typical Kazakh fashion this symbol of nationhood is kept under lock and key in a vault of the National Bank, far away from the public's gaze.

At the western edge of the ceremonial area, on an intersection adorned with a bed of roses, Respublika Alangy meets with a street formerly known as Peace, but since renamed Jeltoqsan (December) to mark the events which took place there. On December 17ᵗʰ 1986, thousands gathered to protest against the long-serving ethnic Kazakh First Secretary of the Communist Party of Kazakhstan being replaced by a Russian. In response to their swelling numbers, the Central Committee ordered the KGB, troops from the Ministry of Interior Affairs and *druzhinki* – "volunteers" – to disperse what the Russian news agency TASS referred to as 'hooligans [and] parasites.'

Estimates of the number killed during clashes which took place over the next three days vary from Moscow's claim of two dead to the US Library of Congress' reports of at least two hundred. Marking these events, the Dawn of Liberty Monument features a maiden with arms outstretched in invocation, seemingly struggling to break free, but tethered to two jagged blocks representing the past and the future.

Dreams of the Sea#1

Finally opened in 2011 after twenty-three years in the making, in the ticket halls of the Almaty Metro, underemployed women in eighties style stewardess uniforms with ridged triangular hats sold plastic tokens. Beyond the turnstiles, vertiginous escalators descended, their handrails giving off static shocks. Long and claustrophobic, the pristine, surveillance camera heavy platforms were decorated in monotonal colours, geometric shapes, chandeliers and strip-lights.

Each of the eight stations boasting a slightly different design, the most striking was named after Baikonur – the Russian Cosmodrome in the middle of the Kazakh steppe - where a clip of a rocket launch played on a loop to a mildly appreciative audience. Tashkent it was not, but unlike Uzbekistan where snap happy punters could wind up in jail, despite photography being prohibited, everyone was busy taking selfies. Currently used largely for joy-rides, local media reports that newlyweds seeking a change of scenery are among the networks most frequent passengers.

A hundred metres from Abay Metro, the sprawling Kazakh National Pedagogical University was the country's first seat of higher learning when it opened in 1928. Alongside signs at its entrance prohibiting the carrying of firearms on campus, posters advertising opportunities to study abroad sported the tagline 'Get out of Kazakhstan.' Given official concern regarding a 'brain drain,' it appeared to be a popular sentiment.

With Stan's dissertation in mind, the overriding goal of our third Central Asian odyssey was to visit the Small Aral Sea and take salinity readings. This data would then be coupled with global satellite images in the near-infrared scale to form the basis of a series of permutations so painstakingly scientific that the thought of them caused the blood to drain from my face.

Celebrating something of a rebirth, the Small Aral is now only twelve kilometres from the city of Aralsk, as opposed to the hundred kilometres it was a decade ago. By way of contrast, in 2014 intensive irrigation coupled with low levels of precipitation in the Pamir Mountains saw the eastern lobe of the Large Aral in Uzbekistan dry up completely for the first time in recorded history.

Entering the labyrinthine interior of the university, we set out in search of Kristopher White, an American geographer ten years an Associate Professor at KIMEP who'd been part of Phillip Micklin's Aral expedition in 2011. Trailing a nimble-footed secretary through spiralling stairwells, we eventually arrived at his office.

'Ah, you found me! How you doing?' the tall, brawny Professor boomed, rising from behind his cluttered desk to clasp our hands.

With all five of the Central Asian nations numbering amongst the worst water wasters on the planet, we talked about the likelihood of any change to the status quo.

'When the region was part of the USSR, upstream states were provided with winter electricity and heat under the centralized Soviet system. Irrigation construction and function was also dictated by Moscow.

At independence this all changed,' White said as he dug through scattered storage boxes. 'Improvements in irrigation efficiency are being tested and implemented at a fairly small and localized scale,' he continued. 'Plenty of international assistance has been directed at this, but for the region's two main cotton producers, Uzbekistan and Turkmenistan, there's no incentive to move away from cotton. The economic repercussions make it a near impossibility.'

Producing a manila envelope, White spread his photos from 2011 over the mélange of documents on his industrial steel desk.

'Man,' he whispered, momentarily transported, 'I just gotta get back to the sea.'

Appleness

Opposite the university, a cul-de-sac led to a cable car which ascended the 1,100 metre Kok-Tobe (Green Hill) above the city. Judging from the queues, we weren't the only ones who'd decided that escaping downtown would be a fine way to see out the afternoon on this sweltering Saturday in July.

Negotiating the melee, we boarded the swinging car, a piped soundtrack of mullet-tastic German band Dschinghis Khan's enthusiastic "Moskau!" broken by jittery gasps every time the *vagon* plummeted from a stanchion. Climbing above barking dogs through the suburbs, the cabin ground to a halt at the top of the mesa, where wrapped in ragged greatcoats despite the heat, a guild of beggars sat rattling scantly-filled receptacles.

The first sight to greet visitors to Kok-Tobe is a granite statue of an apple with water gushing from its core. The closest translation for Almaty - renamed in 1993 for the third time in a century - is 'Appleness,' though practically all the city's orchards have been felled. Beyond this good orb, a plethora of fairground attractions included a shooting gallery with feathered plastic chickens for targets and a hair-raising ride known as the Fast Coaster. Located on the far side of the crest, the only rollercoaster in Kazakhstan involved single occupancy fibreglass cars, which pleasure-seekers clung to the sides of whilst careening over sheer drops. If this wasn't hazardous enough, a climbing area suspended from ropes enticed adrenalin junkies with the promise of plummeting onto the concrete path should a pedestrian's head not break their fall.

Farther into the park was an area known as the Lane of Enamoured Ones. The most popular photo opportunity for women in Almaty, it seemed, was to have your picture taken emerging from various states of entanglement in the bushes here. Cameras dangling from their necks, suitors stood with their lenses at the ready.

On the opposite side of the hill, a rather sad zoo featured scrawny goats and pikat. There were four colly birds, three hens of indeterminate origin and two turtle doves, but the partridge had long since died and the pear tree been put through the wood chipper. At a table loaded with cups filled with rotting cabbage and carrots, an industrious woman attempted to part parent's from their tenge so their children could feed the miserable creatures. From behind the wire mesh fence, a lonely ostrich kicked up clouds of dust.

Saving the best till last, the concluding sight was a cast bronze of the Beatles. Erected in 1997, it once claimed to be the only statue in the world of the "fab four" together. Kissing their metallic likenesses, laughing old dames hung from their necks. It all felt a bit incongruous until I spoke to Gabit Sagatov.

'The spirit of Beatlemania is huge in Almaty,' he told me, 'so it's natural that the first monument to the Beatles to be built in the CIS should be here.'

Gabit Sagatov grew up in Kyzylorda, a sleepy provincial capital in the Kyzyl-Kum Desert, shortly to be our next port of call.

'Ever since I was a child, I loved singing,' he said, pushing his mop-top to one side. 'I sang the songs of Kazakh artists and songs from popular Soviet movies. In 1974, I heard the Beatles for the first time.

I was shocked; it changed my musical perception dramatically. Their music started a craze of young people playing the guitar. You could hear people practising in all the courtyards. Desks in the high school were inscribed with graffiti in English, things like "I Love Beatles." I tried to imitate them in my clothing, in everything. I began to grow long hair. My headmaster chastised me for it.

'In 1975, my friend and I created an English language group, singing Beatles, Rolling Stones and Slade covers. On TV and in the media at the time, there was no information about Western pop music. We listened to Voice of America and the BBC, recorded it on tape and passed it on. I painted a portrait of John Lennon and Paul McCartney and hung it in my room. My father would say to his friends as a joke, "this room belongs to our relative who lives in the city of Liverpool in distant England".'

I asked Gabit how the regime had reacted to this Western phenomena being embraced so wholeheartedly.

'We didn't feel much pressure,' he said. 'Komsomol [the Leninist Youth Communist League] members were Beatles fans themselves. Hundreds of thousands of boys and girls and later millions of people in the USSR succumbed to Beatlemania. The authorities couldn't ignore the stupendous amount of interest. LPs with Beatles songs like "Octopus's garden" and "Come together" began to appear in stores, though it wasn't written on them that they were Beatles songs. I still have those records.'

Sagatov's fifteen minutes of fame came in 1993, courtesy of the BBC documentary series *Holidays in the Danger Zone*, for which his band the Kazakh Beatles were invited to play at the renowned Cavern Club, where his heroes' careers had begun.

'We did two gigs at the Beatle Week Festival in Liverpool. I've played in London and Washington,' he told me proudly. 'I'll email you a photo of me crossing Abbey Road.'

Descending in the crammed *funikulera*, the seventies soundtrack had moved onto Boney M's "Rasputin." Despite the weekend being in full swing, however, the mild sense of excitement found on Kok-Tobe wasn't replicated in the city centre. On Zhibek Zholi - Silk Road - the main nightlife hub, the low streetlights were wasted on one man and his dog. Anchored in an inactive fountain centred on a mossy stork, a redundant sign prohibited swimming, though the stagnant waters were only centimetres deep. In the Tirol Bar, a few men were joylessly watching the World Cup. Only once it became clear which side would prevail did they decide they were Germany fans. Everyone loves a winner.

Heading back to our hotel, we found ourselves drawn towards the only hint of a pulse, the thumping doof escaping from the Keremet - Love is Everything Discotheque. Ascending the stairs and shuffling past a pair of bewildered looking bouncers, we entered a world of vinyl seats and gingham tablecloths beamed in from the seventies. Beneath erratic spotlights and a strobe which poked one in the eyes, a smattering of girls in long flowery dresses and their boyfriends in drainpipes, white shirts and black pencil ties were whirling like dervishes. Three sheets to the wind, we soon cleared the dance floor, raising eyebrows with our moves. The choice of tunes though, couldn't sustain our drunken brio.

'Got any Pixies?' Stan ascended a wooden trellis to ask the confused DJ, but alas, it wasn't to be.

'Well,' I said to Stan as we rolled back down the stairwell to the cries of taksi drivers, 'I'm not much of a fan personally, but in there the Beatles would've been a godsend.'

CHAPTER 22

Red Capital

S wiftly airborne, we soared over the lifeless, cracked ridges of Bet-pak-Dala, the 'Unlucky Plain' of the Hungry Steppe. From the rear of the airbus, a laboured groaning emanated, which one could only hope was somebody having a moment in the tua-let. In front of my over-wing seat, a key protruded from the emergency exit, the tag fastened to it admonishing the cabin crew: 'DANGER. IMPORTANT. REMOVE BEFORE TAKE OFF.' Whilst our Air Astana plane might have been banned in the EU until recently, at least during the last couple of years a clutch of small Kazakh operators whose safety record had led to the collective nickname "Air Maybe" had gone belly up.

A canal snaking into view, the land below arced and swirled like a fingerprint as the city of Kyzylorda emerged from the void. Descending, we skimmed along the tarmac, where a double-winged plane and a snub-nosed helicopter were dwarfed by giant scarecrows reminiscent of *The Wicker Man*. Casting long shadows, eerie and still they stood guarding the empty space.

Inside the terminal building, people in sweatpants, Union Jack and NYC t-shirts milled about reclaiming luggage and relatives. High on the wall above a banner declaring support for the local football team, a plethora of Zhanros Drilling sponsored clocks marked the hour in London, Moscow and Astana, though the time wasn't right on any of them.

Beyond the parking lot, skeletal trees rose from the sand and scrub. Every fifty metres a billboard displayed an image of President Nazarbayev or his militsiya, boom barrier checkpoints tethered by boulders equally as ubiquitous. Approaching the Syr Darya River, a statue of a warrior on horseback welcomed visitors to the city. Across the shimmering lifeline, next to rows of photostat, ostensibly uninhabited pink blocks, horses foraged at the side of the road where plastic tulips five metres tall were set to be illuminated at night. Not content with this, giant flower sculptures were cast in the shape of butterflies, clocks and teapots.

Snatching the taksi sign from his roof with a gnarled hand, our driver, Samad steered with his knees, honking nonchalantly and signalling in acknowledgment when sporadic traffic sped by. Despite having initially said he knew where he was going, it came as no surprise that he didn't have a clue.

Cruising through the low suburbs, we zipped by the Gany Muratbayev Stadium of FC Kaysar, their red and black badge sporting a choleric looking beast which resembled a werewolf. The club having been renamed seven times since being founded in 1968, one couldn't blame them for having an identity crisis.

Drawing towards the centre, dumpy, cubic blocks overlooked clusters of traffic lights on the unerringly flat streets. With Samad alternately circling or reversing at speed as the meter ran wild, giving up on accommodation, we decided to procure supplies and head straight for the train station to wait it out. This proved to be a big mistake.

'*Kazhdyy*,' Samad bawled in mock consternation as I handed him a fistful of tenge. It was the same old story, whatever the meter read, that was the fare per person.

A historic Silk Road centre, briefly the capital of Soviet Kazakhstan in the 1920s, Kyzylorda - meaning 'Red Capital' - is now a provincial backwater, its relative prosperity underpinned by Chinese oil and gas ventures in the desert. These 'middle lands of the yellow steppes,' as revered Kyrgyz author Chingiz Aitmatov described them, are also home to the Baikonur Cosmodrome, the first and largest spaceport in the world.

Originally constructed during the Cold War as a missile test site, it was from Baikonur that Yuri Gagarin became the first man to leave the Earth in 1961. Officially Russian territory on Kazakh soil, Vladimir Putin appoints the mayor of this city leased out at an annual rate of a hundred and fifteen million dollars. Still home to Russian lift-offs despite growing environmental concerns, the Kazakh government recently signed a new deal allowing their neighbour to stay until at least 2050. 'We would like Russia to stay at Baikonur forever,' former cosmonaut and current head of the Aerospace Agency of Kazakhstan, Talgat Musabayev declared.

Reliant on proton fuel, launches from the site cause carcinogens, acid rain, and are conceivably responsible for herds of critically endangered saiga antelope being found dead. Attempting to circumvent Kazakhstan's strict laws, campaigners against the base have taken to staging lone protests, often with a cosmic bent. After Kazakhstan's space chief dismissed demonstrators as 'sick' in January 2013, an activist turned up at the site dressed as an alien in a mock attempt to kidnap the supremo and take him to Mars.

Whilst residents of the oblast have been hospitalized and farmers complain about the debris from rockets crushing their horses, some will be glad to see the spaceport stay. Darting across the desert, the regions scrap metal dealers have built a thriving micro-industry upon scavenging fragments which fall from the sky.

The Vokzal Politsiya

The city centre had a listless quality. A frontier feel to the wide streets, the population of Kyzylorda felt a far cry from the supposed figure of 186,000. Watching us intently from the shade afforded by apartment blocks, gangs of children were amused by our presence. They weren't alone. In a town where a zoo filled with animals fashioned from cement passed as entertainment, this didn't come as a great surprise. Kicking a can along as they tailed us, the kids' interest was a sentiment shared by shopkeepers, none of whom had any change. Out of water, it took multiple attempts in an underground mall where the politsiya smirked malevolently before we found a trader willing to break a banknote.

Arriving at the train station with five hours to spare, we propped ourselves against a wall, settling in for the long haul. Built in 1905 and daubed in the same shade of goldenrod yellow as the lower reaches of the Zenkov Cathedral, the late-imperial architecture of the Kyzylorda Vokzal resembled nothing more than a wedding cake that'd been sat upon. On the side of an adjoining building, a Soviet mural portrayed a heroic peasant couple bearing a scythe and a chaff of wheat as boats which had become increasingly distant sailed by in the background.

Our arrival at the station was met by grinning men with bulging eyes, but at least the peak capped politsiya initially ignored us. Hunkered down in a slither of shade, we peered out across the tracks where metallic sleeper carriages slumbered, waiting for life to arrive. With more wagons being added to trains, it seemed the most interesting thing to do in Kyzylorda was to leave.

In the ticket office-cum-waiting room, pastel paint peeled from the walls. Women fanned themselves to the flat echo of ticking clocks. In a canteen thickset with dead insects in pools of grease, with nothing but time to spend, men wearing Chinese goods - chiefly t-shirts emblazoned with American flags - eyed us suspiciously. Approaching the counter, I ascertained that nothing bar soggy pastries was going to happen.

Back on the platform, our good fortune didn't last. A moon-faced blue shirt with a wooden baton stopping to question us, our inability to understand him led to a rapid deterioration in our situation.

'*Pa idyom sa mnoy,*' he set to bellowing, beckoning for us to follow.

That one of the three tiny rooms in the Vokzal Politsiya Office was a prison cell didn't bode well. From behind his desk, the head of operations sneered as he assessed our dishevelled shapes through bloodshot clay brown eyes.

'*Dayte minya vash pasporta,*' he began with a curdling smile which metastasized to his entourage.

A bowl cut, dirty blonde ethnic Russian in a red and white pinstripe clown suit started chortling, which triggered a fit of the giggles from a man with a pink shirt tucked into his ball hugging nylon blue trousers, his one inch of ginger hair rigid with product.

'Turist? ' the boss continued knowingly as he flicked through our papers.
'Da, turist,' I responded with a false bonhomie.
'Good, good,' he muttered, wiping away beads of sweat which had loosed themselves from beneath his cap.

Shuffling in the limited space, sidekick number one, the Cushingoid-faced simpleton moved to block the exit. His mouth drawn into an 'O' as if astonished, perhaps he couldn't believe his luck in having stumbled upon us.

Directing that our bags be brought to him, overlord had a minion place them on his desk. Beaming as he rifled through our possessions, he wrenched my camera from its pouch, chuckling as he mimicked taking snapshots of his posse. Dismissing the hard case full of Stan's scientific equipment - which looked highly suspect to the layman, but was no doubt far beyond their comprehension - he shoved it to one side. Clearly it didn't look like the path to a quick buck.

Particularly impressive by virtue of their nickel-brass outer circle and cupronickel interior were the British two-pound coins and heptagonal fifty pence pieces lifted from my wallet. These novelties slid off the desk, disappearing into a drawer with a hollow clunk. More stirring still was the fifty dollar bill tucked in the back of my wallet. No sooner had they found the money than there were 'problemy' - multiple problems - overlord flicking his neck with an index finger, an action his monkeys picked up on and replicated. It was quite a sight.

Despite never having seen this gesture before, it was immediately apparent to me what it meant. Legend has it that in the time of Peter the Great there lived a great shipbuilder who happened to be a raging alcoholic. So enamoured was the Tsar with his workmanship, that he awarded the fellow a certificate which shown in any tavern would entitle him to free vodka. The only trouble was that in his drunken state, the souse kept losing the deed.

After inking multiple replacements, Peter became weary of the inconvenience and had his seal branded on the man's neck, thus enabling the craftsman to roll into any establishment and drink his fill free of charge simply by flicking his neck.

Whilst pretty hungover, however, we hadn't touched a drop. This didn't stop them from inviting Stan to enjoy the hospitality of their jail though, its bars painted a fetching shade of ballet slipper pink. Even as 'O' face indicated the cell, we played along, Stan meekly complying.

'*Idty*, go!' they hollered, flaring their nostrils and demanding I leave.

Knowing that my brother had over a thousand dollars hidden in the lining of his equipment case, I grabbed all of our bags, my ridiculously over encumbered form reflected in the frosted window.

'Get a message to Serik, the guy whose meeting us...' Stan trilled as they manhandled me through the door, but once outside I realised I didn't have his number.

I'd barely begun to contemplate what the next stage in this squeeze would entail when it must've dawned on the politsiya that I'd taken the precious dollars with me. Lips pursed as if blowing smoke rings, the misted outline of 'O' face appeared at the glass, his pounding serving as a signal for me to return; and bring the money.

Back in the office, overlord sat in a pose redolent of Rodin's *The Thinker*. Appropriating my pen and ripping a leaf of paper from my notebook, he scratched out '$50', the sum total of all the money they'd found on us. Hissing something at his retinue, they began bobbing up and down with arms outstretched in a most peculiar manner.

'*Pyi'desyat!*' he barked.
'Ah!' I blurted to Stan, apprehending their meaning. 'They want the fifty dollars and they want you to do fifty squats.'

It took less than ten before they lost interest.

'Go!' the boss ordered, waving his hand magnanimously as he delivered his considered verdict that Stan's sentence had been served.

Zhon and the Art of Train Maintenance

Sharp sunlight reflecting off their high-viz jackets, workmen meandered up and down the tracks, hammering the wheels of trains to check their integrity. At the farthest end of the sprawling station, we'd ensconced ourselves at a plastic table and ordered a pot of chay. Swaggering down the platform, chests puffed out like *The A-Team* in victorious formation, the considerably wealthier politsiya and their flunkies took the table behind us, overlord treating his buddies to a lunch consisting largely of vodka.

Oblivious to them and four new blue shirts fingering long, black truncheons as they eyed us, a stocky, sallow-skinned figure approached.

'Ullo, I can sit?' he asked, already seeking out a sweet spot on the folding chair. 'My name is Zhon; I am from Aktau, yes.'

Discovering our nationality, his face lit up and he shook our hands ever more vigorously.

'I meet English last three years ago when Mongolian Rally come through Kazakhstan. I too am driver, truck driver Kazakhstan Turkmenistan, yes, but Turkmenistan many problem,' he groaned, his initial effulgence evaporating. 'Turkmenistan militsiya always money, money, prison.'
'It's the same for us here,' I assured him in a hushed tone, but he didn't absorb this.
'Today I coming to meet my father-in-law,' he continued breathlessly, chair creaking as he leant in close. 'My wife sick, yes, but medicine too

much expensive. So we move to Kyzylorda because services for health better here.'

That didn't say much for Aktau.
Helping himself to chay, Zhon shrugged enduringly.

'God's hand is above all,' he sighed sombrely. 'Aktau has many problems now, yes, because of oil.'

In December 2011, a peaceful occupation of the main square in Aktau's neighbouring *monogorod* – single industry town - of Zhanaozen over mass sackings, pay and conditions for oil workers turned violent. The authorities attempting to move demonstrators on in favour of Independence Day celebrations, security forces opened fire, killing at least fifteen unarmed civilians. Discontent quickly spread throughout the oblast. For daring to report that two-hundred people had been incarcerated and tortured by methods including suffocation and being hung by their hair, the newspaper *Respublika* found itself banned from Kazakhstan on charges of extremism. It remains outlawed to this day.

'I was in Zhanaozen with friend when politsiya start shooting automatic weapon. Many were bleeding, injured and dead. I lie behind bodies and hide there. I go home, but for three days, riots in Aktau,' Zhon shouted injudiciously in order to be heard above the wheeltappers, who'd reached our end of the platform. 'Still though, Aktau good,' he assured us with a grin; 'you should visit.'

He wasn't selling it.
Respublika is one of a string of news outlets banned in recent years, the crux of the government's strategy for addressing public dissatisfaction being to clampdown on dissent. The widening gap between the haves and have not's continuing to fuel fragmented pockets of protest, Kazakhstan's richest fifty people are now worth twenty-four billion dollars, whilst only

twenty-four percent of the country's rural population have access to running water.

On February 11ᵗʰ 2014, a day written in infamy in as "Black Tuesday," the National Bank of Kazakhstan kicked away the crutches with which it had been supporting the economy and devalued the tenge by 18.9 percent. An end to months of fiscal denial, the devaluation – the second in five years – put a serious dent in President Nazarbayev's claim to be the custodian of prosperity. This nosedive, which paralleled the slump of the Russian rouble, saw Kazakh citizens lose one fifth of their savings overnight.

The next morning, activists who descended on the National Bank were summarily arrested, riot police adding to their haul the following day when they frogmarched off seven women wearing racy knickers on their heads. Demonstrating against the Customs Union, a ban on lace and the 'absurdity' of life in Kazakhstan, the so-called "panty protesters" were among thirty-five people tried on charges of hooliganism and breaching public assembly laws. When Nazarbayev dared to show his face in public two days later, he was greeted with unprecedented chants of 'old man out!'

Not a good year for the regime, 2014 also saw the resignation of the government and the detention of multiple officials on embezzlement charges, whilst reports surfaced regarding the retrial of a man convicted of assassinating an opposition leader. At his appeal hearing, the prisoner testified that he was hired by Rakhat Aliyev, who was married to the President's daughter Dariga at the time of the murder. Allegations surfaced that a coup plot had been dreamed up by Aliyev, who was seeking to propel his wife to power. Since fleeing the country in 2007, Aliyev has been divorced by Dariga and sentenced in absentia to forty years.

In line with Central Asia's other dictator's daughters, Dariga has many strings to her bow. One-time head of the state news agency, she also formed the political party All Together, though it soon pledged allegiance to her father. An avid opera singer, despite having no formal training Dariga often performs arias at events and served as a jury member on *SuperStar KZ*, the Kazakh trope of *Pop Idol*. The public airing of these claims constituting a setback to her ambitions to succeed her father, speculation is rife that the timing of the retrial was connected to a power struggle playing out behind the scenes.

My conversation with Zhon turned to events in Ukraine, the crisis there having sent shockwaves through Central Asia, where trepidation regarding new Russian Empire building is widespread.

'I think Putin actions very bad for Russia,' said Zhon. 'Now there is change in thinking toward Russia; but actions in Ukraine bad for Kazakh people too.'

Having had the fear of God put into them, the regions governments have responded in a predictably reactionary manner. In Kazakhstan, new regulations allow for a twenty-four-hour delay on the dissemination of news. In Tajikistan, meanwhile, the twitchy authorities have ordered all old and spare tyres be taken to a dump forty kilometres from Dushanbe, so they can't be used as roadblocks. Not to be outdone, the Uzbek government has placed explosives on the nation's TV and radio transmitters.

Across the Steppe

Unable to leave fast enough, we bolted before the cyan green train had juddered to a halt. Ushering away two boys, with a snarl they vacated our reserved upper *kupe* bunks and we settled in. With no air-con or windows which opened, for the next twenty-five sweltering minutes we lay low, the politsiya milling up and down the platform gawking through the cloudy glass. When we finally pulled away, it was a beautiful thing indeed.

We shared our four-berth compartment with a couple and their two children. The youngsters having befriended every other child on the train, the girls and their new playmates stared at us unblinkingly.

'*Ya dada,*' they shrieked gleefully at their exhausted looking father.

Leaving Kyzylorda, ecru beige scrub swallowed up the last fertile strips of land. Square single storey white buildings with pyramidal metal roofs rose in huddles before the steppe reasserted its dominion once more. The occasional goat and scant pylons bringing flickers of life, any deviation, even discarded goods carriages became a point of interest.

At stations without signs to designate their name, burly men in voluminous shorts and wife-beater vests prowled sluggishly. The locomotive delivering a brief flurry of excitement, middle-aged women behind rickety stands sprung into life, tenge changing hands for cigarettes and embossed *lipeshki* bread. As the train departed, beyond the window a familiar sense of sadness seemed to take hold. Shuffling lumps of unsold dried meat across their stalls, traders returned to spitting out sunflower seeds and staring into the distance.

Zelyony Bazaar at dawn, Almaty.

Golden Man, Monument to Independence, Almaty.

Ascension Cathedral, Almaty.

Cameras not welcome, Aralsk Bazaar.

A boy carries water to the chay stand as Serik and Earwig attempt to get directions, Artesian

The ghosts of sailors haunt a ship graveyard, Zhalanash.

Abandoned ship, Butakov Bay.   *Saviour of the Small Aral Sea, the Kokaral Dam.*

Lilting boats, Tastubek Bay.

Karateren Village.

CHAPTER 23

Dreams of the Sea#2

'Welcome to Aral, David Beckham!' the ruddy-cheeked *provodnik* bellowed, flicking my foppish hair as we disembarked the Moscow-bound train.

The platform at Aralskoe More amounting to little more than a strip of bars, in the waiting room a mural depicted the importance of fishing to the oblast and the Soviet Union as a whole.

In response to a letter from Lenin dated October 1921, the fishermen of Bugun had filled fourteen railcars with their catch, helping to alleviate the famine sweeping across the USSR. The text of Lenin's letter stands immortalised in stone in the main square of Aralsk. Twenty years later, the region came to the empire's rescue once again during the Great Patriotic War, fish processed and canned in the monocity being sent to starving troops. "More fish to the front and to the country," the authorities sloganeered.

Having been closed for decades as the Aral Sea diminished, the cannery in Aralsk has recently been replaced with a brand new facility emblematic of the sense of hope slowly returning. The long-running decline in population seemingly at an end, government figures claim that more than five thousand people have moved back to the area in the past few years.

At the entrance to the station, a wooden statue of a six-sailed brig lay marooned atop a freestanding gate. To the right of this strange sight, on a giant billboard a suited and booted Nazarbayev had been photoshopped in, wading knee deep in the sea and smiling as the water trickled through his fingers.

Met by Serik Dyussenbayev from the Danish co-founded NGO Aral Tenizi, we loaded our rucksacks into his jeep. Dressed in a khaki print t-shirt and shorts, he wore a gold medallion around his neck and a chunky silver wristwatch, dark glasses obscuring his eyes despite the late hour.

'As you can see, we are small town, but we have new asphalt and street-lights. This is because the President was supposed to come last year,' he said as we cruised through the patchily lit streets. 'He didn't come,' he concluded.

Pulling up at metal gates, we were greeted by a coterie of children. Although it had gone midnight, the thoroughfares of Aralsk were still filled with the cries of kids, who introduced themselves with giddy chirps.

Leaving them to their games, I opened the door of the lifeless building; pristine, but unlived in, like a show home. With neither cutlery nor dishes, we ate a supper of boiled potatoes and cold, bony Aral bream from newspaper plates, a black and white photograph of the President staring up at us, his eyebrows arched questioningly.

To the Shore

A faded black t-shirt riding up on the bulge of his hirsute belly, our driver arrived two hours late the next morning. Habitually scratching at the crown of his head as if in a state of considerable confusion, with wingnut ears and puffy cheeks he resembled the children's TV character Pob.

We proceeded into the achromatised centre of the city, each identical house along the way whitewashed with a turquoise trim, as if they'd chipped in for a job lot on paint. A town where junkers had come to perish, the conjoined series of potholes posing as a road attested that any new surfacing had only been laid on the President's prospective route. Observing the submissive mien of residents as they were fleeced, it seemed our circling was part of a well-rehearsed strategy through which we were attempting to avoid the politsiya.

Parking in the shade of a horse statue, we eventually drew to a halt to gather supplies. Constructed of concrete and sheet metal, the sepulchral aisles of the sweltering bazaar were illuminated by bare strip lights. In the fresh produce section, an angry man suffering spasms hopped up and down, his buddy in an urban blue woodlands camo uniform shooting daggers at us. Heavyset women in white headscarves waved muddy bunches of carrots and dill at customers, leaves floating through the fusty air like green snow. Despite their best efforts, sweet biscuits and sausages were the most popular produce.

'Is it okay to take pictures?' Stan asked Serik.
'Well, I suppose so,' he answered at length, an expression as if suffering an angina attack etched across his face; 'just don't say you know me.'

Drawing scowls and grimaces, the camera proved distinctly unwelcome. Shoppers and staff fleeing from the lens, a mini-stampede sent our goods rolling away under pitches.

'There are seventy-two thousand people in the region now, twenty-four villages and eight schools,' Serik explained as we departed. Picking his nose with one hand, he adjusted his sunglasses with the other as we skirted the railway tracks, trailing after a freight train.
'This is new government compound, boarding school, teacher's houses,' he continued with pride, indicating a hulking block which looked as if it'd been placed there by some unearthly being. 'Enjoy the asphalt,' he scoffed as the last of it came into view. 'You won't see it again for days.'

The radio cutting out, the steppe took over. Bouncing along a rutted track, an expanse of desiccated scrub rolled past as if on a loop.

'There were three Russian military bases here,' Serik continued, pointing to a stripped, slate grey building, 'now two are gutted, one is Kazakh militsiya.'

Used as a prison for kulaks - comparatively wealthy peasants designated class enemies - one of these abandoned bases had been fondly christened 'New America' by the KGB.

Abaft of a windswept cemetery and an arch leading nowhere, occasional criss-crossing power lines were the only signs of civilisation to break the uniformity of the Kyzyl-Kum. Small brown Desert Warblers flitting about our jeep, falcons with vast wingspans circled in slow motion overhead. In the distance, beyond mounds from which dried clumps of grass protruded, monolithic cliffs formed by erosion marked the erstwhile location of the coastline.

A single motorbike in the village of Zhalanash marking the sum total of traffic over the next ten hours, battling through furrows past a herd of cows, we came to rest at a ship graveyard. As recently as 2006, there had been twelve boats stranded near Zhalanash, but now, their bones picked clean by scrap metal scavengers, only three remained.

Drained pivo bottles peeking through the sand around them, a caravan of Bactrian camels besieged by flies had sought shade beneath part of the largest husk. Swathed in graffiti, the ship had been coated in black and white spray paint with the ghostly forms of sailors. Evocative against the rust red ruins, some loitered in hammocks, one even urinating beneath a porthole. Across the Central Steppe dotted with the burrows of sand cats, two smaller tugboats were less haunted than tagged.

Reliant on GPS, we thrust on across the manmade desert, passing a blur of low saksaul trees like wisps of smoke. Our skulls smashing into the head-liner with every jounce, mice scuttled from our path. In the *aul* (settlement) of Tastubek, a young boy and girl wearing masks against the insistent dust stared back at us, tentatively raising their hands. All told, Tastubek amounted to twenty dwellings, thirty camels and an upturned chassis. At a remove from the main body of the village, the structures in the cemetery rivalled the abodes of the living.

With Serik and our driver - who'd been introduced as Earwig - having taken on the surrounding quietude, the squall and the sputtering of the engine were amplified. When the Aral came into sight five kilometres later, it was initially unclear whether we were seeing the endorheic basin or a shimmering mirage. The tranquil, warm waters gently lapping against the shore where a pair of rowing boats lilted in the shallows, two years after our first attempt, we'd finally reached the Aral Sea.

The Northernmost Point

Attempting to reach the next set of coordinates, we drifted uncertainly across the scorched wilderness. That the staff of an NGO tasked with saving the Small Aral didn't know where they were going said a lot about how few visitors this area sees.

Having failed to find a route along the seaboard, we backtracked through Tastubek, travelling onto Butakov Bay. In the algae-filled waters, shoals of fry swam in the shade of a beached barge. Wading around it, I managed to slice open my toes on a sheet of serrated metal.

'Shit,' said Stan as I hobbled onto the sand, leaving a trail of blood in the water, 'I hope you got your tetanus shot.'
'I thought that was only for animal bites?' I rejoined.

Still, there was nothing to be done about it, so I just sat there bleeding until it was time to leave.

A few minutes' drive from Butakov Bay, we stopped at the Artesian Well, a hot spring gushing foamy white water. In this isolated setting, a shack no more than two metres square offered pots of chay. Draped in drainpipe denim culottes and a gold chain, a boy scuttled back and forth carrying bottles of the water which cascaded from a fountain resembling a tiered cake. Standing by the well, an old man rubbing the paunch liberated from the confines of his shirt and a babushka in a Stetson were clearly bemused by our presence. Approaching the overpoweringly sulphuric well, I was equally surprised to see a sign written in English.

'This hot water contain many useful minerals, that is deficit to our organizm,' it read. 'It is necessary to swim2 times in 30 minutes.'

Not only would it have been impossible to take a dip in this puddle, but putting my hand in, I determined that one would've boiled to death.

'Read prayer… Withhold negative habits; don't drink bear vodka,' the sign exhorted. 'After meal: empty dishes, rubbish throw away to special dust digs.'

Given the dark clouds rolling in, dust wouldn't be in short supply.

Figures released by Ardanbay Asanbaev, Chief Medical Doctor of Aralsk assert that throughout the 1990s fifty to sixty children a day were admitted to Aralsk hospital with respiratory illnesses. Babies being born with half hearts, without lungs or eyes was also commonplace.

'Are there still large dust storms out here?' I asked Serik.

'Da, very often, very big, very bad,' he replied gravely.

Due north of the well, we stopped in the hamlet of Aksepe to ask for directions. Encircled by camels, horses and malnourished cows, the only three men there couldn't reach agreement. It transpired that none of them had ever travelled farther west than the village of their birth.

A kilometre outside of Aksepe, our уA3 Hunter jeep became stuck on the dunes. In the searing forty-two degree heat, attempting to free the vehicle left burn marks on the palms of one's hands. Marooned, with not a clue how to reach our next port of call, Serik and Earwig looked worried, which wasn't reassuring.

Akbasty

Curling clouds sailed over the distant cliff face. The earth splintered, the clay soil gave way to a quicksand beach where bug-eyed, biting green flies swarmed. At every location we'd visit around the Small Aral, salinity levels between 11.1 and 87.3 percent lower than three years previously would be recorded, an indication that the inflow of water remains above that lost through evaporation. Lumbering from the brackish water shaking a stubborn clump of chara from his measuring stick, Stan confirmed that given our whereabouts in Shevchenko Bay, the Small Aral had also grown during this period, returning by increments so that the spot where we were standing could soon be returned to the sea.

Leaving the bay behind, we were soon lost again, bouncing to an impasse at an embankment where a truck was stranded. Covered in gunk, its crew said they were fishermen, which didn't tally with the shovels and sheets of asbestos piled high upon their vehicle. Thankful to see us, a man with the authoritative air of a foreman explained they had a flat battery and had been there for fourteen hours.

'We were really lucky you came along,' he exclaimed, a mixture of sweat and engine grease smeared across his face. 'Last time this happened, we were stuck for three days.'

Doubling back along the track, Earwig cranked up the stereo. Tolerating ardent Kazakh folk ballads, Serik even let Lionel Ritchie's "Hello" pass - a strange song to hear in the middle of the Kyzyl-Kum - but when the macarena came on, he twisted the dial in agitation, silencing the caterwauling.

Grinding over splattered desert foxes, as the sun disappeared our terminus for the night came into sight. With Earwig shutting the engine off two kilometres outside the former fishing village of Akbasty, a flurry of jalopies appeared. Each new party introducing themselves to their compatriots whilst ignoring us, the menfolk exchanged handshakes and chain-smoked.

'At least there are probably no politsiya out here,' I said to Stan as we sat on a low ridge staring longingly towards our destination.

Arriving in the aul an hour later, we stopped at a standpipe where three generations of men were hosing themselves down in the sulphurous water spouting from its nozzle. The buildings set far part, this was another settlement of low mud-brick domiciles with wooden window frames and corrugated roofs from which thin chimneys protruded. Toddlers drove camels past a silver domed mosque, which glinted in the pink light. Enticing sheep, tufty clumps of vegetation pullulated from the verges of the unsealed main road, plastic and shards of bone jutting through the sandy surface.

On compound walls cobbled together with whatever came to hand - tyres, doors, branches - laundry was laid out to dry. Their suspensions collapsed, Kama3 and yA3 452 forward control vans oxidized, eyeless as if picked clean by birds. Half-collapsed power pylons brought life to satellite dishes, a singular point of contact with the outside world. There was no shop, but a hoarding featuring President Nazarbayev had found its way here.

A long debate with much gesticulating having taken place at the standpipe, we drove to the smartest place in the village. The new double doors swinging open onto a spacious courtyard littered with stag beetles and dead sparrows, a call went out for the head of the household. His head shaved in a number two and short neck morphing in chunky folds, our host shepherded us to a low tapchan laden with kurpachas. Inviting us to take a pew in the *tur* (rear) as the rules of hospitality dictated, he sat facing us in the least secure position, his back to the entrance. Fortunately, his adherence to tradition didn't extend so far as to offer us a sheep's head.

Barking orders at his wife, whose place seemed to be one of domestic servitude, the proud patriarch summoned forth a succession of bowls filled with roach and candy melting in its wrappers. Sitting at his side, his five-year-old son partook of sustenance only when prompted by his father.

As golden as any tooth, chirping birds swooped through the courtyard. Outside, an angry sounding fellow was hollering into a megaphone, camels bellowing their unholy calls as if in response. Above the village, a passing plane cut a contrail through the night sky.

'Akbasty and Bugun have electricity since the nineties; this prosperous times,' Serik commented through a mouthful of nan, although there was no power that night. 'Since Kokaral Dam fish yield has risen and sea has grown a lot. When first Danish project arrived here before the dam, salinity was thirty percent,' he continued, picking at the greasy roach with stubby fingers. 'Back then the only fish were flounders.'

Data from the Research Institute of Fisheries in Aralsk shows that the bulk catch from the Small Aral has grown from 695 metric tons in 2005 to 5,595 metric tons in 2014, whilst the number of species found in the sea – some reintroduced, others naturally migrating - has more than doubled. These figures, however, remain a far cry from the 34,160 tons recorded back in 1961.

Despite this resurgence, Akbasty remains sixteen kilometres – an hour and a half drive - from the current shoreline.

A Black Legacy

At dawn, we were invited into the main house for a breakfast of bread and jam. The familial digs weren't much less sparse than the empty building we'd stayed in, rugs, cushions and a TV the only concessions to furniture. In a colossal painting, three armour-clad horsemen who looked like ZZ Top were posed in an orange grove carrying a sword, a spear and a crossbow. Photographs of babies dressed in elaborate ceremonial costumes adorned a windowsill, long velvet chapans for the boys and *saukele* hats, tall, pointed and festooned with beads and silver for the girls. Blaring from the screen, as if to legitimise itself as a serious source of information, Kazakh TV's news broadcast had stolen the theme music from BBC News 24. An in-depth report from the Cup of Kazakhstan on Bodybuilding followed.

With every meal turning into a protracted social engagement, we ultimately departed some hours later. The morning sunlight imbuing the terrain with a golden hue, we drove towards the bay north of Akbasty, passing desert ships in an area so desiccated that even the hardy saksaul trees were bare and dead.

Kazakhstan has endured the most catastrophic contamination of all the former Soviet Republics. A hundred kilometres south, now joined to the mainland lay Vozrozhdeniya Island, site of plague and anthrax tests. Four hundred kilometres south-west near the village of Say-Utes - a neighbouring hamlet by Kazakh standards - the Soviets had conducted three nuclear explosions in 1969 and 1970.

Between 1949 and 1989, the authorities executed more than 750 nuclear tests in Kazakhstan. The bulk of these, including the USSR's first successful atomic explosion – codenamed Joe-1 - took place in the Semipalatinsk Polygon (closed zone) in the north-east of the country. By far the hardest hit area, Semipalatinsk saw 456 tests, which affected two million people across three hundred square kilometres. Today, people swim in crater lakes left by blasts which dot the steppe, though animals won't go near the water. With all agriculture banned, a vast swathe of land still remains off-limits. Even in inhabited areas, Geiger counters read over 250; the normal level is just fifteen.

Eager to know what to expect in the event of a nuclear war, in 1957 the Soviets secretly opened Dispensary Number Four in Semipalatinsk. Shipping in spectators - teachers were instructed to have their pupils watch explosions - the facility observed and analysed the effects of radiation on the populous and reported their findings back to Moscow. In this post-apocalyptic land, elevated levels of cancer, tuberculosis and mental illness persist. All pregnancies are still screened for possible termination, six percent of babies born "polygon."

In their headlong rush to abandon the empire upon the collapse of the union, the Russians left more than an undetonated payload in the mines of Semipalatinsk. As soldiers rioted over conditions and unpaid wages, upon its birth as a nation Kazakhstan inherited the fourth largest nuclear arsenal in the world. With Libya's Colonel Gaddafi sniffing around, it was widely rumoured that the Iranians, who the CIA publically alleged to be 'actively shopping,' had offered three hundred million dollars for weapons-grade uranium.

Arriving in Kazakhstan post-haste, US Secretary of State James Baker enjoyed a bonding exercise with President Nazarbayev involving drunken singing in a hot tub. Through a combination of threats, the promise of a seat at the international table and hard cash, Nazarbayev was persuaded to give up Kazakhstan's cache, which the Americans duly dismantled and disposed of.

The Kokaral Dam

A three-hour drive around the bleached southern fringe of the sea brought us to the Kokaral Dam. The centerpiece of efforts to save the Small Aral, the dam and its thirteen-kilometre dyke stretch across the Berg Straits. Until

1973, Kokaral was a 270-square-kilometre island, but with the demise of the sea it became an isthmus separating a piece of the endorheic basin from the bulk in the south. The fishing industry collapsed, 45,000 people leaving the Northern Aral region alone between 1980 and 2000.

Completed in 2005 with seventy million dollars in funding from the World Bank, though some environmentalists argue it's another nail in the coffin of what is now known as the Large Aral in Uzbekistan, the dam has seen water levels rise by over twelve meters from their low point in 2003, to now stand at forty-two meters. A long-mooted second phase of the plan to save the sea may progress in the near future.

'The final decision on what to do will be published soon,' Nikolay Aladin of the Russian Academy of Sciences told me. 'Nobody knows which plan will materialise. This information is top secret.'

Attempts to garner information from the Kazakh government bore out the professor's assessment. With the sound of receivers slamming down still ringing in my ears, I thought back to Almaty.

'The main sticking point seems to be the form of the intervention,' Kristopher White had opined during our visit to KIMEP. 'One option involves simply raising the existing dam and dyke, which would raise the entire Northern Aral Sea level by six meters. The other option constructs another dam south of Saryshaganak Bay, which would be at fifty-three meters. In terms of fishing and the overall ecological condition of the sea, raising the existing dam and dyke might be preferable, though observers might rightfully question why the initial design height wasn't forty-eight meters.'

Sandwiched between fervid sandbanks, reeds rose from the murky shallows on the overflow side of the dyke facing the border with Uzbekistan. Back across the embankment, the open waters rippled beneath a stiff wind. Dragonflies with long orange tails darted past, tiny fingerlings nipping at our toes. With Serik and Earwig gambolling like water babies, we headed up to inspect the dam. Belying its age, much of the baby blue and fire red paint had already flaked off the structure. A welcome spray lifting from the tumult and floating through the air, on a series of railings perched a flock of alpine swifts.

Just visible on the horizon lay the Syr Darya Delta, which unlike the Amu Darya in Uzbekistan still feeds the sea for part of the year, water released from Kyrgyz reservoirs finding its way west. Whilst the Kazakhs fear Kyrgyz talk of a new hydroelectric power station, Uzbekistan continues to saber-rattle against Tajik plans to construct the Rogun Dam. Few expect a breakthrough anytime soon.

'Let me put it this way,' Kristopher White had observed, 'the Central Asian republics aren't exactly a model of international cooperation.'

Compound Fractures

A weigh station where anglers sell their catch, the Karateren Fisheries Department was located in a clutch of buildings several kilometres from the village which happened to share its name. Emerging from behind an edifice where they'd been pottering with a wheel-less jeep, the three men of the depot looked perplexed.

'Fish out of season,' explained the eldest, a diaphanous beard trailing from his chin. 'Closed,' he insisted. 'Not for you.'

Despite his protestations, with Serik and Earwig in no hurry to leave, we settled in for the ritual handshakes.

Running low on cigarettes, Earwig turned his attention to Stan's rolling tobacco, tilting his head at a quizzical angle.

'Smoke drugs?' Serik asked, translating his friend's question.

Obviously something which had been bothering them ever since we set off, it was a common misconception, but satisfied at length that the shag didn't contain hallucinogens, the inquisitive Earwig asked if he could try one.

'*Tak plokhoy!*' he spluttered upon taking a drag, hacking like a cat coughing up a hairball.
'I guess not all things better in England,' Serik laughed.

We overnighted in the deserted village of Karateren, where large, sparse compounds were situated ever farther apart as if being pulled by a centrifugal force; not that space was in short supply. Tempering the bitter winter winds and keeping feral dogs at bay, but giving the impression of a colony without a sense of community, each compound sundered its inhabitants, tall walls of brick, mud or salvaged metal indicating disparities in wealth. Although the aul was apparently the scene of annual Fisherman's Day celebrations, it was difficult to imagine a party atmosphere manifesting itself.

By now it had become abundantly clear that we weren't following an itinerary with regard to accommodation, just circling until the most opulent looking digs were spotted, then knocking in the hope of being afforded hospitality. So stopping outside a gate rendered golden in the dying light, after lengthy negotiations we were ushered inside by a waddling babushka in a floppy white chef's hat. A gaggle of toddlers milling at her feet, she guided us to a reception room, where the children wilted under the spell of the television. All those present were soon so absorbed that I wondered what had passed for entertainment here in the days before electricity.

Broken only by the drone of the boob tube and buzzing flies, a pervading silence descended. A soap opera playing, infidelities, hammy expressions and false eyebrows were set against stark backdrops. Following this show, a period drama featured dwarves with swords, the original actor's voices still audible beneath the dubbing. Just when this appeared set to finish, evidently on a loop the same two programmes started over; not that anyone batted an eyelid.

Under surveillance by the matriarch, I took a stroll around. Aside from thick rugs, gaudy curtains and the widescreen TV, there were no other fixtures, fittings or appliances. Did they enjoy the clutter-free life, I wondered, or was it as a chatty young mother in Khorog had told me;

'People think we don't like furniture, but it's just we can't afford it.'

To the sound of stomach's rumbling, at ten PM dinner was served. With Earwig scarfing down the whole caboodle, one's main concern was to get some sustenance before he polished it all off. As the meal concluded and dishes were being piled, a power cut struck. Herded into a room, we were instructed to stay put. Serik having hidden the jeep beneath brush and twigs, perhaps our presence would have alerted an unwelcome authority figure.

Our sleeping mats spread on the floor, the Kazakh's were believers in the firm spine. I opened the frilly curtains to reveal windows which had been nailed shut, sealing in the heat. Whether this was for keeping out insects, the sun or for added privacy it was difficult to say, though it seemed as if most of the creepy-crawlies were indoors already.

Returning home as the clock struck midnight, the stumbling patriarch passed out alone in the living room, the women bedding down with the children as had been the case in Akbasty. From the adjacent room, we listened as his mouth breathing snore thundered through the house.

Conservation

'Seven - one!' Serik greeted us with an unprecedented jocularity.

Seeing confusion writ upon our caffeine-starved countenances, he clarified his statement.

'World Cup,' he chirped, 'Germany seven, Brazil one, ba ha ha!'
'Oh! How did you find out?' I asked, doubting the veracity of his account; 'internet?'

In spite of the unwieldy satellite dishes hanging from the compound, the game hadn't been on TV, the Kazsports network preferring to focus on wrestling.

'Internet!' Serik scoffed, 'there's only one internet café in province.'
'Telephone?' Stan inquired.
'Telephone?' Serik hissed incredulously. 'No signal outside Aralsk!'
'Well, how then?' I pressed, the internet and telephone reception belonging to a barely conceivable future.
'Ah!' he smirked mischievously, 'paperboy.'

Given our remoteness, this sounded even more absurd.

Setting out for Bugun, we approached a second dam built as part of a hydropower project which had never reached fruition. The structure still boasted a checkpoint, though, a sure sign we were back within reach of the regime. Stirring as if to flag down our vehicle, we watched from a great distance - which gave the impression of events unfolding in slow-motion - as the politsiya argued amongst themselves as to who should spoliate us. Keen for them not to spot our rosy, dollar sign mugs, as we drew closer Stan and I ducked down, but the heat overpowering them, the officers slunk back into their chairs. Subsequently, our thoughts turned to avoiding a repeat of the Kyzylorda Vokzal performance. We were nearing the end of the road.

Our last stop on the shores of the Aral, Bugun Bay was, unsurprisingly, nowhere near Bugun. Relative to the GPS coordinates from 2011, however, the sea had inundated the land by two and a half kilometres, creating an impassable marsh. By the time we'd spent an hour trying to find a way across this biting ant infested swamp, our supplies of bottled water were exhausted. Reeling back to the jeep, we found our crew loafing in the shade of the vehicle, chuckling at our bedraggled state. The offer of Serik's frozen tap water too good to refuse, I gulped it down, giardia be damned.

Stopping up the coast, we waded through a slippery, stagnant pool of floating camel turds to reach a coarse, cockle shell sandbank where a picnicking family had pitched up a small white yurt reminiscent of the one offered for sale on the noticeboard in Bishkek.

'*Zdravst*,' they chorused coolly, looking slightly vexed to have been discovered by foreign interlopers.

Our scientific equipment baffling them, two teenagers with faces like melted plastic - most likely a product of nuclear testing –observed intently from the darkened doorway.

Taking leave of the sea, we drove on through a salt flat to Bugun, where as if reemerging from the sand, the asphalt returned. By a building site replete with cranes, we stopped at a petrol station and shop, stocking up on a limited array of junk food and sodas which felt like luxury goods.

'She really like your sunglasses,' Serik said to Stan, nodding to indicate the counter girl who'd followed us outside. 'She ask, can she have them?'

With Stan squinting in the fulgent light, we crossed a bridge dotted with coal black crows. On the banks of Lake Kambash, a construction crew were erecting a gigantic new hotel. Taking a wrong turn, we got a close-up of its skeletal dome, drills and swinging hoists. How anyone was supposed to get here or quite why they'd want to remained a mystery.

Passing a contiguous graveyard, we came to a halt on the beach, where splashing each other affectionately, Serik and Earwig made good use of the next four hours. When they finally tired, they discarded the litter they'd accumulated onto the sand, which was already strewn with waste. The idea of conservation, it seemed, was yet to truly take hold.

Hitting the main highway, a menagerie of animals coalesced in the shade of an underpass. Billboards showed Nazarbayev surrounded by smiling schoolgirls with orchids in their hair, the sky awash with two-dimensional sketches of doves. Lifting from the steppe, the outskirts of Aralsk abruptly engulfed us, women in bright, calf-length outfits lugging groceries whilst men in culottes, socks and sandals skulked on street corners.

With Serik disappearing, Mrs. Earwig invited us into her home and switched on the TV. That a particularly gory zombie flick was playing didn't faze her brood, who giggled at us and the onscreen eviscerations in equal measure. Summoned to the table for a final meal, Earwig joined us, the bench groaning under his weight. Visibly glad to be home, he smiled contentedly, the lines falling from his face.

'Eat,' he said, his first and only word in English.

Epilogue

Do svidaniya Central Asia

Hiding in an unlit nook outside the station, with just seconds to spare we made a dash for the train. That we boarded without incident was more than could be said for a Spanish couple I met a few months later. Arrested and separated in Aralsk, in addition to being extorted for every last tenge, they'd been forced to hand over their shoes. Clearly the shakedown was commonplace, for when I'd told Serik what had taken place in Kyzylorda, he just shrugged.

'It happens to the best of us,' head of the biggest independent travel agency in the region, David Berghof conceded.

Wriggling through a sliding compartment door determined to dismember him, a knock-kneed militsiyaman in a flat cap was on hand to scrutinise our tickets and passports.

'*Niet problema*,' he declared after a pregnant pause, much to my surprise.

Pulling into Kyzylorda eight hours later, we made a beeline for a taksi. Cruising through the uniform city of pink tuff blocks, rubble and open squares, the sound of grinding gears rose up, disturbing the morning still.

Arriving at the airport at six AM, we found the shutters down, padlocked chains around the door handles.

'*Zakrytiy*,' a security guard yelled upon spotting us.

Marching purposefully towards us, he emphasized the point by positioning his muscular forearms in the shape of an 'X'.

Its entrance creaking open at noon, the terminal building offered a welcome respite from the oppressive heat. At the handful of sleepy magazine and concession stands, sales assistants outnumbered punters. Despite having only just pulled up their blinds, by one PM all the kiosks and most of the ticket windows had closed for lunch.

Pooling the last of our funds, we shared an *omlet* and a kofe in the sole eatery. Yanking open the tua-let door, I found it'd been converted into a staff smoking area, a gaggle of women in white aprons spilling onto the floor as their cigarette fumes escaped.

For the next five hours as I stared into space, snapshots of Central Asia surfaced in my mind like elliptical pieces of a giant jigsaw puzzle. From my initial discombobulation, the culture, history and politics of this fascinating region had developed into something of an obsession. For the next three years, we kept returning, yet any attempt to reach conclusions about these countries remained elusive and ultimately futile. Waiting to board the flight now, it seemed to me that these travels had been about more than the sum of my impressions; in the end, it was the journey itself that mattered most. It was about the people and places, the trials and tribulations, and how despite the difficulties, I'd come to love the Stans.

'*Do svidaniya*,' the sloe-eyed stewardess soughed as she ripped our boarding passes at the gate.

Goodbye, for now, Central Asia. With a stopover in Astana to look forward to, we began our voyage to Baku, the next stage in our Post-Soviet odyssey. Soon enough I'd find myself banned from Azerbaijan; but that's another story.

Selected Bibliography

History of Civilizations of Central Asia Volume VI – Chahryar Adle, Madhavan K. Palat & Anara Tabyshalieva

The day lasts more than a hundred years- Chingiz Aitmatov

A Carpet Ride to Khiva- Christopher Aslan Alexander

Soviet and Post-Soviet Identities – Mark Bassin & Catriona Kelly

Chasing the Sea- Tom Bissell

Tradition and Society in Turkmenistan – Carole Blackwell

Social and Economic Change in the Pamirs – Frank Bliss

Turkmenistan – Paul Brummell

Central Asia in Focus – Lydia Buyers

No Holiday: 80 Places You Don't Want to Visit - Martin Cohen

The Forsaken People – Robin Cohen & Francis Mading Deng

Ghost Wars – Steve Coll

Weapons of Mass Destruction: An Encyclopedia of Worldwide Policy, Technology and History Volume One – Eric A. Croddy & James J. Wirtz

Writing on the Edge: Great Contemporary Writers on the Front Line of Crisis – Ed. Dan Crowe & Tom Craig

Ethnic Conflict in the Post-Soviet World – Ed. Leokadia Drobizheva, Rose Gottemoeller, Catherine McArdle Kelleher & Lee Walker

Revolution Baby: Motherhood and Anarchy in Kyrgyzstan – Saffia Farr

The Devil and the Disappearing Sea- Rob Ferguson

Kyrgyzstan: 20 years of independence- Giorgio Fiacconi

Collapse of an Empire: Lessons for Modern Russia – Yegor Gaidar

Creeping Environmental Problems and Sustainable Development in the Aral Sea Basin – ed. Michael Glantz

Soviet Bus Stops – Christopher Herwig & Damon Murray

Inside Central Asia- Dilip Hiro

The Great Game: On Secret Service in High Asia – Peter Hopkirk

Tajikistan- Loosening the Knot- Ross Howard

Freedom's Ordeal – Peter Juviler

Kyrgyzstan – David C. King

Nations in Transition: Central Asian Republics – Michael Kort

Unknown Sands – John W. Kropf

A Game of Polo with a Headless Goat- Emma Levine

The Oil and the Glory - Steve Levine

Vodka Cola – Charles Levinson

The Temptations of Tyranny in Central Asia- David Lewis

Eastern Approaches- Fitzroy Maclean

Central Asia Lonely Planet Fifth Edition- Bradley Mayhew et al

The Aral Sea: The devastation and partial rebirth of a Great Lake – Phillip Micklin, N. V. Aladin &Igor Plotnikov

Murder in Samarkand- Colin Murray

Tajikistan: The Rise of a Narco-State – Letizia Paoli, Irina Rabkov, Victoria A. Greenfield & Peter Reuter

Silk Road to Ruin: Why Central Asia is the Next Middle East – Ted Rall

Love Me Turkmenistan- Nicolas Righetti

In search of Kazakhstan: The Land that Disappeared- Christopher Robbins

Friendly Steppes: A Silk Road Journey – Nick Rowan

Central Asia at the End of the Transition – Ed. Boris Rumer

Moscow's Muslim Challenge – Michael Rywkin

Everyday Life in Central Asia – ed. Jeff Sahadeo & Russell Zanca

Restless Valley: Revolution, Murder and Intrigue in the Heart of Central Asia - Philip Shishkin

The Places In Between – Rory Stewart

Daily Life in Turmenbashy's Golden Age- Sam Tranum

The Caucasus: an introduction – Thomas de Waal

Beyond the Oxus- Monica Whitlock

Narrative of a Mission to Bokhara in the Years 1843 – 1845 – Joseph Wolff

HERTFORDSHIRE PRESS

Title List

Igor Savitsky: Artist, Collector, Museum Founder
by Marinika Babanazarova (2011)

Since the early 2000s, Igor Savitsky's life and accomplishments have earned increasing international recognition. He and the museum he founded in Nukus, the capital of Karakalpakstan in the far northwest of Uzbekistan. Marinika Babanazarova's memoir is based on her 1990 graduate dissertation at the Tashkent Theatre and Art Institute. It draws upon correspondence, official records, and other documents about the Savitsky family that have become available during the last few years, as well as the recollections of a wide range of people who knew Igor Savitsky personally.

Игорь Савитский: художник, собиратель, основатель музея

С начала 2000-х годов, жизнь и достижения Игоря Савицкого получили широкое признание во всем мире. Он и его музей, основанный в Нукусе, столице Каракалпакстана, стали предметом многочисленных статей в мировых газетах и журналах, таких как TheGuardian и NewYorkTimes, телевизионных программ в Австралии, Германии и Японии. Книга издана на русском, английском и французском языках.

Igor Savitski: Peintre, collectionneur, fondateur du Musée (French), (2012)

Le mémoire de Mme Babanazarova, basé sur sa thèse de 1990 à l'Institut de Théâtre et D'art de Tachkent, s'appuie sur la correspondance, les dossiers officiels et d'autres documents d'Igor Savitsky et de sa famille, qui sont devenus disponibles dernièrement, ainsi que sur les souvenirs de nombreuses personnes ayant connu Savistky personellement, ainsi que sur sa propre expérience de travail a ses cotés, en tant que successeur designé. son nom a titre posthume.

LANGUAGE: **ENG, RUS, FR**   ISBN: **978-0955754999**   RRP: **£10.00**
AVAILABLE ON **KINDLE**

Savitsky Collection Selected Masterpieces.
Poster set of 8 posters (2014)

Limited edition of prints from the world-renowned Museum of Igor Savitsky in Nukus, Uzbekistan. The set includs nine of the most famous works from the Savitsky collection wrapped in a colourful envelope. Selected Masterpieces of the Savitsky Collection.

[Cover] BullVasily Lysenko 1. Oriental Café Aleksei Isupov 2. Rendezvous Sergei Luppov 3. By the Sea. Marie-LouiseKliment Red'ko 4. Apocalypse Aleksei Rybnikov 5. Rain Irina Shtange 6. Purple Autumn Ural Tansykbayaev 7. To the Train Viktor Ufimtsev 8. Brigade to the fields Alexander Volkov This museum, also known as the Nukus Museum or the Savitsky

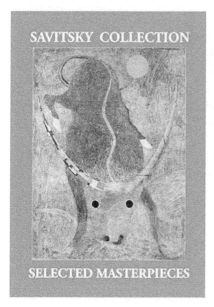
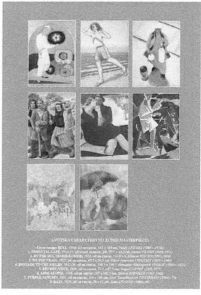

ISBN: **9780992787387**
RRP: **£25.00**

Friendly Steppes. A Silk Road Journey
by Nick Rowan

This is the chronicle of an extraordinary adventure that led Nick Rowan to some of the world's most incredible and hidden places. Intertwined with the magic of 2,000 years of Silk Road history, he recounts his experiences coupled with a remarkable realisation of just what an impact this trade route has had on our society as we know it today. Containing colourful stories, beautiful photography and vivid characters, and wrapped in the local myths and legends told by the people Nick met and who live along the route, this is both a travelogue and an education of a part of the world that has remained hidden for hundreds of years.

HARD BACK ISBN: **978-0-9927873-4-9**
PAPERBACK ISBN: **978-0-9557549-4-4**
RRP: **£14.95**
AVAILABLE ON **KINDLE**

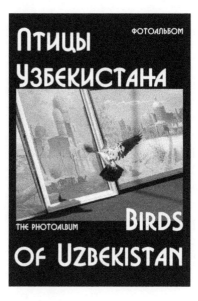

Birds of Uzbeksitan
by Nedosekov (2012)

FIRST AND ONLY PHOTOALBUM
OF UZBEKISTAN BIRDS!

This book, which provides an introduction to the birdlife of Uzbekistan, is a welcome addition to the tools available to those working to conserve the natural heritage of the country. In addition to being the first photographic guide to the birds of Uzbekistan, the book is unique in only using photographs taken within the country. The compilers are to be congratulated on preparing an attractive and accessible work which hopefully will encourage more people to discover the rich birdlife of the country and want to protect it for future generations

HARD BACK
ISBN: **978-0-955754913**
RRP: **£25.00**

Pool of Stars
by Olesya Petrova, Askar Urmanov,
English Edition (2007)

It is the first publication of a young writer Olesya Petrova, a talented and creative person. Fairy-tale characters dwell on this book's pages. Lovely illustrations make this book even more interesting to kids, thanks to a remarkable artist Askar Urmanov. We hope that our young readers will be very happy with such a gift. It's a book that everyone will appreciate. For the young, innocent ones - it's a good source of lessons they'll need in life. For the not-so-young but young at heart, it's a great book to remind us that life is so much more than work.

ISBN: **978-0955754906** **ENGLISH** AVAILABLE ON **KINDLE**

«Звёздная лужица»

Первая книга для детей, изданная британским издательством Hertfordshire Press. Это также первая публикация молодой талантливой писательницы Олеси Петровой. Сказочные персонажи живут на страницах этой книги. Прекрасные иллюстрации делают книгу еще более интересной и красочной для детей, благодаря замечательному художнику Аскару Урманову. Вместе Аскар и Олеся составляют удивительный творческий тандем, который привнес жизнь в эту маленькую книгу

ISBN: **978-0955754906** **RUSSIAN**
RRP: **£4.95**

Buyuk Temurhon (Tamerlane)
by C. Marlowe, Uzbek Edition (2010)

Hertfordshire based publisher Silk Road Media, run by Marat Akhmedjanov, and the BBC Uzbek Service have published one of Christopher Marlowe's famous plays, Tamburlaine the Great, translated into the Uzbek language. It is the first of Christopher Marlowe's plays to be translated into Uzbek, which is Tamburlaine's native language. Translated by Hamid Ismailov, the current BBC World Service Writer-in-Residence, this new publication seeks to introduce English classics to Uzbek readers worldwide.

PAPERBACK
ISBN: **9780955754982**
RRP: **£10.00**
AVAILABLE ON **KINDLE**

Kairat Zakiryanov

Under the Wolf nest.
Turkic Rhapsody

Көкжал белгісімен. Түркі рапсодиясы

Under Wolf's Nest
by KairatZakiryanov
English –Kazakh edition

Were the origins of Islam, Christianity and the legend of King Arthur all influenced by steppe nomads from Kazakhstan? Ranging through thousands of years of history, and drawing on sources from Herodotus through to contemporary Kazakh and Russian research, the crucial role in the creation of modern civilisation played by the Turkic people is revealed in this detailed yet highly accessible work. Professor Kairat Zakiryanov, President of the Kazakh Academy of Sport and Tourism, explains how generations of steppe nomads, including Genghis Khan, have helped shape the language, culture and populations of Asia, Europe, the Middle East and America through migrations taking place over millennia.

HARD BACK
ISBN: **9780957480728**
RRP: **£17.50**
AVAILABLE ON **KINDLE**

BEGENAS SARTOV

WHEN THE EDELWEISS
FLOWERS FLOURISH
INCLUDING FURTHER SIX SHORT STORIES

When Edelweiss flowers flourish
by Begenas Saratov
English edition (2012)

A spectacular insight into life in the Soviet Union in the late 1960's made all the more intriguing by its setting within the Sovet Republic of Kyrgyzstan. The story explores Soviet life, traditional Kyrgyz life and life on planet Earth through a Science Fiction story based around an alien nations plundering of the planet for life giving herbs. The author reveals far sighted thoughts and concerns for conservation, management of natural resources and dialogue to achieve peace yet at the same time shows extraordinary foresight with ideas for future technologies and the progress of science. The whole style of the writing gives a fascinating insight into the many facets of life in a highly civilised yet rarely known part of the world.

ISBN: **978-0955754951** PAPERBACK AVAILABLE ON **KINDLE**

Mamyry gyldogon maalda

Это фантастический рассказ, повествующий о советской жизни, жизни кыргызского народа и о жизни на планете в целом. Автор рассказывает об инопланетных народах, которые пришли на нашу планету, чтобы разграбить ее. Автор раскрывает дальновидность мысли о сохранение и рациональном использовании природных ресурсов, а также диалога для достижения мира и в то же время показывает необычайную дальновидность с идеями для будущих технологий и прогресса науки. Книга также издана на **кыргызском языке**.

ISBN: **97809555754951**
RRP: **£12.95**

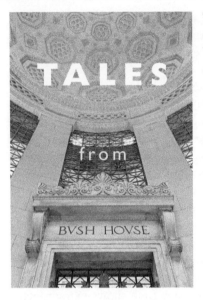

Tales from Bush House
(BBC Wolrd Service)
by Hamid Ismailov
(2012)

Tales From Bush House is a collection of short narratives about working lives, mostly real and comic, sometimes poignant or apocryphal, gifted to the editors by former and current BBC World Service employees. They are tales from inside Bush House - the home of the World Service since 1941 - escaping through its marble-clad walls at a time when its staff begin their departure to new premises in Portland Place. In July 2012, the grand doors of this imposing building will close on a vibrant chapter in the history of Britain's most cosmopolitan organisation. So this is a timely book.

PAPERBACK
ISBN: **9780955754975**
RRP: **£12.95**
AVAILABLE ON **KINDLE**

Жулдуз Байзакова

Песни темного огня

Chants of Dark Fire
(Песни темного огня)
by Zhulduz Baizakova
Russian edition (2012)

This contemporary work of poetry contains the deep and inspirational rhythms of the ancient Steppe. It combines the nomad, modern, postmodern influences in Kazakhstani culture in the early 21st century, and reveals the hidden depths of contrasts, darkness, and longing for light that breathes both ice and fire to inspire a rich form of poetry worthy of reading and contemplating. It is also distinguished by the uniqueness of its style and substance. Simply sublime, it has to be read and felt for real.

ISBN: **978-0957480711**
RRP: **£10.00**

Kamila
by R. Karimov
Kyrgyz – Uzbek Edition (2013)

«Камила» - это история о сироте,
растущей на юге Кыргызстана.
Наряду с личной трагедией Камилы и ее
родителей, Рахим Каримов описывает
очень реалистично и подробно местный
образ жизни. Роман выиграл конкурс
"Искусство книги-2005" в Бишкеке
и был признан национальным
бестселлером Книжной палаты
Кыргызской Республики.

PAPERBACK
ISBN: **978-0957480773**
RRP: **£10.00**

Gods of the Middle World
by Galina Dolgaya (2013)

The Gods of the Middle World tells the story of Sima, a student of archaeology for whom the old lore and ways of the Central Asian steppe peoples are as vivid as the present. When she joints a group of archaeologists in southern Kazakhstan, asking all the time whether it is really possible to 'commune with the spirits', she soon discovers the answer first hand, setting in motion events in the spirit world that have been frozen for centuries. Meanwhile three millennia earlier, on the same spot, a young woman and her companion struggle to survive and amend wrongs that have caused the neighbouring tribe to take revenge. The two narratives mirror one another, and Sima's destiny is to resolve the ancient wrongs in her own lifetime and so restore the proper balance of the forces of good and evil

PAPERBACK
ISBN: **978-0957480797**
RRP: **£14.95**
AVAILABLE ON **KINDLE**

Jazz Book, poetry
by Alma Sharipova , Russian Edition

Сборник стихов Алмы Шариповой JazzCafé, в котором предлагаются стихотворения, написанные в разное время и посвященые различным событиям из жизни автора. Стихотворения Алмы содержательные и эмоциональные одновременно, отражают философию ее отношения к происходящему. Почти каждое стихотворение представляет собой законченный рассказ в миниатюре. Сюжет разворачивается последовательно и завершается небольшим резюме в последних строках. Стихотворения раскрываются, как готовые «формулы» жизни. Читатель невольно задумывается над ними и может найти как что-то знакомое, так и новое для себя.

ISBN: 978-0-957480797
RRP: £10.00

13 steps of Erika Klaus
by Kazat Akmatov (2013)

The story involves the harrowing experiences of a young and very naïve Norwegian woman who has come to Kyrgyzstan to teach English to schoolchildren in a remote mountain outpost. Governed by the megalomaniac Colonel Bronza, the community barely survives under a cruel and unjust neo-fascist regime. Immersed in the local culture, Erika is initially both enchanted and apprehensive but soon becomes disillusioned as day after day, she is forbidden to teach. Alongside Erika's story, are the personal tragedies experienced by former soldier Sovietbek , Stalbek, the local policeman, the Principal of the school and a young man who has married a Kyrgyz refugee from Afghanistan . Each tries in vain, to challenge and change the corrupt political situation in which they are forced to live.

PAPERBACK
ISBN: **978-0957480766**
RRP: **£12.95**
AVAILABLE ON **KINDLE**

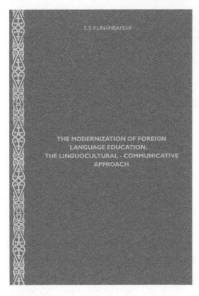

The Modernization of Foreign Language Education: The Linguocultural - Communicative Approach
by SalimaKunanbayeva (2013)

Professor S. S. Kunanbayeva - Rector of Ablai Khan Kazakh University of International Relations and World Languages This textbook is the first of its kind in Kazakhstan to be devoted to the theory and practice of foreign language education. It has been written primarily for future teachers of foreign languages and in a wider sense for all those who to be interested in the question (in the problems?) of the study and use of foreign languages. This book outlines an integrated theory of modern foreign language learning (FLL) which has been drawn up and approved under the auspices of the school of science and methodology of Kazakhstan's Ablai Khan University of International Relations and World Languages.

PAPERBACK
ISBN: **978-0957480780**
RRP: **£19.95**
AVAILABLE ON **KINDLE**

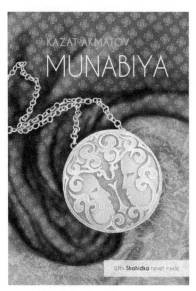

Shahidka/ Munabia
by KazatAkmatov (2013)

Munabiya and Shahidka by Kazat Akmatov National Writer of Kyrgyzstan Recently translated into English Akmatov's two love stories are set in rural Kyrgyzstan, where the natural environment, local culture, traditions and political climate all play an integral part in the dramas which unfold. Munabiya is a tale of a family's frustration, fury, sadness and eventual acceptance of a long term love affair between the widowed father and his mistress. In contrast, Shahidka is a multi-stranded story which focuses on the ties which bind a series of individuals to the tragic and ill-fated union between a local Russian girl and her Chechen lover, within a multi-cultural community where violence, corruption and propaganda are part of everyday life.

PAPERBACK
ISBN: **978-0957480759**
RRP: **£12.95**
AVAILABLE ON **KINDLE**

Howl *novel*
by Kazat Akmatov (2014)
English –Russian

The "Howl" by Kazat Akmatov is a beautifully crafted novel centred on life in rural Kyrgyzstan. Characteristic of the country's national writer, the simple plot is imbued with descriptions of the spectacular landscape, wildlife and local customs. The theme however, is universal and the contradictory emotions experienced by Kalen the shepherd must surely ring true to young men, and their parents, the world over. Here is a haunting and sensitively written story of a bitter -sweet rite of passage from boyhood to manhood.

PAPERBACK
ISBN: **978-0993044410**
RRP: **£12.50**
AVAILABLE ON **KINDLE**

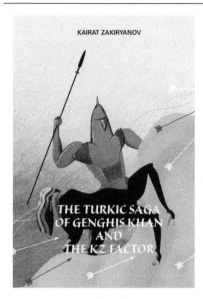

The Turkic Saga
of Genghis Khan and the KZ Factor
by Dr.Kairat Zakiryanov (2014)

An in-depth study of Genghis Khan from a Kazakh perspective, The Turkic Saga of Genghis Khan presupposes that the great Mongol leader and his tribal setting had more in common with the ancestors of the Kazakhs than with the people who today identify as Mongols. This idea is growing in currency in both western and eastern scholarship and is challenging both old Western assumptions and the long-obsolete Soviet perspective. This is an academic work that draws on many Central Asian and Russian sources and often has a Eurasianist bias - while also paying attention to new accounts by Western authors such as Jack Weatherford and John Man. It bears the mark of an independent, unorthodox and passionate scholar.

HARD BACK
ISBN: **978-0992787370**
RRP: **£17.50**
AVAILABLE ON **KINDLE**

Alphabet Game
by Paul Wilson (2014)

Travelling around the world may appear as easy as ABC, but looks can be deceptive: there is no 'X' for a start. Not since Xidakistan was struck from the map. Yet post 9/11, with the War on Terror going global, could 'The Valley' be about to regain its place on the political stage? Xidakistan's fate is inextricably linked with that of Graham Ruff, founder of Ruff Guides. Setting sail where Around the World in Eighty Days and Lost Horizon weighed anchor, our not-quite-a-hero suffers all in pursuit of his golden triangle: The Game, The Guidebook, The Girl. With the future of printed Guidebooks increasingly in question, As Evelyn Waugh's Scoop did for Foreign Correspondents the world over, so this novel lifts the lid on Travel Writers for good.

PAPERBACK
ISBN: **978-0-992787325**
RRP: **£14.95**
AVAILABLE ON **KINDLE**

Life over pain and desperation
by Marziya Zakiryanova (2014)

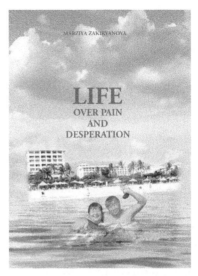

This book was written by someone on the fringe of death. Her life had been split in two: before and after the first day of August 1991 when she, a mother of two small children and full of hopes and plans for the future, became disabled in a single twist of fate. Narrating her tale of self-conquest, the author speaks about how she managed to hold her family together, win the respect and recognition of people around her and above all, protect the fragile concept of 'love' from fortune's cruel turns. By the time the book was submitted to print, Marziya Zakiryanova had passed away. She died after making the last correction to her script. We bid farewell to this remarkable and powerfully creative woman.

HARD BACK
ISBN: **978-0-99278733-2**
RRP: **£14.95**
AVAILABLE ON **KINDLE**

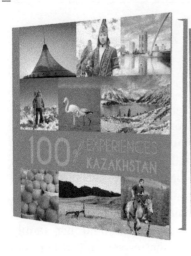

100 experiences of Kazakhstan
by Vitaly Shuptar, Nick Rowan
and Dagmar Schreiber (2014)

The original land of the nomads,
landlocked Kazakhstan and its expansive
steppes present an intriguing border
between Europe and Asia. Dispel
the notion of oil barons and Borat and be
prepared for a warm welcome into a land
full of contrasts. A visit to this newly
independent country will transport you
to a bygone era to discover a country
full of legends and wonders. Whether
searching for the descendants of Genghis Khan - who left his mark on this
land seven hundred years ago - or looking to discover the futuristic
architecture of its capital Astana, visitors cannot fail but be impressed
by what they experience. For those seeking adventure, the formidable Altai
and Tien Shan mountains provide challenges for novices and experts alike

ISBN: 978-0-992787356
RRP: £19.95

Dance of Devils , Jinlar Bazmi
by AbdulhamidIsmoil
and Hamid Ismailov
(Uzbek language),
E-book (2012)

'Dance of Devils' is a novel about the life of a great Uzbek writer Abdulla Qadyri (incidentally, 'Dance of Devils' is the name of one of his earliest short stories). In 1937, Qadyri was going to write a novel, which he said was to make his readers to stop reading his iconic novels "Days Bygone" and "Scorpion from the altar," so beautiful it would have been. The novel would've told about a certain maid, who became a wife of three Khans - a kind of Uzbek Helen of Troy. He told everyone: "I will sit down this winter and finish this novel - I have done my preparatory work, it remains only to write. Then people will stop reading my previous books". He began writing this novel, but on the December 31, 1937 he was arrested.

AVAILABLE ON **KINDLE**
ASIN: B009ZBPV2M

Vanished Khans and Empty Steppes
by Robert Wight (2014)

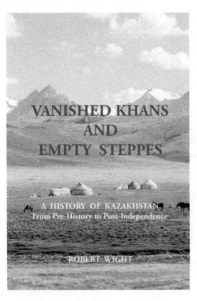

The book opens with an outline of the history of Almaty, from its nineteenth-century origins as a remote outpost of the Russian empire, up to its present status as the thriving second city of modern-day Kazakhstan. The story then goes back to the Neolithic and early Bronze Ages, and the sensational discovery of the famous Golden Man of the Scythian empire. The transition has been difficult and tumultuous for millions of people, but Vanished Khans and Empty Steppes illustrates how Kazakhstan has emerged as one of the world's most successful post-communist countries.

HARD BACK
ISBN: **978-0-9930444-0-3**
RRP: **£24.95**

PAPERBACK
ISBSN: **978-1-910886-05-2**
RRP: **£14.50**
AVAILABLE ON **KINDLE**

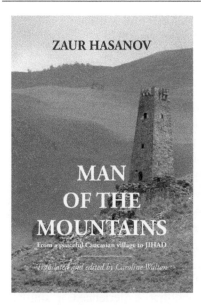

Man of the Mountains
by Abudlla Isa (2014)
(OCABF 2013 Winner)

Man of the Mountains" is a book about a young Muslim Chechen boy, Zaur who becomes a central figure representing the fight of local indigenous people against both the Russians invading the country and Islamic radicals trying to take a leverage of the situation, using it to push their narrow political agenda on the eve of collapse of the USSR. After 9/11 and the invasion of Iraq and Afghanistan by coalition forces, the subject of the Islamic jihadi movement has become an important subject for the Western readers. But few know about the resistance movement from the local intellectuals and moderates against radical Islamists taking strong hold in the area.

PAPERBACK
ISBN: **978-0-9930444-5-8**
RRP: **£14.95**
AVAILABLE ON **KINDLE**

Silk, Spice, Veils and Vodka
by Felicity Timcke (2014)

Felicity Timcke's missive publication, "Silk, Spices, Veils and Vodka" brings both a refreshing and new approach to life on the expat trail. South African by origin, Timcke has lived in some very exotic places, mostly along the more challenging countries of the Silk Road. Although the book's content, which is entirely composed of letters to the author's friends and family, is directed primarily at this group, it provides "20 years of musings" that will enthral and delight those who have either experienced a similar expatriate existence or who are nervously about to depart for one.

PAPERBACK
ISBN: **978-0992787318**
RRP: **£12.50**
AVAILABLE ON **KINDLE**

Finding the Holy Path
by Shahsanem Murray (2014)

"Murray's first book provides an enticing and novel link between her adopted home town of Edinburgh and her origins form Central Asia. Beginning with an investigation into a mysterious lamp that turns up in an antiques shop in Edinburgh, and is bought on impulse, we are quickly brought to the fertile Ferghana valley in Uzbekistan to witness the birth of Kara-Choro, and the start of an enthralling story that links past and present. Told through a vivid and passionate dialogue, this is a tale of parallel discovery and intrigue. The beautifully translated text, interspersed by regional poetry, cannot fail to impress any reader, especially those new to the region who will be affectionately drawn into its heart in this page-turning cultural thriller."

В поисках святого перевала – удивительный приключенческий роман, основанный на исторических источниках. Произведение Мюррей – это временной мостик между эпохами, который помогает нам переместиться в прошлое и уносит нас далеко в 16 век. Закрученный сюжет предоставляет нам уникальную возможность, познакомиться с историейи культурой Центральной Азии. «Первая книга Мюррей предлагает заманчивый роман, связывающий между её приемным городом Эдинбургом и Центральной Азией, откуда настоящее происхождение автора.

RUS ISBN: **978-0-9930444-8-9**
ENGL ISBN: **978-0992787394**
PAPERBACK
RRP: **£12.50**

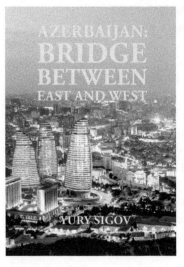

Azerbaijan:
Bridge between East and West
by Yury Sigov, 2015

Azerbaijan: Bridge between East and West, Yury Sigov narrates a comprehensive and compelling story about Azerbaijan. He balances the country's rich cultural heritage, wonderful people and vibrant environment with its modern political and economic strategies. Readers will get the chance to thoroughly explore Azerbaijan from many different perspectives and discover a plethora of innovations and idea, including the recipe for Azerbaijan's success as a nation and its strategies for the future. The book also explores the history of relationships between United Kingdom and Azerbaijan.

HARD BACK
ISBN: **978-0-9930444-9-6**
RRP: **£24.50**
AVAILABLE ON **KINDLE**

Kashmir Song
by Sharaf Rashidov
(translation by Alexey Ulko, OCABF 2014 Winner). 2015

This beautiful illustrated novella offers a sensitive reworking of an ancient and enchanting folk story which although rooted in Kashmir is, by nature of its theme, universal in its appeal.

Alternative interpretations of this tale are explored by Alexey Ulko in his introduction, with references to both politics and contemporary literature, and the author's epilogue further reiterates its philosophical dimension.

The Kashmir Song is a timeless tale, which true to the tradition of classical folklore, can be enjoyed on a number of levels by readers of all ages.

COMING SOON!!!
ISBN: 978-0-9930444-2-7
RRP: £29.50

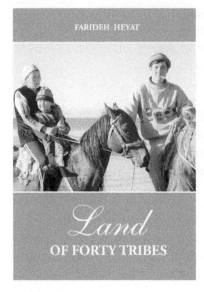

Land of forty tribes
by Farideh Heyat, 2015

Sima Omid, a British-Iranian anthropologist in search of her Turkic roots, takes on a university teaching post in Kyrgyzstan. It is the year following 9/11, when the US is asserting its influence in the region. Disillusioned with her long-standing relationship, Sima is looking for a new man in her life. But the foreign men she meets are mostly involved in relationships with local women half their age, and the Central Asian men she finds highly male chauvinist and aggressive towards women.

PAPERBACK
ISBN: **978-0-9930444-4-1**
RRP: **£14.95**

Terror: events, facts, evidence.
by Eldar Samadov, 2015

This book is based on research carried out since 1988 on territorial claims of Armenia against Azerbaijan, which led to the escalation of the conflict over Nagorno-Karabakh. This escalation included acts of terror by Armanian terrorist and other armed gangs not only in areas where intensive armed confrontations took place but also away from the fighting zones. This book, not for the first time, reflects upon the results of numerous acts of premeditated murder, robbery, armed attack and other crimes through collected material related to criminal cases which have been opened at various stages following such crimes. The book is meant for political scientists, historians, lawyers, diplomats and a broader audience.

PAPERBACK
ISBN: **978-1-910886-00-7**
RRP: **£9.99**
AVAILABLE ON **KINDLE**

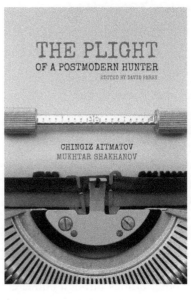

THE PLIGHT
OF A POSTMODERN HUNTER
EDITED BY DAVID PARRY

CHINGIZ AITMATOV
MUKHTAR SHAKHANOV

THE PLIGHT OF A POSTMODERN HUNTER

Chlngiz Aitmatov □
Mukhtar Shakhanov
(2015)

"Delusion of civilization" by M. Shakhanov is an epochal poem, rich in prudence and nobility – as is his foremother steppe. It is the voice of the Earth, which raised itself in defense of the human soul. This is a new genre of spiritual ecology. As such, this book is written from the heart of a former tractor driver, who knows all the "scars and wrinkles" of the soil - its thirst for human intimacy. This book is also authored from the perspective of an outstanding intellectual whose love for national traditions has grown as universal as our common great motherland.

I dare say, this book is a spiritual instrument of patriotism for all humankind. Hence, there is something gentle, kind, and sad, about the old swan-song of Mukhtar's brave ancestors. Those who for six months fought to the death to protect Grand Otrar - famous worldwide for its philosophers and rich library, from the hordes of Genghis Khan.

LANGUAGES ENG
HARDBACK
ISBN: **978-1-910886-11-3**

Raushan Burkitbayeva – Nukenova

The Wormwood Wind
Raushan
Burkitbayeva- Nukenova (2015)

A single unstated assertion runs throughout The Wormwood Wind, arguing, amid its lyrical nooks and crannies, we are only fully human when our imaginations are free. Possibly this is the primary glittering insight behind Nukenova's collaboration with hidden Restorative Powers above her pen. No one would doubt, for example, when she hints that the moment schoolchildren read about their surrounding environment they are acting in a healthy and developmental manner. Likewise, when she implies any adult who has the courage to think "outside the box" quickly gains a reputation for adaptability in their private affairs – hardly anyone would doubt her. General affirmations demonstrating this sublime and liberating contribution to Global Text will prove dangerous to unwary readers, while its intoxicating rhythms and rhymes will lead a grateful few to elative revolutions inside their own souls. Thus, I unreservedly recommend this ingenious work to Western readers.

HARD BACK
ISBN: **978-1-910886-12-0**
RRP: **£14.95**

My Homeland, Oh My Crimea
by Lenifer Mambetova
(2015)

Mambetova's delightful poems, exploring the hopes and fates of Crimean Tartars, are a timely and evocative reminder of how deep a people's roots can be, but also how adaptable and embracing foreigners can be of their adopted country, its people and its traditions.

LANGUAGES ENG / RUS
HARDBACK
ISBN: **978-1-910886-04-5**

GOETHE AND ABAI
by Herold Belger
2015

In this highly original extended essay, renowned author and critic Herold Belger explores an uncanny similarity between the life and career of that great genius of the Weimar Republic Johann Wolfgang von Goethe, and the legendary wordsmith from the Central Asian steppes, Abay. A resemblance previously ignored by most mainstream critics, even though a comparison that is bound to delight enlightened readers. As such, this rare and lyrical discussion examines the poetry, music, and prose of this golden period, while the author takes a number of biographical steps on a personal journey into the Germanic side of his own ethnic and cultural heritage. As such, Belger shamelessly plays with notions of shared influence, common sources, and possible pathways whereby the reading circles developed in this region are clearly revealed as mechanisms for the dispersion of high art and culture.

LANGUAGES ENG
HARDBACK
ISBN: 978-1-910886-16-8
RRP: £19.95

"The true story of immigration"
— Paul Wilson is a long-time writer on the Silk Road —

CRANES
IN
SPRING
TOLIBSHOHI DAVLAT

The best work in the literary competition
"Open Central Asia Book Forum and Literature Festival - 2014"

"Cranes in Spring"
by Tolibshohi Davlat
(2015)

This novel highlights a complex issue that millions of Tajiks face when becoming working migrants in Russia due to lack of opportunities at home. Fresh out of school, Saidakbar decides to go to Russia as he hopes to earn money to pay for his university tuition. His parents reluctantly let him go providing he is accompanied by his uncle, Mustakim, an experienced migrant. And so begins this tale of adventure and heartache that reflects the reality of life faced by many Central Asian migrants. Mistreatment, harassment and backstabbing join the Tajik migrants as they try to pull through in a foreign country. Davlat vividly narrates the brutality of the law enforcement officers but also draws attention to kindness and help of several ordinary people in Russia. How will Mustakim and Saidakbar's journey end? Intrigued by the story starting from the first page, one cannot put the book down until it's finished.

LANGUAGES ENG / RUS
HARDBACK
ISBN: **978-1-910886-06-9**
RRP: **£14.50**

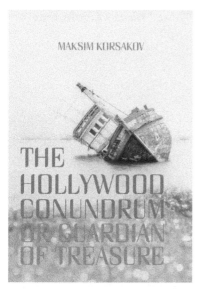

The Hollywood Conundrum or Guardian of Treasure
Maksim Korsakov
(2015)

In this groundbreaking experimental novella, Maxim Korsakov breaks all the preconceived rules of genre and literary convention to deliver a work rich in humour, style, and fantasy. Starting with a so-called "biographical" account of the horrors lurking beneath marriages of convenience and the self-delusions necessary to maintain these relationships, he then speedily moves to a screenplay, which would put most James Bond movies to shame. As if international espionage were not enough, the author teases his readers with lost treasure maps, revived Khanates, sports car jousting, ancient aliens who possess the very secrets of immortality, and the lineal descendants of legendary Genghis Khan. All in all, an ingenious book, as well as s clear critique of traditional English narrative convention.

LANGUAGES ENG / RUS
PAPERBACK
ISBN: **978-1-910886-14-4**
RRP: **£24.95**

The City Where Dreams Come True
Gulsifat Shahidi
(2016)

Viewed from the perspective of three generations, Shahidi presents a rare and poignant insight into the impact which Tajikistan'sterrible civil war had on its people and its culture during the early '90s. Informed partly by her own experiences as a journalist, these beautifully interwoven stories are imbued with both her affection for her native land and her hopes for its future. The narrators – Horosho, his granddaughter Nekbaht ,her husband Ali and his cousin Shernazar – each endure harrowing episodes of loss, injustice and violence but against all odds, remain driven by a will to survive, and restore peace, prosperity and new opportunities for themselves and fellow citizens.

LANGUAGES ENG / RUS
PAPERBACK
ISBN: **978-1-910886-20-5**
RRP: **£12.50**

Crane

Abu-Sufyan

(2016)

In this remarkable collection of prose poems, author Abu Sufyan takes readers through a series of fairy tale scenarios, wherein are hidden a number of sour existential truths. Indeed, from the bewilderment felt by anthropomorphised cranes, to the self-sacrifice of mares galloping towards their (potential) salvation, all the way to the bittersweet biographies experienced by a girl and her frustrated mother, this book weaves darkly enchanted frame stories into highly illustrative fables. Structured, as they are, in the style of unfolding dialogues, Sufyan's haunting literary technique serves to unveil a story within a storyline. An almost Postmodern strategy, whereby an introductory, or main narrative, is presented (at least in part), for the sole purpose of sharing uncomfortable anecdotes. As such, critics have observed that emphasized secondary yarns allow readers to find themselves - so to speak - stepping from one theme into another - while simultaneously being carried into ever-smaller plots. Certainly, as adventures take place between named and memorable characters, each exchange is saturated with wit, practical jokes, and life lessons contributing to an overall Central Asian literary mosaic. All in all, this tiny volume is both a delight and a warning to its admirers.

LANGUAGES ENG
PAPERBACK
ISBN: **978-1-910886-23-6**
RRP: **£12.50**

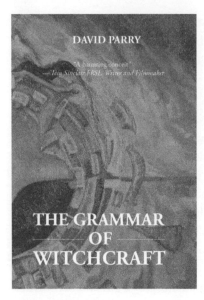

The Grammar of Witchcraft
David Parry
(2016)

In this collection of Mini-Sagas and poems, Parry narrates the final journey taken
by his alter ego Caliban from the surreal
delights of a lesbian wedding in Liverpool,
all the way back to a non-existent city of
London. In himself, the author is aiming
to resolve lyrical contradictions existing
between different levels of consciousness:
betwixt reality and the dreaming state.
And as such, unnervingly illogical scenar-
ios emerge out of a stream of consciousness wherein bewildering theatrical
landscapes actively compete with notions of Anglo-Saxon witchcraft, Radical Traditionalism, and a lack of British authenticity. Each analysis pointing
towards those Jungian Spirits haunting an endlessly benevolent Archetypal
world.

LANGUAGES ENG
PAPERBACK
ISBN: **978-1-910886-25-0**
RRP: **£9.95**

COLD SHADOWS
Shahsanem Murray
(2016)

The story, set at the end of the 1980's, revolves around a group of disparate individuals living seemingly unconnected lives in various countries.

But then a strange incident on the Moscow to Frunze train leads to the gradual exposure of complex web in which their lives, loves and profession's have long been entangled.

Bound together by an intriguing series of incidents, each struggles to survive the hardships and challenges that life throws at them, from radical changes in the political climate to the murky antics of spies and double agents. But behind everything lies love…

LANGUAGES ENG
PAPERBACK
ISBN: 978-1-910886-27-4
RRP: **£12.50**

Lightning Source UK Ltd.
Milton Keynes UK
UKHW040340281219
355981UK00002BA/457/P